FORMATIVE FICTIONS

signale
modern german letters, cultures, and thought

Series editor: Peter Uwe Hohendahl, Cornell University

Signale: Modern German Letters, Cultures, and Thought publishes new English-language books in literary studies, criticism, cultural studies, and intellectual history pertaining to the German-speaking world, as well as translations of important German-language works. *Signale* construes "modern" in the broadest terms: the series covers topics ranging from the early modern period to the present. *Signale* books are published under a joint imprint of Cornell University Press and Cornell University Library in electronic and print formats. Please see http://signale.cornell.edu/.

FORMATIVE FICTIONS

Nationalism, Cosmopolitanism, and the Bildungsroman

TOBIAS BOES

A Signale Book

CORNELL UNIVERSITY PRESS AND CORNELL UNIVERSITY LIBRARY
ITHACA, NEW YORK

Cornell University Press and Cornell University Library gratefully acknowledge The Andrew W. Mellon Foundation and the College of Arts and Sciences, Cornell University, for support of the Signale series.

Copyright © 2012 by Cornell University

All rights reserved. Except for brief quotations in a review, this book, or parts thereof, must not be reproduced in any form without permission in writing from the publisher. For information, address Cornell University Press, Sage House, 512 East State Street, Ithaca, New York 14850.

First published 2012 by Cornell University Press and Cornell University Library

Printed in the United States of America

Library of Congress Cataloging-in-Publication Data

Boes, Tobias, 1976–
 Formative fictions : nationalism, cosmopolitanism, and the Bildungsroman / Tobias Boes.
   p. cm. — (Signale : modern German letters, cultures, and thought)
 Includes bibliographical references and index.
 ISBN 978-0-8014-5177-5 (cloth : alk. paper)
 ISBN 978-0-8014-7803-1 (pbk. : alk. paper)
 1. Bildungsromans—History and criticism. 2. German fiction—History and criticism. 3. European fiction—History and criticism. 4. Nationalism and literature. 5. City and town life in literature. 6. Comparative literature—German and European. 7. Comparative literature—European and German   I. Title.   II. Series: Signale (Ithaca, N.Y.)
  PN3448.B54B64   2012
  809.3'9354—dc23   2012016137

Cloth printing   10 9 8 7 6 5 4 3 2
Paperback printing 10 9 8 7 6 5 4 3 2 1

Contents

A Note on Translations — vii

Acknowledgments — ix

Introduction — 1

Part I Methodological Background

1. The Limits of National Form: Normativity and Performativity in *Bildungsroman* Criticism — 13

2. Apprenticeship of the Novel: Goethe and the Invention of History — 43

Part II Comparative Studies

3. Epigonal Consciousness: Stendhal, Immermann, and the "Problem of Generations" around 1830 — 73

4. Long-Distance Fantasies: Freytag, Eliot, and National Literature in the Age of Empire — 101

5. Urban Vernaculars: Joyce, Döblin, and the "Individuating Rhythm" of Modernity — 128

Conclusion: *Apocalipsis cum figuris*: Thomas Mann and the *Bildungsroman* at the Ends of Time — 155

Bibliography — 183

Index — 193

A Note on Translations

Most quotations are in English only. I have included the original German only where a translation seemed insufficient to illustrate my point. References are to standard English editions wherever possible, although I have sometimes silently modified existing translations. All uncredited translations are my own.

The original publication date of each primary source is given on its first appearance in the text. For some of the less common sources, I have also indicated the German title.

Acknowledgments

As anyone who has ever written a scholarly book will be able to confirm, the acknowledgments section is the academic's equivalent of a *Bildungsroman*. Far more than a catalog of accumulated debts and favors, it also reveals the story of an intellectual formation and maturation. One major argument of this study is that formative trajectories are rarely uncomplicated, and that they usually traverse multiple possible communities, multiple ways of conceptualizing historical time. This has certainly been my own experience.

My interest in the *Bildungsroman* was sparked by an undergraduate thesis on James Joyce's *A Portrait of the Artist* that I wrote under the supervision of Ellen Stauder in the English Department at Reed College. Several years later, I returned to the topic when I began work on a dissertation that I eventually submitted to the Department of Comparative Literature at Yale University. Pericles Lewis and Carol Jacobs provided unfailing support and expert advice as my official advisers; Katie Trumpener gave just as much of her time without the satisfaction of seeing her name on the project's title page. I also benefited from many productive discussions with the other two members of my dissertation committee, Barry McCrea and the late Cyrus Hamlin. At Yale, Gregory Byala, Maria Fackler, Colin Gillis, Megan Quigley, Leonardo Lisi, and Johannes Türk provided additional feedback on individual chapters, as did audience members of the Modernist Studies Colloquium and the Comparative Literature Open Forum Lecture Series.

I significantly reworked the project at the University of Notre Dame, where my colleagues Alys George, Vittorio Hösle, Robert Norton, and Mark Roche provided especially valuable comments. I am also grateful to Sarah Bearzi, Nicole Knight, Erik Larsen, I-Mei Ling, Javier Mocarquer, Abigail Palko, and Sara Troyani for their feedback during our spring 2010 graduate seminar "Fictions of Development." An early version of my third chapter benefited from the kind attention of the Literature and Revolution Working Group at Notre Dame's Nanovic Institute for European Studies, and I would like to thank both the institute and the group's participants (Julia Douthwaite, Robert Fishman, Alex Martin, Pierpaolo Polzonetti, and Lesley Walker) for their support.

I owe much of the most valuable feedback on my writing to scholars who kindly gave their time and attention without being prejudiced by shared institutional affiliations. Audience members at presentations that I gave to the German Studies Association, the American Comparative Literature Association, the International Society for the Study of Narrative, and the Modernist Studies Association helped me sharpen crucial portions of my argument, as did the faculty of the Department of Modern and Classical Languages at George Mason University. Eric Downing, Stephen Kern, Todd Kontje, and Dennis Mahoney provided additional feedback in personal or written conversations.

In the spring of 2007, I had the opportunity to cohost a seminar on contemporary approaches to the novel of formation at the annual conference of the American Comparative Literature Association. Those three days in Puebla, Mexico, were among the intellectually most stimulating of my life, and I would like to thank all my fellow seminar participants: Ericka Beckman, Rita Berman, Maria Fackler, Enrique Lima, Maria Lima, Doug Mao, Joseph Slaughter, and especially Jed Esty, who has been a professional role model and mentor for the past six years.

At Cornell, Kizer Walker and the editorial board of the Signale series gave early and continuous support for my work, while Marian Rogers helped me put the final form to what I had written. I am also grateful to the anonymous reviewers of my manuscript.

I would like to thank the Institute for Scholarship in the Liberal Arts at the University of Notre Dame for its support of the indexing and publication of this book. The Institute also provided research funding for my project during the summer of 2008.

An early version of my second chapter won the 2007 A. Owen Aldridge Essay Prize of the American Comparative Literature Association and subsequently appeared in *Comparative Literature Studies*, where it also won the 2009 Article Prize of the Goethe Society of North America. I would like to thank both the ACLA jury, chaired by Thomas Beebee, and the GSNA jury, chaired by Astrida Tantillo. An early version of the fifth chapter appeared in *ELH: English Literary History*. The introduction and opening chapter also incorporate some ideas I first formulated in a slightly different form in my critical translation of Karl Morgenstern's "On the Nature of the *Bildungsroman*," which was published in *PMLA*.

One way in which *Bildungsromane* differ from acknowledgments sections is that the former by their very nature delineate individual lives in sharp contrast to everything that surrounds them. Fortunately, actual lives are rarely this solitary. My parents and friends, central among them Aaron Carico, Denise Della Rossa, Johannes Göransson, Stuart Greene, Kate Marshall, Joyelle McSweeney, Ian Newman, Joseph Rosenberg, Jason Ruiz, and Yasmin Solomonescu at Notre Dame, provided me with the emotional support necessary to complete this project. Nothing that they did, however, can match the strength and companionship of Tracy Bergstrom, to whom I dedicate this book.

Formative Fictions

Introduction

On December 12, 1819, in an auditorium at the University of Dorpat (now Tartu in Estonia), an obscure professor of rhetoric by the name of Karl Morgenstern coined what would become one of the central terms not merely of German, but of world literary study: *Bildungsroman*.[1] The *Bildungsroman*, or "novel of formation," is a kind of novel that focuses on the spiritual and intellectual maturation of its protagonist; for Morgenstern, as for almost every other critic since him, the paradigmatic example of the genre was Goethe's *Wilhelm Meister's Apprenticeship* (1795–96). Morgenstern's lecture is suffused with the spirit of romantic nationalism that erupted throughout Europe after the fall of Napoleon. Hopes of some sort of national unification, most likely under the leadership of the Prussian king Frederick William III, were then running high in Germany, and Morgenstern celebrated *Wilhelm Meister* for "presenting German life, German thought and the morals of

---

1. Technically speaking, Morgenstern had already used the term in a lecture titled "Concerning the Spirit and Cohesion of a Number of Philosophical Novels" that he had delivered almost a decade earlier, on December 12, 1810. But it was only in the later lecture that Morgenstern advanced toward a systematic definition of the *Bildungsroman* as a literary genre, and only in the later lecture that he treated his new invention as a valuable new term for literary study. Indeed, Morgenstern begins the 1819 lecture with the disclaimer "You will permit me to call [the novel of which I am about to speak] by a name that has to my knowledge never been used before, namely that of the *Bildungsroman*." Karl Morgenstern, "On the Nature of the *Bildungsroman*," trans. Tobias Boes, *PMLA* 124 (2009): 647.

our time through its hero, its scenery and environment." In a none-too-subtle jab at Enlightenment culture, he also claimed that the eighteenth-century novelist Christoph Martin Wieland had failed where Goethe had succeeded because Wieland "lived in an earlier period in which German *Bildung* could not yet hold its own against meddlesome foreign influences."[2]

A closer look at the context of Morgenstern's lecture, however, reveals a number of facts that are difficult to reconcile with the nationalist swagger of these quotations. Although Morgenstern was a native of Magdeburg, and German was the official language of instruction in Dorpat, the town was nevertheless part of imperial Russia, and its university a brainchild of Tsar Alexander I. Nor could this fact have been far from anyone's mind on that December day, for Morgenstern's audience had assembled to commemorate the founding of the university, which coincided with the tsar's birthday. And while Morgenstern may have officially derided the intellectual heritage of the Enlightenment, his own biography tells a different story. A student of the philologist Friedrich August Wolf, who helped give birth to the modern specialized university, Morgenstern found permanent academic employment in Danzig (Gdansk, Poland), but soon quit this position out of frustration with the pedagogic routine that it thrust on him. At the new University of Dorpat, which Alexander was aggressively staffing with Western academics, Morgenstern reinvented himself as a universal humanist in the eighteenth-century mold, not only lecturing on rhetoric, but also founding the library, art museum, and botanical garden.

In more ways than one, Morgenstern's life thus demonstrates the condition that we have nowadays come to refer to as globalization. Geographically, he (like an ever-increasing number of German intellectuals after him) belonged not to any nation, but to what Arjun Appadurai has called the "transnation": a community "which retains a special ideological link to a putative place of origin but is otherwise a thoroughly diasporic collectivity."[3] Historically, he found himself swept up in revolutionary currents whose allure was impossible to resist, even as they hollowed out the foundations of the very life he had built for himself. Although he is sometimes depicted as a boring and out-of-touch pedant, Morgenstern embodied the forces of global modernity to a greater degree than many of his more famous contemporaries.

In the following study, I use the contradictory elements of Morgenstern's biography as the starting point for a cosmopolitan interpretation of the German *Bildungsroman*. By this I mean a critical approach that will pay particular attention

---

2. Morgenstern, "On the Nature," 655. For further information on Morgenstern and his context, see my critical introduction to this translation, as well as Wilhelm Süss, "Karl Morgenstern: Ein kulturhistorischer Versuch," *Acta et Commentationes Universitatis Tartuensis (Dorpatensis)* 16.B (1929): 1–160.

3. Arjun Appadurai, *Modernity at Large: Cultural Dimensions of Globalization* (Minneapolis: University of Minnesota Press, 1996), 172.

to the ways in which individual novels repeatedly run into difficulties when they attempt to fulfill Morgenstern's dictum and link national experience to the life of their hero. The premise of my argument is that the *Bildungsroman* is a genre connected more than any other to the rise of modern nationalism. But repeatedly and consistently, the knot that ties literature to politics comes undone in precisely those cases where the stakes are the highest. The five German novels that I examine over the course of this study—Goethe's *Wilhelm Meister's Apprenticeship*, Karl Leberecht Immermann's *The Epigones* (1836), Gustav Freytag's *Debit and Credit* (1855), Alfred Döblin's *Berlin Alexanderplatz* (1929), and Thomas Mann's *Doctor Faustus* (1947)—all respond to turning points in the history of German nationalism in precisely the way that Morgenstern argued they should: by trying to give what I shall henceforth call a "national form" to the narrative trajectories of their protagonists. Yet despite the fact that harmony and teleology are among the most-often enumerated qualities of traditional *Bildungsromane*, none of these novels ultimately succeed in giving a definitive form to the collective experience that they articulate. There is always some kind of remainder, some identity claim that resists nationalism's aim for closure in what (following a host of political theorists from Hegel to Ernest Gellner) we can identify as the normative regime of the nation-state. These remainders are the novels' "cosmopolitan" elements.

The three chapters that stand at the heart of this study are comparative in nature, each linking a German novel to a roughly contemporary work from the French, English, and Irish traditions. The connections—between *The Epigones* and Stendhal's *The Red and the Black* (1830), *Debit and Credit* and George Eliot's *Daniel Deronda* (1876), *Berlin Alexanderplatz* and James Joyce's *A Portrait of the Artist as a Young Man* (1914)—will sometimes seem surprising, both because the novels being compared are stylistically dissimilar and because they occupy different places in their respective national canons. But this is precisely the point. By paying attention to the cosmopolitan remainders of these works (remainders generated, to reiterate, by the search for a "national" form), we can discover new grounds for literary comparisons that cut across national borders without negating these boundaries altogether.

Such new grounds for literary comparison seem to me sorely needed in the case of *Bildungsroman* criticism, which has for far too long been caught between the Scylla of national essentialism and the Charybdis of an empty universalism. In the first camp, we can place those critics who regard the *Bildungsroman* as a "peculiarly German species" of novel devoted to expressing a "German ideology" or "German way of interpreting the world."[4] The genre, so these critics agree, provides a

---

4. The first of these quotes is taken from Nicholas Boyle's biography of Goethe, as quoted in Jeffrey L. Sammons, "Heuristic Definition and the Constraints of Literary History: Some Recent Discourses on the *Bildungsroman* in English and German," in *Dazwischen: Zum transitorischen Denken in Literatur- und Kulturwissenschaft*, ed. Andreas Härter et al. (Göttingen: Vandenhoeck & Ruprecht, 2003), 174,

narrative response to the provincial and politically repressive atmosphere that prevailed in central Europe throughout the nineteenth century. It could therefore not have flourished in any other national context. Contrasting with this first camp is a second one that approaches the *Bildungsroman* as a universal marker of modernity, a literary response to changing times in which individuals have to secure their own place in the world rather than find it pre-given by tradition or inheritance.

Common to both of these schools is the assumption that the rise of the *Bildungsroman* in the late eighteenth century is closely connected to the simultaneous ascent of German idealism. Indeed, the very name of the genre pays tribute to the concept of *Bildung*, a central term within this philosophical tradition that refers to the organic and teleological growth of an individual. The problem with such an assumption, however, is that hardly any actual novel bears it out, as Jeffrey L. Sammons showed in a withering article published in 1981.[5] The *Bildungsroman*, many critics came to agree over the following years, is in fact an elaborate hoax first perpetrated during the Wilhelmine period by nationalist scholars who were eager to elevate the influence of German thinkers and distinguish German literary production from that of the Western European countries.[6] Much to Sammons's chagrin, however, his published findings did little to halt the actual usage of the term. Indeed, in the wake of poststructuralism, critics began to build elaborate theories around the "phantom" or "spectral" character of the *Bildungsroman*, or around the ways in which it generates "fictions" of moral personhood.[7]

It is my belief that this debate over what must on first sight seem a trivial technical matter actually has far larger methodological implications for literary study. I first conceived this book when I left a graduate program in comparative literature in order to take up a position as an assistant professor of German at a large research university, where my central duty was to promote interest in a single national culture. In adjusting to my new disciplinary environment, I was struck by a strange incongruity. As a graduate student during the early years of the new millennium, I had experienced firsthand an exciting shift in direction that affected the field of comparative literature. In those years, my discipline was profoundly transformed

---

while the other two are partial translations of the titles of Louis Dumont, *Homo aequalis II: L'idéologie allemande; France-Allemagne et retour* (Paris: Éditions Gallimard, 1991), and Georg Bollenbeck, *Bildung und Kultur: Glanz und Elend eines deutschen Deutungsmusters* (Frankfurt am Main: Suhrkamp, 1996).

5. Jeffrey L. Sammons, "The Mystery of the Missing *Bildungsroman*, or: What Happened to Wilhelm Meister's Legacy?" *Genre* 14.1 (1981): 229–46.

6. Todd Kontje, in his comprehensive survey of *Bildungsroman* criticism, logically concludes that the novel of formation exists not as a collection of actual textual objects, but only as the "history of a discourse" that is specific to the German critical tradition. See Todd Kontje, *The German Bildungsroman: History of a National Genre* (Columbia, SC: Camden House, 1993), ix.

7. The first two quotations refer to the titles of Marc Redfield, *Phantom Formations: Aesthetic Ideology and the Bildungsroman* (Ithaca, NY: Cornell University Press, 1996), as well as Pheng Cheah, *Spectral Nationality: Passages of Freedom from Kant to Postcolonial Literatures of Liberation* (New York: Columbia University Press, 2004). For the third quote, see Joseph R. Slaughter, *Human Rights, Inc.: The World Novel, Narrative Form, and International Law* (New York: Fordham University Press, 2007), 19.

by the call of "world literature," a mode of criticism defined by what one of my teachers called the search for "a different map, a different time scale, predating and outlasting the birth and death of any nation."[8] To "do" world literature on this model meant to look for grand patterns, to trace ideas, themes, or motifs through texts produced in different cultures at oftentimes radically asynchronous points in time. Another manifesto called this the art of "uncanny reading," of looking for the strange-yet-familiar in new texts.[9] The new critical paradigm went hand in hand with a related rise in interest in translation studies, an understandable parallelism, since few if any scholars could be expected to master all the languages necessary to draw up a truly comprehensive new map or time scale for literary study.

As I took up my new job in a national literature department, I came to realize that the new criticism in many ways stood at odds with the foundations of the discipline that I had entered. In the wake of the global recession of 2008, several German departments at large state universities were forced to close their doors; others were integrated into departments of modern languages. Simultaneously, traditional study-abroad programs increasingly gave way to "global campuses," where American students could study American curricula while maintaining an expatriate lifestyle that allowed for little meaningful contact with the exotic (but often politically problematic) locations to which they had moved. Was "world literature," I couldn't help but ask myself, unintentionally advancing the corporatization of the university by providing a new program for literary study that (taken to a reductive extreme) required neither advanced language expertise nor immersion in cultural nuance and difference?

The current state of *Bildungsroman* criticism, so I came to believe, reflected the issues afflicting literary studies as a whole: on the one hand, a no longer timely insistence on national essentialism; on the other hand, a grand leap to very broad claims about temporally and geographically diverse novels and their supposed relationship to abstract concepts such as "modernity" or "humanity." Was there a way to mediate between these two extremes?

It was around this time that I discovered Karl Morgenstern's rarely read lecture on the novel of formation. What immediately fascinated me about Morgenstern was his conceptual distance from the problematic definition of the *Bildungsroman* as a genre that stages the development of an individual toward a normative ideal. Instead, Morgenstern foregrounds three separate elements: an emphasis on change in the protagonist, a relationship between this change and the specific national setting in which the protagonist moves, and the positive effect that the depiction of this change will have on the reader. Here, in other words, was what I shall henceforth call a "performative" understanding of *Bildung*. Morgenstern's praise of *Wilhelm*

---

8. Wai Chee Dimock, "Literature for the Planet," *PMLA* 116 (2001): 175.
9. Vilashini Cooppan, "Ghosts in the Disciplinary Machine: The Uncanny Life of World Literature," *Comparative Literature Studies* 41:1 (2004): 10–36.

Meister also brought to mind Friedrich Schlegel's much better known eulogy of the work as a novel that "represents the greatest tendency of the age."[10] Both of their statements reveal an attitude toward historical time that seems mundane to us now but was in fact radically new in the late eighteenth century, namely the notion that *things change*, and that individual epochs might have a character that is radically different from that of preceding eras. I began to wonder whether it would not be possible to advance a definition of the genre based on its response to this new understanding of time, which would later come to be known as "historicism."

The advantage of such an approach is twofold. First, it moves discussions of the genre away from the realm of phantoms, specters, and fictional personalities, and toward a consideration of what narrative actually does, namely offer a coherent account of events as they exist in time. At the same time, it maintains the specificity of the genre by insisting on its link to the conceptual history of *Bildung*, even as it presents a slightly different "origin story" than has traditionally been offered. *Bildung* and *Bildungsroman* can now be interpreted as twin responses to the rise of historicism: both are essentially strategies of emplotment, the one philosophical, the other narrative in nature.

The idea that the novel of formation is a literary response to a changing conception of historical time isn't new. Mikhail Bakhtin had already argued as much in the 1930s, when he defined the *Bildungsroman* as a type of novel that constructs "an image of *man growing* in *national-historical time*."[11] Karl Morgenstern's lecture allows us to question some of the premises of Bakhtin's argument, however. After all, what did Morgenstern really understand about the "German time" that Goethe was supposedly depicting? It certainly did not exist in any institutional sense, for there was no unified German nation-state in either 1796 or 1819. The German-speaking principalities weren't even united in a common time zone. "German time" existed in an imagined, aspirational sense only, and for this reason was able to find a powerful rhetorical expression in the work of an expatriate in provincial Russia, lecturing to a group of students of whom few would ever have traveled west of Riga. The "German time" that Morgenstern was celebrating was imaginary and aspirational in a second sense as well, however, for it was radically asynchronous with actual events as they transpired in central Europe. Morgenstern's lecture is full of revolutionary fervor, and he was clearly unaware (or at least ignorant of the full impact) of the Carlsbad Decrees that had been imposed on the German Confederation three months earlier, stifling the intellect and voices of an entire generation.

---

10. Friedrich Schlegel, *Philosophical Fragments*, trans. Peter Firchow (Minneapolis: University of Minnesota Press, 1991), 46.

11. Mikhail Bakhtin, "The *Bildungsroman* and Its Significance in the History of Realism," in *Speech Genres and Other Late Essays*, trans. Vern W. McGee and ed. Caryl Emerson and Michael Holquist (Austin: University of Texas Press, 1986), 25 (emphasis in original).

The argument of this book will be that Morgenstern's situation, though clearly extreme, nevertheless contains instructive lessons that can be applied to the *Bildungsroman* tradition as a whole. That is, any attempts to give a national form to the life of a protagonist will always resist fulfillment in institutional structures, thereby violating the demands for finality and normative closure that are constitutive of traditional *Bildungsroman* criticism, and they will always remain internally asynchronous, thereby revealing a cosmopolitan character. For these reasons, interpretive approaches to the novel of formation must not only pay attention to the concrete historical circumstances that are depicted in these novels, but must also and especially watch out for the ways in which these novels transgress against the ordering structures—both geographical and temporal—by which we ordinarily impose meaning on these circumstances. The *Bildungsroman*, in short, is neither the product of an aberrant national tradition, nor is it a specter that wanders through world literature.

My study comprises three parts that are in turn divided into a total of six chapters. The first part serves as an extended methodological introduction and contains a theoretical chapter as well as an analysis of the rise of historicism and its impact on *Wilhelm Meister's Apprenticeship*. The second part contains three comparative studies, each pairing a German novel with one from another Western European tradition. The final part, an analysis of Thomas Mann's allegorical novel of formation, *Doctor Faustus*, serves as a conclusion to the project and returns to themes first raised in the previous two parts.

My opening chapter, "The Limits of National Form," expands on the central claims that I presented in this introduction. I first examine how traditional *Bildungsroman* criticism is built on the premise of the protagonist's fulfillment in a normative ideal, and then advance an alternative understanding of the genre based on *Bildung* as a performative response to a crisis in historical understanding. I then relate this new model to nationalism on the one hand, and to cosmopolitanism on the other. The chapter concludes with a reflection on the relevance of the novel of formation to contemporary discourses of world literature, as well as a discussion of the uses and pitfalls of genre-based criticism.

The second chapter, "Apprenticeship of the Novel," complements the first by providing an intellectual history of *Bildung* in the eighteenth century, paying special attention to the ways in which the concept departs from alternate models that emphasize finality, such as *kalokagathia* and "evolutionism." I then relate the birth of a new historical sensibility to the rise of the novel on the one hand, and to the rise of national thinking on the other. A detailed reading of *Wilhelm Meister's Apprenticeship* reveals that that text indeed displays many of the hallmarks of the new national thinking but refuses to find closure in an allegory of the state. Instead, Goethe's Tower Society reinvents itself as an explicitly cosmopolitan organization.

My goal throughout the second part is to trace how the imposition of new forms of historical emplotment onto diverging national traditions creates previously unnoticed connections between disparate texts. The third chapter, "Epigonal Consciousness," focuses on *The Red and the Black* and *The Epigones*, and shows how a new pan-European effort to "possess the past" (Peter Fritzsche) in the wake of the Napoleonic Wars interacted with the differing political geographies in the French Hexagon and the German Confederation. In France, where the Bourbon Restoration created a unified state and a common public sphere, citizens nevertheless perceived reality quite differently, often depending on when they were born and what their formative experiences had been. Stendhal pays tribute to this with a novel in which characters impose different plots onto the same events. The internal division of Germany, on the other hand, meant that such plots could be safely segregated in one and the same novel, resulting in a more picaresque approach to the *Bildungsroman*.

The fourth chapter, "Long-Distance Fantasies," examines two novels that were written in response to a crisis in liberal-national ideology in the middle of the nineteenth century: Gustav Freytag's *Debit and Credit* and George Eliot's *Daniel Deronda*. This pairing is unusual, not the least because Freytag's anti-Semitism starkly contrasts with Eliot's proto-Zionism. However, both these texts can be read as responses to the rise of modern imperialism, a political development that was frequently justified with new forms of historical emplotment, such as Social Darwinism. Imperialism poses a significant threat to liberal-national ideology, because it unites different ethnic and cultural groups within a single state, and thereby challenges the traditional foundations of national communities.

The fifth chapter, "Urban Vernaculars," examines the notion that the modernist city texts of the early twentieth century put an end to the *Bildungsroman* tradition, because urban environments provide neither the temporal continuity nor the cultural homogeneity demanded by traditional historicism. As I point out, however, novels of formation and modernist city texts have a dialectically intertwined relationship during the modernist period. In *A Portrait of the Artist as a Young Man*, Joyce used the *Bildungsroman* tradition to impose a poetic structure on colonial Dublin. Fifteen years later, Döblin adopted many of Joyce's advances for his own depiction of an imperial metropolis in *Berlin Alexanderplatz*. My readings in this chapter focus on the ways in which both texts use poetic means to create a temporal "rhythm" in which the modern city emerges as a rivaling site of identity formation to the nation-state.

The conclusion, "*Apocalipsis cum figuris*," returns to the themes of the first two chapters by providing an in-depth reading of Thomas Mann's *Doctor Faustus*, a novel that, I argue, responds explicitly to the "crisis of historicism" debate that raged in Germany during the interwar years. A large part of the chapter is given to a comparison of Mann's thought to that of Friedrich Meinecke, who was Mann's close contemporary and perhaps the last great practitioner of classical historicism in Germany. At the same time, Mann's high-modernist style is undeniably allegorical in nature, which allows me to contrast my model of the "performative nationalism" at work in the nineteenth-century *Bildungsroman* with competing claims on the genre as a "national allegory" that have been advanced by Fredric Jameson and Jed Esty.

In a movement that recapitulates the structure of several classic studies in the field, this book thus begins with Johann Wolfgang von Goethe, the poet who inaugurated the age of "Weimar Classicism," and concludes with Thomas Mann, the twentieth-century novelist who self-identified not only as Goethe's successor, but also as the conscience and voice of the German nation in times of war and totalitarian terror. As the nature of the three intervening chapters will make clear, however, my intention isn't to once again retrace the outlines of a canonical corpus within German letters, but rather to sketch the genealogy of a certain intersection between narrative and communal identity. "Genealogy," as I will explain in greater detail in the first chapter, here refers to a chain of literary influence by which formal and thematic solutions to recurring social problems are passed down through time and acquire cultural solidity. Genealogy, however, is only one way of conceptualizing diachronic relationships and, in the modern world, stands in strict opposition to "history," understood as a process of temporal change that repeatedly undoes precisely the inherited forms that are passed down through genealogical links. The great advantage of the *Bildungsroman* is that it models for us a kind of temporal existence that speaks equally to both of these two ordering systems: to the preservation and further refinement of established identities, and to an embrace of the novelty and contingency of an ever-changing world. For this reason, the novel of formation is perhaps better suited than any other literary genre of the modern era to shed new light on the methodological debates that surround the birth of what we now call "world literature."

PART I

Methodological Background

1

THE LIMITS OF NATIONAL FORM: NORMATIVITY AND PERFORMATIVITY IN *BILDUNGSROMAN* CRITICISM

When Morgenstern gave his *Bildungsroman* lecture in Dorpat, he could not know that roughly seven hundred miles to the west, another academic who was his exact contemporary was working on the first (and some would say the only) great aesthetic theory of the nineteenth century. Georg Wilhelm Friedrich Hegel and Karl Morgenstern were born within one day of one another, but though briefly joined by this historical coincidence their lives followed different trajectories ever after. Morgenstern's career took him further and further toward geographical and intellectual obscurity when he accepted job offers in Danzig and Dorpat. Hegel, on the other hand, enjoyed increasing renown in Jena, Nuremberg, and Heidelberg and in 1818 was offered Johann Gottlieb Fichte's former chair in philosophy at the University of Berlin. It was here, at the center of German political life, that Hegel began giving his lectures on aesthetics during the winter of 1820–21.

Hegel was far from the first German intellectual to reflect on the status of the new literary form that had come into being in the twenty-five years since the publication of Goethe's *Wilhelm Meister's Apprenticeship*.[1] But he was the first to integrate his thoughts into a systematic theory of aesthetics. Eighteenth-century theorists of

---

1. For a detailed discussion of German romantic novel theory and how it relates to the *Bildungsroman*, see Todd Kontje, *The German Bildungsroman: History of a National Genre* (Columbia, SC: Camden House, 1993), 1–22.

the novel, such as Friedrich von Blanckenburg, took an essentially rhetorical approach to their task: they tried to give a technical account of how the new genre worked, how it differed from established literary forms such as the epic or the drama, and how aspiring writers might produce successful novels of their own. For Hegel, by contrast, novels (and indeed artistic objects of any kind) were interesting not in and of themselves, but because of the service they provided to systematic philosophy, whose ultimate task was to trace the unfolding of world spirit. As he puts it at the very outset of his lectures, "Art liberates the true content of phenomena from the pure appearance and deception of this bad, transitory world, and gives them a higher actuality, born of the spirit."[2]

Poetic literature (*Poesie*) occupies a privileged position in Hegel's aesthetic system, because it is uniquely suited to mediate between the "content" and "artistic form" of the external world, imposing on both the necessary sense of closure or "totality" that is a precondition for ascent into the world of the spirit.[3] In his discussion of poetic literature, however, Hegel formulates a crucial distinction between the ancient Greek epic and the novel, which he terms "a modern bourgeois epic" (2:1092). The former encounters totality as an external given, in the "total world of a nation and epoch" (2:1044); the latter, on the other hand, takes as its subject the collision between the "poetry of the heart and the opposing prose of external circumstances" (2:1092). To illustrate what Hegel has in mind, it is useful to contrast Homer's Achilles with Goethe's Wilhelm Meister. Achilles' life is characterized by a fundamental congruity between form and content: he *is* a warrior, and all his actions can be related to this basic fact. At the same time, his destiny is inseparable from that of the people whom he leads, and it would have never occurred to an ancient bard to question whether Achilles might perhaps better serve the Achaians by being something other than he actually is. By contrast, Wilhelm Meister's nature and calling are far from clear throughout much of his development. He *believes* himself to be born for the theater, and most of Goethe's plot is given over to a series of trials in which this belief collides with the actual life of an actor. How Meister's life relates to that of the people around him is also far from certain, and the novel tries out various forms of the social contract before eventually giving preference to the Tower Society.

In Hegel's novel theory, then, totality does not exist as something that is pregiven. Instead, it comes about over the course of the work as the protagonist

---

2. G. W. F. Hegel, *Aesthetics: Lectures on Fine Art*, trans. T. M. Knox (Oxford: Clarendon Press, 1975), 1:9. Further references to this work appear in parentheses in the text.

3. In Hegel's words, "Poetry can harbor the entire content of art and all the forms of art. This too we have to regard as a struggle for a totality, a struggle that can be demonstrated philosophically only as a sublimation of the limits placed upon the particular" (2:968). For my understanding of this and the following passages from Hegel, I am indebted to Wilhelm Vosskamp, "Bildung und Roman—Hegels Romantheorie als Poetik des Bildungsromans?" in *Der Roman des Lebens: Die Aktualität der Bildung und ihre Geschichte im Bildungsroman* (Berlin: Berlin University Press, 2009), 143–61.

struggles for a compromise between the poetic form within and the prosaic reality without. This process is teleological, because everything that happens finds its ultimate justification in the endpoint of the narrative. In Hegel's words, "In the modern world [the hero's] struggles are nothing more than years of apprenticeship [*Lehrjahre*] . . . and thereby acquire their true significance" (1:593).[4] The very next sentence makes clear, however, that Hegel regards this "true significance" with great skepticism, judging it as falling short of a true reconciliation between poetic form and prosaic content. More often than not, he claims, the protagonist will simply submit to the pressures of external reality: "The end of such apprenticeship consists in this, that the subject sows his wild oats, accommodates himself with his wishes and opinions to existing relationships and their rationality, enters the concatenation of the world, and acquires for himself an appropriate attitude to it" (1:593).

Hegel remained skeptical of the novel because, unlike the classical epic with its divine, semidivine, or at least nobly born heroes, the novel is condemned to search for a redemptive totality in the life of a more or less random individual. It can therefore offer only a "subjective" perspective on the world. An "objective" perspective that would have universal meaning is reserved for the philosophical sciences, which is why "poetry [appears] as that particular art in which art itself begins at the same time to dissolve and acquire in the eyes of philosophy its point of transition to religious pictorial thinking as such, as well as to the prose of scientific thought" (2:968). Indeed, it is by now a bit of a critical commonplace to refer to various other parts of Hegel's philosophical system, especially the *Phenomenology of Mind*, as a "*Bildungsroman* of the spirit."[5]

The three characteristics of Hegel's novel theory that I have just outlined (the search for totality in the life of an individual, the staging of this struggle in a teleological narrative, and the yearning for an objective supplement to the merely subjective totality supplied by artistic description) all tie his aesthetic system to the philosophical concept of *Bildung* as it was articulated in German idealism during the late eighteenth and early nineteenth centuries.[6] In the second chapter of this book, I will outline a revisionist model of *Bildung* that detaches it from its idealist interpretations and restores it to its roots in the mid-eighteenth century. First,

---

4. Hartmut Steinecke has pointed out that Hegel's appeal to an "apprenticeship" in this passage strongly suggests that he was influenced by *Wilhelm Meister*, and indeed, Hegel's whole theory seems much better suited to the *Bildungsroman* than to the novel genre as a whole. See Steinecke's essay "The Novel and the Individual: The Significance of Goethe's *Wilhelm Meister* in the Debate about the *Bildungsroman*," in *Reflection and Action: Essays on the Bildungsroman*, ed. James Hardin (Columbia: University of South Carolina Press, 1991), 77.

5. See, e.g., Vosskamp, "Bildung und Roman," 145.

6. This link would be made explicit by Hegel's pupil Karl Rosenkranz, who wrote in the opening paragraph of his 1827 "Introduction to the Novel" that "*Bildung* is the real object of the novel." See Karl Rosenkranz, "Einleitung über den Roman," in *Zur Geschichte des deutschen Bildungsromans*, ed. Rolf Selbmann (Darmstadt: Wissenschaftliche Buchgesellschaft, 1988), 100.

however, I will outline how an implicit commitment to totality, teleology, and normativity has shaped the critical discourse on the *Bildungsroman* for the past two centuries, and what an alternate approach to the genre might look like. On the basis of such an alternate model, I will then develop some larger hypotheses about the purpose of literary study, and derive from them some methodological strictures that I intend to follow in this book.

Novel Criticism and the "Unchanging Unity of the Ideal"

One of the foundational texts for all idealist theories of *Bildung* is Friedrich Schiller's *Letters on the Aesthetic Education of Man*, published in 1795, the year that also saw the publication of *Wilhelm Meister's Apprenticeship*. In the fourth letter of this collection, Schiller argues that "every individual human being . . . carries within him, potentially and prescriptively, an ideal man, the archetype of a human being, and it is his life's task to be, through all his changing manifestations, in harmony with the unchanging unity of this ideal."[7] This statement expresses two of the three characteristics that I highlighted about Hegel's aesthetic theory: that all human beings carry within themselves the prescription for an "ideal" existence, and that the realization of this ideal presents itself teleologically, as a "life's task." Soon after, Schiller addresses the third characteristic as well, providing an "objective form" to complement the merely subjective dimensions of *Bildung*: "This archetype, which is to be discerned more or less clearly in every individual, is represented by the *state*, the objective and, as it were, canonical form in which all the diversity of individual subjects strive to unite" (93). Already in Schiller's account then, written at a time when Germany was still paralyzed by the provincial sectionalism of the Holy Roman Empire, the state emerges as the "objective and canonical" form of the inner potential of man. In order to achieve subjective completion, individual human beings must strive for some kind of "harmony" with its unalterable unity.

It quickly becomes apparent, however, that Schiller's understanding of the state differs from our contemporary approach to the term. As he explains, the correspondence between individual subject and state can be achieved in one of two ways: "either by the ideal man suppressing empirical man, and the state annulling individuals; or else by the individual himself *becoming* the state, and man in time being *ennobled to the stature* of man as idea" (93, emphasis in original). The first of these possibilities ("the state annulling individuals") emits an undeniably totalitarian odor, and present-day readers of Schiller will no doubt be reminded of Fascist Germany or Stalinist Russia by his claims that the diversity of human subjects invariably strives to gain a canonical form in the state. Schiller is well aware of the

---

7. Friedrich Schiller, *Letters on the Aesthetic Education of Man*, trans. Elizabeth M. Wilkinson and L. A. Willoughby, in *Essays*, ed. Walter Hinderer and Daniel O. Dahlstrom (New York: Continuum, 1993), 93. Further references to this work appear in parentheses in the text.

dangers that lie ahead down this road, and consequently advocates for the second alternative: "A political constitution will still be very imperfect if it is to achieve unity only by suppressing variety. The state should not only respect the objective and generic character in its individual subjects; it should also honor their subjective and specific character" (94). "Once man is inwardly at one with himself," Schiller continues, "he will be able to preserve his individuality however much he may universalize his conduct, and the state will be merely the interpreter of his own finest instinct, a clearer formulation of his own sense of what is right" (94–95). The bulk of Schiller's study is then concerned with elucidating how man might become "inwardly at one with himself" through a process of aesthetic education in which "sense impulse" (mutable life) and "form impulse" (eternal shape) are united with one another in a process of free play of the mental faculties.

The early reception history of *Letters on the Aesthetic Education of Man* coincided with a tumultuous period in German history that witnessed, first, heated intellectual debates about the significance of the French Revolution and the rise of Napoleon, and then the dissolution of the Holy Roman Empire and the first stirrings of genuine nationalism during the Wars of Liberation. Schiller's notion that human beings might give the law unto the state rather than vice versa if they only developed their inner faculties to a sufficient extent was quickly seized on by German intellectuals and developed into a programmatic alternative to the French Revolution. Almost immediately, this discourse also became linked with *Wilhelm Meister's Apprenticeship*, a book that Goethe's contemporaries now read not only as an exemplary depiction of a man's aesthetic education, but also as a veiled political program.[8] The romantics began writing novels in the *Meister* tradition, and as Todd Kontje has shown, almost all the enduring examples of their kind (e.g., Ludwig Tieck's *Franz Sternbald's Wanderings* [1798], Novalis's *Heinrich von Ofterdingen* [1800], and Jean Paul's *The Awkward Age* [*Flegeljahre*, 1804]) feature protagonists who seek to improve themselves through the medium of literature.[9] As Kontje also remarks, however, the phase of optimistic trust in the possibilities of an aesthetic education—a *Bildung* that might discover its ideal purpose in literature—was comparatively short-lived. Already satirized in Jean Paul's *The Awkward Age*, it was thoroughly deconstructed by E. T. A. Hoffmann in his *The Life and Opinions of the Tomcat Murr* (1819–21).

Hegel's lectures, with their distrust of literary description as a merely "subjective" realization of the ideal, can be read as the final step of this reversal. Hegel's call

---

8. Daniel Jenisch, for instance, in a 1797 review of the novel, praised it as "a story that we all partake of; in Wilhelm Meister we can see . . . our own true self"; Jenisch also proclaimed that "the more mankind develops and perfects its faculties, the less it will need great revolutions and violent upheavals of things." Quoted in Wilhelm Vosskamp, "Der Bildungsroman als literarisch-soziale Institution," in *Der Roman des Lebens: Die Aktualität der Bildung und ihre Geschichte im Bildungsroman* (Berlin: Berlin University Press, 2009), 123–25.

9. Todd Kontje, *Private Lives in the Public Sphere: The German Bildungsroman as Metafiction* (University Park: Pennsylvania State University Press, 1992).

for an "objective" ground for the manifestation of spirit was prefigured by other thinkers, however, and this suggests that the romantic enthusiasm for aesthetic education always coexisted with concurrent and more general proposals for how the gulf between empirical and ideal existence might be bridged. Unlike Schiller's aesthetic theories, these rival proposals have what I shall henceforth call a "normative" character, in the sense that they subordinate the *Bildung* of the individual to the manifestation of a universal ideal. Thus Immanuel Kant, in several political essays written in the immediate aftermath of the French Revolution, proposed a cosmopolitan commonwealth of nations as the ultimate telos of man's striving for freedom and self-actualization. Johann Gottlieb Fichte, in his *Addresses to the German Nation* (1808), delivered shortly after the battle of Jena-Auerstedt and the dissolution of the Holy Roman Empire, reserved a similar status for the German nation. Hegel himself, finally, lecturing in the wake of the Congress of Vienna, assigned this purpose to the constitutional state.[10] The late work of Wilhelm von Humboldt provides another example that is less known than the previous three. Humboldt begins his 1821 essay "On the Task of the Historian" with the audacious thesis that the work of the artist can provide methodological inspiration to the historian: "Historical presentation, like artistic presentation, is an imitation of nature. The basis of both is the recognition of the true form, the discovery of the necessary, the exclusion of the accidental. We must therefore have no regrets in applying the more readily recognizable method of the artist to an understanding of the more dubious method employed by the historian."[11] In striking parallel to Schiller's exposition of the aesthetic education, Humboldt further regards the ultimate purpose of the historian as the formal elucidation of an ideal underlying reality, to which he gives the name "history as such" (*die Geschichte überhaupt*): "The historian worthy of his title must show every event as part of a whole, or, what amounts to the same thing, must show the form of history as such in every event described" (1:8).

In short, the purpose of Humboldt's essay is to appropriate for the historian (and thus for the narrator of a collective destiny) the task that Schiller would have reserved for the artist and for the aesthetic education of an individual. Tellingly, when Humboldt proceeds to describe the methods by which the form of "history as such" might be uncovered in empirical events, he introduces the nation as a third term that mediates between the individual and history:

All understanding presupposes in the person who understands, as a condition of its possibility, an analogue of that which will actually be understood later; an antecedent

---

10. All three of these thinkers are discussed at length in Pheng Cheah, *Spectral Nationality: Passages of Freedom from Kant to Postcolonial Literatures of Liberation* (New York: Columbia University Press, 2003).

11. Wilhelm von Humboldt, "Über die Aufgabe des Geschichtsschreibers," in *Gesammelte Werke*, ed. Alexander von Humboldt and Carl Brandes (photomechanical repr., Berlin: Walter de Gruyter, 1988), 1:8. Further references to this work appear in parentheses in the text.

and original correspondence between subject and object.... In the case of history this antecedent of understanding is quite obvious, since everything that is active in world history also moves within man. The more deeply, therefore, the soul of a nation feels everything human, and the more tenderly, purely, and diversely it is moved by this, the greater will be its chance to produce historians in the true sense of the word. (1:14–15)

What Humboldt here describes as an "original correspondence between subject and object" is, of course, the logic of *Bildung*, in which the human subject discovers itself to be an aesthetic object that has not yet quite come into being. The historian, Humboldt continues, recognizes that there is a fundamental homology between this purely personal formation and the development of the world at large. The intermediary step between the individual and world history is the nation; by fostering the inner formation of its citizens, the nation will produce sensitive historians who are capable of depicting the process by which history animates the "soul" of the community into which they have been born.

This "normative" strain of German idealism, according to which individuals who freely develop their faculties will ultimately discover that their development reveals a universal rather than merely singular telos, would become constitutive of modern *Bildungsroman* theory as it came into being during the years after 1850. The bulk of said theory can be divided into two camps, which I called the "essentialist" and the "universalist" in the introduction to this study. The essentialist camp believes that *Wilhelm Meister's Apprenticeship*, as well as the other novels of formation that were more or less directly inspired by it, reveals something specific about the character of the German nation. Thus Julian Schmidt (the founder of German realist novel theory, about whom I will have more to say when I discuss Gustav Freytag's 1855 novel, *Debit and Credit*) argued that *Wilhelm Meister* expresses "the spiritual orientation [*Geistesrichtung*] of the entire nation ... the destiny of the German people."[12] Wilhelm Dilthey, in his 1906 work, *Poetry and Experience*, similarly wrote that "the *Bildungsroman* gave expression to the individualism of a culture whose sphere of interest was limited to private life."[13] By this, of course, he was referring to the political impotence and internal division of the German middle classes, which, unlike their French and British neighbors, were denied union in a national public sphere. Thomas Mann helped spread the same idea to a wider audience with a 1916 lecture on the novel of development, in which he referred to the *Bildungsroman* as a "typically German and legitimately national" novel "intimately connected with the German concept of humanity, which, since it is the product of

---

12. Quoted in Vosskamp, "Der Bildungsroman als literarisch-soziale Institution," 133.
13. Wilhelm Dilthey, *Selected Works*, ed. Rudolf A. Makkreel and Frithjof Rodi, vol. 5, *Poetry and Experience* (Princeton, NJ: Princeton University Press, 1985), 335. For a comprehensive study of how German literary criticism helped construct a German national identity during the second half of the nineteenth century, see Peter Uwe Hohendahl, *Building a National Literature: The Case of Germany, 1830–1870*, trans. Renate Baron Franciscono (Ithaca, NY: Cornell University Press, 1989).

an era in which society disintegrated into atoms and turned every human being into a citizen, was lacking a political element all along."[14]

Needless to say, in the century since Mann spoke these words, attitudes toward German nationalism and the "lack of a political element" in the ideas that undergird it have changed completely. The period between 1945 and 1980 was thus especially rich in studies that questioned the problematic legacy of the *Bildungsroman* without, however, thereby rejecting the fundamental thesis that the genre communicated a specifically German national essence.[15] The general weariness with political readings that befell German studies after the ideological wars of the 1970s, along with the challenges to the so-called *Sonderweg* hypothesis that arose in the 1980s, brought a momentary lull to this debate. Nevertheless, the basic question has not gone away, as Wilhelm Vosskamp demonstrates when he attempts to reconcile the contradictory positions: "The *Bildungsroman* presents an allegory of the German bourgeoisie [*Bürgertum*], since it combines the dual nature of self-affirming homogenization and critical self-reflexion in its history."[16]

Before I describe the competing "universalist" approach to the novel of formation, I want to examine briefly the term "allegory," which occurs in the quotation from Vosskamp. Most immediately, Vosskamp is arguing that the history of *Bildungsroman* criticism, at times affirmative and at times critically reflective of bourgeois identity, presents an allegory of German national consciousness. However, a closer reading of his essay reveals that Vosskamp detects the same affirmative and reflective tendencies within literature itself, and it would therefore be equally correct to speak of the German novel of formation as an essentially allegorical genre. A similar claim is made by Fredric Jameson and Jed Esty, two critics from the "universalist" camp who describe the *Bildungsroman* as a "national allegory" and a "soul-nation allegory," respectively.[17] Jameson's account has found especially broad resonance among critics of postcolonial literatures, and it is not at all uncommon now to hear the *Bildungsroman* referred to as an allegorical genre. Jameson never explicitly defines what he means by this term, but presumably he would agree with Esty's claim that "nationhood ... gives a finished form to modern societies in the same way that adulthood gives a finished form to the modern subject."[18] If one adds to this observation the poststructuralist insight that "allegory" gives a name to the arbitrary signifier-signified relationship underlying all language, then it is once again possible to see the *Bildungsroman* as a literary genre in which the idealized

---

14. Thomas Mann, "Der Entwicklungsroman," in *Gesammelte Werke in dreizehn Bänden*, ed. Peter de Mendelssohn (Frankfurt am Main: Fischer, 1990), 11:702.
15. See Kontje, *The German Bildungsroman*, 44–68.
16. Vosskamp, "Der Bildungsroman als literarisch-soziale Institution," 141.
17. I borrow these characterizations from Fredric Jameson, "Third-World Literature in the Age of Multi-National Capitalism," *Social Text* 15 (1986): 65, as well as from Jed Esty *Unseasonable Youth: Modernism, Colonialism, and the Fiction of Development* (New York: Oxford University Press, 2011), 24.
18. Esty, *Unseasonable Youth*, 4.

shape of the nation comes into being through the essentially arbitrary vessel of an individual life—or, to put it slightly differently, in which the normative expresses itself through the contingent.

As Esty correctly points out, allegory expresses its meaning not through its content, but rather through the final form toward which it strives. Wilhelm Meister could, in theory, have been a baker's apprentice (though Goethe's novel would then lack the metareflective elements of the theatrical chapters); what matters for an allegorical reading is the conclusion of the novel, in which Wilhelm discovers the underlying form of his life in the Tower Society. Marc Redfield glosses this relationship in the following manner:

> The "content" of the *Bildungsroman* instantly becomes a question of form, precisely because the content is the forming-of-content, *Bildung*—the formation of the human as the producer of itself as form. Wilhelm Dilthey's seemingly content-oriented definition of the *Bildungsroman* as a "regular development . . . in the life of the individual," in which each stage of development "has its own intrinsic value and is at the same time the basis for a higher stage," is animated by a formal principle that undermines the content's specificity.[19]

I will have more to say about the "allegorical" nature of the *Bildungsroman* in the conclusion of this study, in which I examine Thomas Mann's *Doctor Faustus*, a novel written with explicitly allegorical intentions. For the moment, however, I merely wish to point out that traditional theories of the novel of formation, regardless of whether they are drawn from the "essentialist" (Vosskamp) or "universalist" (Jameson, Esty, Redfield) camp, define the *Bildungsroman* via the question of form rather than content, and thus also via its ultimate telos.

In contrast to the "essentialist" camp, which approaches the *Bildungsroman* on the premise that the genre communicates something about Germany's special path into modernity, the "universalist" camp detects themes of universal human significance in the novel of formation. The modern origins of this tradition can be found in Georg Lukács's *The Theory of the Novel* (1916), written roughly simultaneously with (and in stark contrast to) both Dilthey's explication of the genre in *Poetry and Experience* and Mann's wartime lectures on autobiographical fiction. Finished before Lukács's conversion to Marxism, *The Theory of the Novel* borrows many of its central concepts from Hegel's aesthetic lectures. Lukács defines the novel as one of the two subcategories of "great epic literature" (*die große Epik*), the other one being epic poetry (*die Epopöe*).[20] His explication of the differences between the two

---

19. Marc Redfield, *Phantom Formations: Aesthetic Ideology and the Bildungsroman* (Ithaca, NY: Cornell University Press, 1996), 42.
20. Georg Lukács, *The Theory of the Novel: A Historico-Philosophical Essay on the Epic Forms of Great Literature*, trans. Anna Bostock (Cambridge, MA: MIT Press, 1971). Subsequent references to

borrows from Hegel as well, as do his references to "immanence" and "totality." Interestingly, Lukács defines totality through a problem of reference, thus relating it to the question of allegory; totality, according to him, implies that "something closed within itself can be completed; completed because everything occurs within it, nothing is excluded from it and *nothing points at a higher reality outside it*; completed because everything within it ripens to its own perfection and, by attaining itself, submits to limitations" (34, emphasis mine).

Lukács differentiates the novel from other kinds of literature by highlighting its preoccupation with biographical form. "The inner form of the novel," he explains, "has been understood as the process of the problematic individual's journeying toward himself, the road from dull captivity within a merely present reality—a reality that is heterogeneous in itself and meaningless to the individual—toward clear recognition" (80). "After such self-recognition has been attained," Lukács continues, "the ideal thus formed irradiates the individual's life as its immanent meaning; but the conflict between what is and what should be has not been abolished and cannot be abolished in the life sphere of the novel, wherein these events take place; only a maximum conciliation—the profound and intensive irradiation of a man by his life's meaning—is attainable" (80). Lukács's claim that the novel can never entirely abolish "the conflict between what is and what should be" recalls Hegel's pessimistic stance, but the second half of *The Theory of the Novel* illuminates how the merely subjective side of the "profound and intensive irradiation of a man by his life's meaning" can be overcome. *Wilhelm Meister*, Lukács argues there, takes as its central theme "the reconciliation of the problematic individual, guided by his lived experience of the ideal, with concrete social reality" (132).

The twentieth century has seen a number of competing *Bildungsroman* theories that draw either implicitly or explicitly on Lukács's thesis that the self-realization of the individual ultimately sheds some light also on "social reality." Franco Moretti, for instance, has advanced a complex account in which he argues that "youth" (for Moretti the defining feature of the novel of formation) "is, so to speak, modernity's 'essence,' the sign of a world that seeks its meaning in the *future* rather than in the

---

The Theory of the Novel will appear in parentheses in the text. Lukács's classification system is far from transparent, and matters aren't helped by the fact that the English translation by Anna Bostock simply elides any differences between his terms *die Epik* and *die Epopöe*, rendering both indifferently as "epic." David Midgley has recently argued that Lukács is using the term *die Epopöe* in the sense of the Greek noun "hē epopoieia" to refer to the "active making of an epic account of the world," rather than to any finished literary product. See David Midgley, *Writing Weimar: Critical Realism in German Literature, 1918–1933* (New York: Oxford University Press, 2000), 143. But this thesis cannot stand up in the light of statements such as the following: "Epic poetry and novel [*Epopöe und Roman*], these two major forms of great epic literature, differ from one another not by their author's fundamental intentions but by the given historico-philosophical realities with which the authors were confronted" (Lukács, *The Theory of the Novel*, 56). Clearly Lukács regards *Epopöe* and *Roman* as two different forms of writing; I therefore propose that *Epopöe* should consistently be rendered as "epic poetry," and I have implemented this change in all my quotations from Bostock's translation.

past."[21] The events of an individual youth are therefore merely signifiers ("signs") for the underlying story of modernity. Furthermore, the endpoint of this allegory, in which youth gives way to adulthood, is especially privileged. In order to become a "form," "youth must be endowed with a very different, almost opposite feature to those already mentioned: the very simple and slightly philistine notion that youth 'does not last forever.' Youth is brief, or at any rate circumscribed, and this enables, or rather *forces* the *a priori* establishment of a formal constraint on the portrayal of modernity."[22]

Jed Esty has pointed out that Moretti's account of youth as the "symbolic form of modernity" can be easily read to prefigure Esty's own theories about the "nation-soul allegory" that underlies the novel of formation:

> But if the standard novel of socialization figures modernity's endless revolution in the master trope of youth, then what is the social referent for the counter-trope of adulthood, that containment device upon which everything, in the end, depends? If capitalism never rests, what allegorical correspondence can explain the capacity of the form itself to put the brakes on development, thereby preventing the *Bildungsroman* from becoming a never-ending story? Here we arrive at a possibility that remains a bit buried in Moretti: that nationhood supplies the *Bildungsroman* with a language of historical stability, a final form amidst the vast changes of industrialization.[23]

A number of other theorists join Esty in seeing the modern nation-state as the "final form" revealed by the biographical trajectory of the hero.[24] The difference between these theories and the ones drawn from the "essentialist" camp is that the "universalist" accounts aim to theorize the nation-state *as such*, rather than just in its particularized German expression. An insuperable difficulty in this regard, however, is that *Wilhelm Meister's Apprenticeship* predates both the creation of a unified nation-state on German soil and even the formulation of coherent theories for what such a

---

21. Franco Moretti, *The Way of the World: The Bildungsroman in European Culture*, trans. Albert Sbragia, new ed. (London: Verso, 2000), 5–6.
22. Moretti, *The Way of the World*, 5–6.
23. Jed Esty, "The Colonial *Bildungsroman*: *The Story of an African Farm* and the Ghost of Goethe," *Victorian Studies* 49:3 (2007): 413.
24. Pheng Cheah, for instance, argues that an "exemplary lesson about the imperativity of national *Bildung* [is] invariably personified in the [colonial *Bildungsroman*'s] protagonist whose formation or *Bildung* parallels and symbolizes that of the emergent nation because he is its first patriot and ideal citizen" (*Spectral Nationality,* 239). Similarly, Joseph R. Slaughter argues: "[Both] human rights law and the *Bildungsroman* posit the nation-state as the highest form of expression of human sociality and the citizen as the highest form of expression of human personality. With the 'state/citizen bind' posited as the ultimate horizon of human personality development, the nation-state consistently emerges as a problem for the abstract universalism under which both human rights and *Bildung* are theorized." See Joseph R. Slaughter, *Human Rights, Inc.: The World Novel, Narrative Form, and International Law* (New York: Fordham University Press, 2007), 94.

state might look like. The supposedly foundational example of the *Bildungsroman* genre thus has to be written out of the canon.[25]

Other critics use the novel of formation to articulate even broader claims. Moretti speaks of the *Bildungsroman* as the "symbolic form of modernity," once again linking it to the idealist tradition by means of Ernst Cassirer's concept of a "symbolic form," in which "a particular spiritual content . . . is connected to a specific material sign . . . and intimately identified with it."[26] Joseph R. Slaughter argues that the contemporary *Bildungsroman* illustrates the "tropological configuration of the human person through . . . the figural habituation of the individual to the norms and forms of international citizenship," thereby relating literature to international human rights law.[27] And in perhaps the most far-reaching claim of all, both Michael Beddow and Marc Redfield link the novel of formation to the production of "humanity" as such. For Beddow, these works testify "to a conviction that there is something about imaginative fiction, and something about authentic humanity, which makes the former an especially suitable medium of insight into the latter," while for Redfield, their referent is "the self-positing consciousness of the human."[28] Clearly, a lot is at stake in *Bildungsroman* criticism!

Bildung in Dorpat

The problem with all of these claims, however, is that they provide a poor fit for the empirical evidence. It is surprisingly hard to discover novels that fulfill the strictures of totality, teleology, and normativity demanded by the idealist understanding of *Bildung*, even if one consults works that were written in immediate temporal vicinity to *Wilhelm Meister's Apprenticeship*. The romantic novels of Novalis and Joseph von Eichendorff place their hero squarely outside of what they regard as a fallen social world, something that is true also of Adalbert Stifter's later *Indian Summer* (1857). Heinrich Lee, the protagonist of Gottfried Keller's *Green Henry* (revised version 1879–80) renounces his earlier strivings and accepts a position as a civil servant, while Hans Castorp, the hero of Thomas Mann's *The Magic Mountain* (1924), staggers beyond the bounds of his own story and is presumably blown

---

25. This problem is especially apparent in Cheah's account, since he links the German idealist tradition to modern novels of decolonization by means of Germany's status as an early decolonized state that won a sense of its own identity only after the experience of being occupied by a foreign empire. *Wilhelm Meister's Apprenticeship* warrants only a single passing reference in his study.

26. Moretti, *The Way of the World*, 5. Moretti is quoting a gloss on Cassirer by Erwin Panofsky.

27. Slaughter, *Human Rights, Inc.*, 22. The form of Slaughter's claim that literary and legal texts are, as it were, diegetic and exegetic expressions of the same underlying allegory strikingly mirrors Vosskamp's contention that both the *Bildungsroman* and the history of its criticism provide allegories of the German bourgeoisie, and thereby affirms the close connection between the "essentialist" and "universalist" camps against strenuous objections from either side.

28. Michael Beddow, *The Fiction of Humanity: Studies in the Bildungsroman from Wieland to Thomas Mann* (Cambridge: Cambridge University Press, 1982), 6; Redfield, *Phantom Formations*, 55.

up on some unknown battlefield in World War I. Looking beyond Germany, we find that the French and British novels of formation provide a very similar sight. Julien Sorel, the hero of Stendhal's *The Red and the Black* (1830), ends on the guillotine; George Eliot's Tom and Maggie Tulliver (*The Mill on the Floss*, 1860) drown in a flood. Gustave Flaubert's Madame Bovary (*Madame Bovary*, 1856), like so many other female protagonists, starts to develop as a person only after her marriage, while Charles Dickens's Pip (*Great Expectations*, 1860–61) needs to relinquish his social expectations before he can truly come into his own. Thomas Hardy's Jude (*Jude the Obscure*, 1895) ends his days in a loveless marriage after losing his children to murder and suicide, while Joyce's Stephen Dedalus (*A Portrait of the Artist as a Young Man*, 1914) vanishes from the purview of his novel much as Hans Castorp would ten years later. How any of these texts could be read as expressions of a normative ideal remains a mystery.

Critics first noticed these contradictions in the 1970s, and Jeffrey L. Sammons launched a methodical attack against the genre in his 1981 article "The Mystery of the Missing *Bildungsroman*."[29] Although Sammons's observations have done little to halt actual usage of the term, they have at least forced subsequent critics to defend their faith in the novel of formation as an organizing category. In such defenses, Sammons is sometimes chastised for his "conservative generic formalism" or his "typological" inclinations.[30] A more productive response, however, is offered by Jed Esty, who points out: "The concept of *Bildung* has shaped literary criticism and practice for generations—a fact not altered by its nonfulfillment in any given text. Indeed, genres are almost always empty sets that shape literary history by their negation, deviation, variation, and mutation. Such deviations can themselves be tracked, grouped, and historicized."[31] This is undoubtedly true; the most interesting thing about the *Bildungsroman*, however, is that the fact of its "nonfulfillment" isn't merely accidental to, but rather constitutive of, the critical tradition that it has spawned. This was first made explicit by Marc Redfield (to whom Esty responds in the quotation above), who argued that the critical desire to uncover plenitude and wholeness at the end of developmental narratives was constitutive of "aesthetic ideology."[32] Redfield calls the *Bildungsroman* a "phantom formation," and indeed the form has taken on a ghostly afterlife in many subsequent studies, especially those that share Redfield's poststructuralist orientation. For Pheng Cheah, the organicist

---

29. Jeffrey L. Sammons, "The Mystery of the Missing *Bildungsroman*, or: What Happened to Wilhelm Meister's Legacy?" *Genre* 14:1 (1981): 229–46. See also Jeffrey L. Sammons, "The Bildungsroman for Nonspecialists: An Attempt at a Clarification," in *Reflection and Action: Essays on the Bildungsroman*, ed. James N. Hardin (Columbia: University of South Carolina Press, 1991), 26–45. For earlier work on the same topic, see Jürgen Jacobs, *Wilhelm Meister und seine Brüder: Untersuchungen zum deutschen Bildungsroman* (Munich: Fink, 1972), which speaks of the *Bildungsroman* as an "unfulfilled genre."
30. I take the first phrase from Gregory Castle, *Reading the Modernist Bildungsroman* (Gainesville: University Press of Florida, 2006), 13, and the second from Slaughter, *Human Rights Inc.*, 7.
31. Esty, *Unseasonable Youth*, 18.
32. Redfield, *Phantom Formations*, viii.

notion of the nation as a self-enclosed totality is a "specter" that "haunts" postcolonial discourses of liberation.[33] For Joseph R. Slaughter, the subject of human rights law remains a *"persona ficta."*[34] Michael Beddow similarly speaks of the "fiction" of humanity. And Esty's own account of colonial development draws exclusively on novels in which the protagonists fail to develop in a regular pattern.

Throughout the history of criticism, there have always been attempts to approach the *Bildungsroman* as a merely "taxonomic" category, that is, to separate it from the underlying philosophical discourse altogether and reclassify it as simply a kind of novel focused on the acculturation of a central protagonist.[35] Left unexamined, however, is the question of whether it might not also be possible to arrive at a more satisfactory understanding of the novel of formation if one starts out with a different set of premises about *Bildung*. For instance, Thomas Pfau has pointed out that the obsession with "ends and endings" in much *Bildungsroman* criticism really rests on a historical misunderstanding, an instrumentalization of the notion of teleology that came about only in the late nineteenth century. The organicist and dialectical thought of the late eighteenth and early nineteenth centuries, Pfau notes, instead "grasps narrative as an open-ended, variational sequence of so many 'positions,' 'states,' or 'moments.'"[36] I will provide my own revisionist history of *Bildung* in the next chapter; here, I want to focus instead on the methodological, rather than historical, foundations on which a comprehensive critique of *Bildung* as a totalizing and teleological mode of thinking might be built.

A natural starting point for such a critique is the so-called expressionism debate of the 1930s, in which Marxist philosophers and critics such as Ernst Bloch, Bertolt Brecht, and Walter Benjamin turned against Lukács and denounced his excessive dependency on the intellectual legacy of German idealism. Ernst Bloch was especially forthright, arguing: "Lukács's thought takes for granted a closed and integrated reality that does indeed exclude the subjectivity of Idealism, but not the seamless 'totality' which has always thriven best in idealist systems, including those of classical German philosophy. Whether such a totality in fact constitutes reality, is open to question.... What if authentic reality is also discontinuity?"[37] Bloch had already presented a Marxist theory of discontinuous reality in his *Heritage of Our*

---

33. Cheah, *Spectral Nationality*, 269–80.
34. Slaughter, *Human Rights, Inc.*, 19.
35. The merits and pitfalls of such an approach are discussed in Martin Swales, *The German Bildungsroman from Wieland to Hesse* (Princeton, NJ: Princeton University Press, 1978). For a highly original attempt to detach novels of formation from the discourse of *Bildung*, see Michael Minden, *The German Bildungsroman: Incest and Inheritance* (Cambridge: Cambridge University Press, 1997), which rejects traditional notions of *Bildung* because of their linearity, arguing that the form of eight canonical German novels of formation is actually circular, and marked by the desire for a return to origins.
36. Thomas Pfau, "Of Ends and Endings: Teleological and Variational Models of Romantic Narrative," *European Romantic Review* 18:2 (April 2007): 237.
37. Ernst Bloch, "Discussing Expressionism," in *Aesthetics and Politics*, ed. Ronald Taylor (London: Verso, 1980), 22.

Times, published in 1934. In this book, he utilized the concept of the "synchronicity of the non-synchronous" (*Gleichzeitigkeit des Ungleichzeitigen*)—the notion that different historical strata that would be expected to follow on one another in a strictly teleological model of modernity actually coexist with one another in time.[38] Marxist theory had gone wrong, Bloch insisted, in viewing contemporary Germany as simply an industrialized nation in the late phase of monopoly capitalism. In reality, the nation was deeply divided between urban industrial and rural agrarian tendencies. And while modernization in Germany had created a proletarian underclass congruent to the one predicted by Marx and Engels, it had done little to touch the middle classes, the nobility, or the peasantry, which were essentially still locked in a feudal ideology. It was fascism, not communism, so Bloch realized, that had learned to utilize these historical nonsynchronicities and exploit them for its ascent to power.

Bloch's model of nonsynchronicity brings to mind Karl Morgenstern, the man who invented the term *Bildungsroman* from an intellectual vantage point that quite literally placed him "out of time." Morgenstern had left Halle, one of the centers of European intellectual life, in 1798, and thus at the very moment when the vocabulary and ideology of German idealism were falling into place. His views of both *Bildung* and the novel were conditioned by the eighteenth century, especially the aesthetic theory of Friedrich von Blanckenburg, and his definition of the new genre displays an obvious debt to his training as a rhetorician: "We may call a novel a *Bildungsroman* first and foremost on account of its content, because it represents the development of the hero in its beginning and progress to a certain stage of completion, but also, second, because this depiction promotes the development of the reader to a greater extent than any other kind of novel."[39] Interestingly, Morgenstern speaks only of progress "to a certain stage of completion," without making any appeal to totality or finality. *Bildung* for him is exactly what Pfau also claims it is, a "variational sequence" of different states or moments, and not yet the operative logic for the revelation of "world spirit," "humanity," or any other similarly grand concept.

Morgenstern's thesis that any *Bildungsroman* should further the development of the reader also puts him at odds with the literary theories of his own time and reveals his roots in the rhetorical tradition of the eighteenth century.[40] It is impossible

---

38. Bloch's speculations on nonsynchronism have been translated into English as Ernst Bloch, "Non-Synchronism and the Obligation to Its Dialectics," trans. Mark Ritter, *New German Critique* 11 (Spring 1977): 22–38. The idea of a "synchronicity of the non-synchronous" was first formulated by the art historian Wilhelm Pinder a few years before Bloch popularized the term. See Frederic J. Schwartz, "Ernst Bloch and Wilhelm Pinder: Out of Sync," *Grey Room* 3 (Spring 2001): 54–89.

39. Karl Morgenstern, "On the Nature of the *Bildungsroman*," trans. Tobias Boes, *PMLA* 124 (2009): 654. All further references to this work will appear in parentheses in the text.

40. For a longer explication of this aspect of Morgenstern's theory, see Dennis Mahoney, "The Apprenticeship of the Reader: The *Bildungsroman* of the 'Age of Goethe,'" in *Reflection and Action: Essays on the Bildungsroman*, ed. James Hardin (Columbia: University of South Carolina Press, 1991), 97–117.

not to wonder, however, whether this unusual demand does not also reflect Morgenstern's peculiar situation as an expatriate intellectual, lecturing on the most important German novel of his time to a transnational audience in Dorpat that self-identified as German but owed political allegiance to the tsar of Russia. After all, Morgenstern's very task in Russia was to "promote the development" of his listeners by introducing them to (what he understood to be) the most advanced intellectual currents flowing out of central Europe. This context is also important to keep in mind when one tries to evaluate Morgenstern's claim that *Wilhelm Meister* presents "German life, German thought and the morals of our time through its hero, its scenery and environment" (655). Juxtaposed with the earlier definition of the *Bildungsroman*, this sentence reveals Morgenstern at his contradictory and asynchronous best: a cosmopolitan product of the eighteenth century who is nevertheless enkindled by the romantic nationalism of his own time.

Morgenstern's theory of the relationship between literature and nationalism is completely different from the one postulated by German idealism. For him, "the nation" isn't some sort of essential ground, as it is for Johann Gottlieb Fichte or Wilhelm von Humboldt, nor is the *Bildungsroman* an allegorical genre in which the struggles of the hero are but "signs" for an underlying "symbolic form." Morgenstern instead understands nationalism as a kind of performance, and his theory of the novel can therefore be called "performative" rather than "normative." Rather than *revealing* it at the end of its plot, the novel of formation *produces* a national form by means of its mimetic capacities as well as its direct rhetorical address to the reader. As such, the most important aspect of the genre is that it takes place in and through time, not that it aspires to take the reader outside of time by means of its totalizing conclusion: "I just now called *Wilhelm Meister's Apprenticeship* a model of its kind, from our time and for our time. But Chronos marches quickly, leaving ruins behind and gazing toward new edifices that rise up before him. How much has changed in Germany and in the rest of Europe during the twenty-five years that have passed since the publication of the *Apprenticeship*!" (658). In the last paragraph of his lecture, Morgenstern exhorts his readers to turn away from *Wilhelm Meister*, the product of a time that has already passed, and instead turn to the "many other marvelous trees with beautiful flowers and ripe fruits [that] flourish in the infinitely large garden of novel writing" (659). Perhaps, the implied claim seems to be, some of these new novels will even be written by members of his audience.

Once we decenter German novel theory by taking Dorpat, rather than Weimar, Jena, or Berlin, as its natural starting point, it becomes possible to write a completely new genealogy of *Bildungsroman* criticism. Thus we find Novalis, in a letter to his friend Caroline Schlegel dated February 27, 1799, confessing his ardent desire "to devote my whole life to a novel that ... would perhaps contain the apprentice years of a nation."[41] In this description, the nation itself undergoes the apprenticeship

---

41. Quoted in Rüdiger Safranski, *Romantik: Eine deutsche Affäre* (Munich: Hanser, 2007), 111.

rather than being revealed at the end of it; national form thus submits to the turbulences of history. And in 1833, Wilhelm Mundt, one of the leading minds of the "Young Germany" movement, praised Goethe's ability to harmoniously combine Meister's individual development with the broader tapestry of a developing national consciousness. He simultaneously warns of approaches to the *Bildungsroman* that postulate "an entire world knotted up in the actions and personality of a single creative individual."[42]

The critic who comes closest to articulating a comprehensive modern theory of the novel of formation that improves upon themes also present in Morgenstern is Mikhail Bakhtin, who describes the genre as one in which "[man] emerges along with the world and . . . reflects the historical emergence of the world itself." Somewhat more cryptically, Bakhtin further argues that "the image of the emerging man begins to surmount its private nature (within certain limits, of course) and enters into a completely new, *spatial* sphere of historical existence."[43] The idea that "historical existence" might somehow acquire a spatial form is reminiscent of Benedict Anderson's famous analysis, in his *Imagined Communities*, of novels by José Rizal and José Joaquín Fernandez de Lizardi. Anderson focuses on the ability of literary works to synchronize spatially diverse events by "[fusing] the world inside the novel with the world outside."[44] On his account, a reader reads a novel, recognizes the formal unity of the world depicted therein, and moves on from this to the secondary recognition of a corresponding unity in the real world, which is depicted with such stunning likeness in the literary text. Henceforth, historical events are understood to contribute to a geographically shared destiny—a "spatial sphere" that for Anderson coincides neatly with that of the classical nation-state.

Indeed, Bakhtin soon puts forth the claim that the *Bildungsroman* constructs "an image of *man growing* in *national-historical time*" (25, emphasis in original). Here, however, he enters dangerous ground. Bakhtin's analysis of Goethe's works in the remaining thirty pages of the essay (the rest of the book-length manuscript was destroyed during the Second World War) is largely confined to extracts from the *Italian Journey* (1817, but describing a journey that took place from 1786 to 1788). Neither Germany nor Italy, however, was a functioning nation-state in the late eighteenth century, and it is important to keep this in mind when reading Bakhtin's analysis of the following passage from Goethe:

---

42. Quoted in Hartmut Steinecke, "Die 'Zeitgemässe' Gattung: Neubewertung und Neubestimmung des Romans in der jungdeutschen Kritik," in *Untersuchungen zur Literatur als Geschichte*, ed. Vincent J. Günther (Berlin: Erich Schmidt Verlag, 1973), 332–33.
43. Mikhail Bakhtin, "The *Bildungsroman* and Its Significance in the History of Realism," in *Speech Genres and Other Late Essays*, trans. Vern W. McGee and ed. Caryl Emerson and Michael Holquist (Austin: University of Texas Press, 1986), 24 (emphasis in original). All further references to this work appear in parentheses in the text.
44. Benedict Anderson, *Imagined Communities: Reflections on the Origin and Spread of Nationalism* (London: Verso, 1983), 30.

> We Cimmerians hardly know the real meaning of day. With our perpetual fogs and cloudy skies we do not care if it is day or night, since we are so little given to take walks and enjoy ourselves out of doors. But here, when night falls, the day consisting of evening and morning is definitely over, twenty-four hours have been spent, and time begins afresh. The bells ring, the rosary is said, the maid enters the room with a lighted lamp and says: "*Felicissima notte!*" This period of time varies in length according to season, and people who live here are so full of vitality that this does not confuse them, because the pleasures of their existence are related not to the precise hour, but to the time of day. If one were to force a German clock hand on them, they would be at a loss, for their own method of time measurement is closely bound up with their nature. (31)

Bakhtin is correct when he claims that this passage illustrates Goethe's fascination with the incongruities between "organic" time (rooted in cyclical practices, such as pealing church bells and circadian prayers) and abstract "historical" time (confirmed only by clock hands and calendars). But things get more complicated when he identifies the transition from organic to historical time with the rise of a national identity ("a German clock hand"). In fact, there *was* no national German time in 1786, and it would not be until 1893 that such a uniform time would be created. Before that, there were many German clocks that measured abstract historical time, but each ticked to a beat dictated by the will of the local potentate.

Because of their ability to synchronize collective experience, clocks and calendars certainly play an important part in the performative creation of national consciousness. But before they can assume this function, state power must first impose them on the people, and in Germany, nation and state would not overlap with one another until much later in the century. Nationalism, precisely because it is a product of the imagination rather than of reason (and thus of the same inchoate forces that Bloch understood to contradict the totalizing logic of Lukácsian Marxism), is inherently asynchronous. The enthusiasm with which Morgenstern put eighteenth-century aesthetics into the service of nineteenth-century nationalism is evidence of this; as, for that matter, is one of the more famous quotations from Goethe, a couplet that he wrote for the 1797 *Xenias*, published jointly with Schiller:

> Germany? But where is that? I don't know how to find the country.
> Where the learned one begins, the political one ends.
>
> Deutschland? Aber wo liegt es? Ich weiss das Land nicht zu finden.
> Wo das gelehrte beginnt, hört das politische auf.[45]

---

45. Johann Wolfgang von Goethe, *Xenien und Votivtaveln*, in *Werke: Weimarer Ausgabe*, vol. I/5.1, *Gedichte, Fünfter Theil, Erste Abtheilung* (Weimar: Böhlau, 1893), 218.

These lines are sometimes read as a document of Goethe's fundamentally antinational outlook, but a closer reading reveals that what the poet is attacking is not so much the idea of nationhood, as the assumption that state and nation need invariably be coextensive: both the political and the "learned" (i.e., cultural) Germany exist for Goethe; they merely occupy different places.

The hero's emergence into "national-historical time"—a performative process that takes place both within the mimetic confines of the novel and outside of them, in the sense that *Bildungsromane* strive to create a national form in the minds of their readers—thus has to be strictly separated from state power. Indeed, the very reference to a "nation" may be out of place here, for as Ernest Gellner reminds us, nations are inherently instable concepts that necessarily strive for completion in the hyphenated identity of the "nation-state": "Not only is our definition of nationalism parasitic on a prior and assumed definition of the state: it also seems to be the case that nationalism emerges only in milieux in which the existence of the state is already very much taken for granted."[46] Nations, in other words, contain within their very fabric a desire for teleology, totality, and normativity, qualities that, as we have already seen, are difficult to adduce in actual *Bildungsromane*. A more supple concept is needed, one that does justice to the often asynchronous nature of literature.

Vernacular Cosmopolitanism and the Compromises of World Literature

Cosmopolitanism is commonly yet erroneously understood to imply the opposite of nationalism, an intellectual and emotional commitment to a deracinated existence outside the fold of any particular ethnic or cultural community. Understood in this commonsensical fashion, furthermore, cosmopolitanism is inherently a totalizing discourse. After all, there can be only one worldwide community of human beings, one cosmos, of which an individual might be a citizen. Recently, theorists of cosmopolitanism have turned against such a reading, however. As Pheng Cheah has pointed out, the philosophical cornerstone of all modern cosmopolitan theory, Immanuel Kant's "An Idea towards a Universal History in a Cosmopolitan Sense," was written in 1784, at a time when the spirit of nationalism had yet to enkindle the European imagination. The proper antonym of "cosmopolitanism" is "statism," rather than "nationalism," and Kant was writing primarily against the European political order that had been laid down in the Treaty of Westphalia 140 years earlier.[47] He was, in other words, arguing for a universal federal state (*allgemeiner*

---

46. Ernest Gellner, *Nations and Nationalism* (Ithaca, NY: Cornell University Press, 1983), 4.
47. Pheng Cheah, "Introduction Part II: The Cosmopolitical–Today," in *Cosmopolitics: Thinking and Feeling beyond the Nation*, ed. Pheng Cheah and Bruce Robbins (Minneapolis: University of Minnesota Press, 1998), 23.

Völkerstaat) that would take the business of adjudicating interstate relationships out of the hands of individual sovereigns.

The idea that cosmopolitanism is a universalizing discourse presents more substantial challenges. No doubt Kant approached it as such. More recently, however, as cosmopolitanism has become a topic in anthropology, sociology, and even literary studies, the definition has shifted. Current theories of cosmopolitanism tend to focus no longer on "the world" in its planetary sense, but rather on "worlds" in the plural—on shifting spaces (both actual and conceptual) that cut across national borders and provide a home to the cosmopolitan individual.[48] On this account, road warrior business travelers who navigate the halls of Schiphol and Narita airports with equal ease are cosmopolitans, as are (at least potentially) the participants in global social networks such as Facebook or Twitter. The Iranian protesters who used these social networking sites to dispute the outcome of the 2009 presidential election in their country were thus performing a cosmopolitan intervention in the newer sense of the term—an intervention that draws on technological resources beyond the reach of official Iranian state apparatuses but that is nevertheless (and contrary to the claims of neoconservative talking heads) meant as an affirmation of a specific national identity, rather than as an expression of a humanitarian universalism.

No commonly agreed-on name exists as yet that would distinguish this new multifaceted understanding of cosmopolitanism from the old universalizing kind. Rebecca Walkowitz, working from within literary studies, has proposed the term "critical cosmopolitanism," an appellation derived partially from Max Horkheimer's distinction between traditional and critical social theory.[49] The cultural anthropologist James Clifford, attempting to distance himself from the "overly global vision of a capitalist or technocratic monoculture," has invoked the term "discrepant cosmopolitanisms" to describe "cultures of displacement and transplantation" that are "inseparable from specific, often violent, histories of economic, political, and cultural interaction."[50] Both of these contributions have shaped my own attempts to come to terms with cosmopolitanism, but the cultural formations that I am describing are neither inevitably the result of displacement and transplantation, nor can they always be said to be critically self-reflective. I have therefore found the greatest value in Homi K. Bhabha's methodological sketches for the study of what he terms "vernacular cosmopolitanism."

---

48. As Kwame Anthony Appiah argues, cosmopolitanism thus "begins with the simple idea that in the human community, as in national communities, we need to develop habits of coexistence." See Kwame Anthony Appiah, *Cosmopolitanism: Ethics in a World of Strangers* (New York: Norton, 2006), xix.

49. Rebecca Walkowitz, *Cosmopolitan Style: Modernism beyond the Nation* (New York: Columbia University Press, 2008), 3.

50. James Clifford, *Routes: Travel and Translation in the Twentieth Century* (Cambridge, MA: Harvard University Press, 1997), 36.

The phrase "vernacular cosmopolitanism" may well seem like a contradiction in terms, and indeed some theorists have identified the "vernacular" as the opposite of the "cosmopolitan."[51] After the fall of the Western Roman Empire, for instance, the cosmopolitan Latin tongue splintered into many vernacular dialects that eventually became the present-day Romance languages. If such an opposition exists, however, it is surely a dialectical one. Consider Martin Luther's translation of the Bible from cosmopolitan Greek into the German vernacular. The resulting text elevated Luther's North German dialect to "standard" German and would eventually go on to play an important role in the formation of a national consciousness. More immediately, however, it also created a new sense of "protestant cosmopolitanism"—a common identity that cut across the hundreds of sovereign principalities grouped together in the Holy Roman Empire, in most of which people spoke variants of German that were rather different from that found in Luther's Bible. For present purposes, then, "the vernacular" is best understood as a system that arises from the day-to-day practices of ordinary peoples, rather than being imposed from above. If language, as the old aphorism holds, is "a dialect plus an army and a navy," and thus represents an intervention of state power through dictionaries, academies, and credentialed experts, then the term "vernacular" encompasses all those forms of expression that flourish in opposition to the normative linguistic rules. Not only do languages never entirely contain preexisting vernaculars; they also breed new vernaculars that frequently cut across state borders and thus become cosmopolitan.

Bhabha's inquiries proceed from a marked dissatisfaction with what he calls the "rhetoric of continuance and inheritance in which the articulation of past and present is affected [and which] Walter Benjamin describes as the historicist (not *historical*) causality represented in a 'sequence of events like the beads of a rosary'—an essentially additive process of 'events' enacted in a homogeneous empty time."[52] Benedict Anderson has shown that precisely this model of historical causality is an indispensable prerequisite of modern nationhood. Against this additive and sequential understanding of history, Bhabha pits an approach to time that is based on quotidian habit and thereby emphasizes the "iterative structuring of the historical event and [of] political pedagogy" (40). Historical time, he reminds us, does not merely flow sequentially from the future into the past; it also possesses an asynchronous character derived from the many inherited rituals that structure everyday existence. Bhabha concludes: "National consciousness, which is not nationalism, is the only thing that will give us an international dimension" (40). Cosmopolitanism,

---

51. Alexander Beecroft, "World Literature without a Hyphen: Towards a Typology of Literary Systems," *New Left Review* 54 (2008): 96.

52. Homi K. Bhabha, "Unsatisfied: Notes on Vernacular Cosmopolitanism," in *Postcolonial Discourses: An Anthology*, ed. Gregory Castle (Oxford: Blackwell, 2001), 39. All further references to this work will appear in parentheses in the text. The quote about historicist causality as a "sequence of events like the beads of a rosary" is taken from Walter Benjamin's "Theses on the Philosophy of History," in *Illuminations*, trans. Harry Zohn and ed. Hannah Arendt (New York: Schocken, 1968), 264.

on this account, is much more than an abstract exercise in intellectual deracination. Instead, it involves the ability to leave behind a merely sequential model of history and forge links between the vernacular realities of different peoples—their "thick" sense of time with all its contradictory rituals and practices.[53]

The *Bildungsroman* presents an especially interesting example on which to test Bhabha's theory of vernacular cosmopolitanism, because, as I will show in greater detail in the next chapter, the genre arose in the eighteenth century as a narrative response to precisely the kind of historicist logic that Bhabha is here attacking. Novels of formation differ from previous realist novels primarily in the way in which they give a poetic shape to a world that is newly felt to be in flux, and in which events succeed one another in empty homogeneous time. To do this, the *Bildungsroman* pioneered a wealth of literary techniques whose startling variety is ignored in many studies that focus exclusively on the linear and forward-moving dimensions of the protagonist's development. Such approaches overlook that the narrative logic of *Bildung* is organic rather than mechanical in nature, which means among other things that experiences and insights from early points in the hero's life tend to resurface in modified shapes at later stages of the formative process. Historical time in the *Bildungsroman* thus acquires an iterative as well as a sequential character, and the resulting asynchronicities undermine simplistic narratives about national consciousness and its putative quest for closure in the normative ideal of the nation-state.

Bruce Robbins puts it best when he points out that the word "'cosmos' (world) in 'cosmopolitan' originally meant simply 'order' or 'adornment'—as in cosmetics—and was only later extended metaphorically to refer to 'the world'. Cosmetics preceded totality."[54] All too often, studies of the novel of formation lose sight of the "cosmetic" dimensions of their chosen texts as they attempt to elucidate the totalizing logic that underlies the hero's development. If, on the other hand, *Bildungsromane* become *Bildungsromane* precisely because of the performative work that they do (i.e., because they surround their protagonists with a compelling world and invite the reader to participate in the interplay between the two as both hero and world respond to changes in historical time), then the seemingly random and repetitive elements of those novels acquire a central interest. Indeed, developmental dynamics that had seemed to indicate failure when looked at from a purely teleological perspective can now be seen as successful responses to internally

---

53. Bhabha's cosmopolitan project owes an unmistakable debt to Ernst Bloch in addition to Walter Benjamin. As Bloch argued in *Heritage of Our Times*, "History is not an essence advancing linearly, but is rather a polyrhythmic and multi-spatial entity with enough unmastered and as yet by no means revealed and resolved corners." See Ernst Bloch, *Heritage of Our Times*, trans. Neville Plaice and Stephen Plaice (Berkeley: University of California Press, 1990), 62. I here adopt the translation by Schwartz, "Ernst Bloch and Wilhelm Pinder," 65.

54. Bruce Robbins, *Secular Vocations: Intellectuals, Professionalism, Culture* (New York: Verso, 1993), 188.

contradictory imaginative worlds. A powerful example of this is Julien Sorel's death on the guillotine at the end of *The Red and the Black*, which concludes no less than three historically asynchronous narratives: Julien's understanding of himself as a post-Napoleonic renegade, the Marquis de la Mole's conception of him as an eighteenth-century Jacobin, and Mathilde's gothic reveries, in which she imagines Julien as the reincarnation of her sixteenth-century ancestor.

Cosmopolitan readings of the kind that I have just described have methodological implications that reach far outside the admittedly rarified realm of *Bildungsroman* studies. Previous approaches to the novel of formation can, as I have suggested, largely be separated into "essentialist" and "universalist" camps, a division that neatly parallels current debates between adherents of "national" and "world" literature traditions within contemporary criticism. Defenders of national literatures as the principal organizing categories of both academic life and intellectual inquiry rightly point out that the responsible study of foreign texts requires a prior immersion in the historical, sociological, and formal particulars that give these artifacts meaning. Proponents of world literature, on the other hand, generally tend to dismiss national traditions in their search for more general connections among texts. Almost invariably, this method is justified with a quotation from Goethe, taken from the 1827 *Conversations with Eckermann*: "I am more and more convinced that poetry is the universal possession of mankind, revealing itself everywhere and at all times in hundreds and hundreds of men. . . . National literature is now a rather unmeaning term; the epoch of world literature is at hand, and everyone must strive to hasten its approach."[55]

Neither of these two methods of studying literature is without its problems. National literature scholars have traditionally been able to draw resources from foreign language and area studies departments, which were able to attract both adequate funding and broad student interest during the time of the Cold War. The spread of "global English" over the last twenty years, however, combined with a more general attack on the humanities in the wake of the 2008 recession, has left many of these departments struggling for financial support, tenure lines, and student enrollment. Increasingly, scholars of national literatures find themselves integrated into departments of modern languages, which cannot possibly offer either students or researchers the same thematic and diachronic breadth that characterized the older structures. Scholars of world literature, on the other hand, are ideally placed to benefit from these institutional changes, both because their training makes them highly adaptable to the new interdisciplinary environments, and because they can actively collaborate with colleagues from a wide variety of subject backgrounds. Their problem is a different one. The nagging question remains

---

55. Johann Wolfgang von Goethe, *Conversations with Eckermann (1823–1832)*, trans. John Oxenford (San Francisco: North Point, 1984), 132.

whether world literature, in its search for common denominators between texts from radically different historical or cultural traditions, doesn't actually serve as a mask for ideological positions that the academy has yet to submit to a fully adequate critique. Wai Chee Dimock's suggestion that literary works are best viewed across "deep time," for instance, bears a remarkable resemblance to Philippe de Montebello's argument that Western encyclopedic museums (like the Metropolitan Museum of Art, in New York, which he directed from 1977 to 2008) are better stewards of antiquities than some of the nation-states that are now besieging them with repatriation claims: "All great works of art have, in addition to their historical and other learned contexts, an aesthetic context as well. Which is why an appreciation of the aesthetic quality of works of art is . . . most likely to be the primary and most exalted feature in the confrontation of the visitor with the work of art."[56] Within the art market, the legal tussles that sparked this comment have led to penetrating inquiries into the ideological functions served by large art museums, which often depend heavily on corporate sponsorship and (despite their stated missions of inclusiveness) usually attract very homogeneous audiences. World literature textbooks serve ideological purposes as well, and while these certainly include such laudable endeavors as increased intercultural communication, their ultimate impact remains far from certain.

In this context, it is useful to remember that Goethe's version of world literature, viewed in its proper context, is not the swan song of nationalism that some comparatists have taken it to represent. The age of nationalism, after all, had barely begun in Germany in 1827. What Goethe instead seems to mean by *Weltliteratur* is an approach to literature from a cosmopolitan perspective, that is, one that is decoupled from state institutions and from the influence that they attempt to exert on the public sphere. (It may be worth pointing out at this point that the German word for "cosmopolitan" is *Weltbürger*; it seems only natural that such a citizen of the world would find *Weltliteratur* an appropriate field of interest.) *Conversations with Eckermann* was published in an age in which a proliferating number of customs unions sought to govern interstate commerce in Germany. The ostensible purpose of these unions was economic in nature, but they always served a political function as well, repressing the circulation of unwelcome ideas. Goethe's project is directed against such repressive state power. Epistolary exchanges as well as philological training allow his ideal reader to remain connected to the corners of the world and to find intellectual fulfillment in wider regions than would be possible in the German principalities alone.

An utterly original approach to world literature, one that detaches it from its frequent universalizing implications, is spelled out by Franco Moretti in his essay

---

56. Philippe de Montebello, "'And What Do You Propose Should Be Done with Those Objects?'" in *Whose Culture Is It? The Promise of Museums and the Debate over Antiquities*, ed. James Cuno (Princeton, NJ: Princeton University Press, 2009), 65. The Dimock quote is taken from Wai Chee Dimock, "Literature for the Planet," *PMLA* 116 (2001): 175.

"Conjectures on World Literature." There, Moretti advances a general theory of global literary diffusion that conceives of the relationship between form and content in literary works (and specifically in the novel) as one of constant and ever-repeated "compromise." Cultural export, Moretti insists, does not happen on the level of "works," but rather on the level of "forms," which then undergo an inevitable process of adaptation and transformation as they are forced to adjust to previously unforeseen social relations:

> For me, [the relationship between form and content is] more of a triangle: foreign form, local material—*and local form*. Simplifying somewhat: foreign *plot*; local *characters*; and then, local *narrative voice*: and it's precisely in this third dimension that these novels seem to be most unstable.... Which makes sense: the narrator is the pole of comment, of explanation, of evaluation, and when foreign "formal patterns" (or actual foreign presence, for that matter) make characters behave in strange ways..., then of course comment becomes uneasy—garrulous, erratic, rudderless.[57]

Moretti's conjectures have interesting implications for the study of the *Bildungsroman*, because the narrator of traditional novels of formation is frequently said to represent the very virtues that also characterize successful development: certainty, wholeness, and an ironic awareness of the protagonist's shortcomings. Oftentimes (as in *Jane Eyre*, *Great Expectations*, or *Green Henry*) the narrator is identical with the hero, and now looks back on past errors from a certain magnanimous distance. In other examples (such as *Wilhelm Meister's Apprenticeship* or Hermann Hesse's 1946 novel, *The Glass Bead Game*) he or she appears to be a benevolent scribe writing from within a perfect society or from a distant future. But on closer examination, this equation always breaks down: Jane, Pip, and Henry are all more or less broken individuals; both the Tower Society and Castalia have more than a hint of the totalitarian about them.

For Moretti, by contrast, the voice of the narrator is never a source of wholeness and completion. It represents, instead, a compromise formation, an attempt to smooth over the difficulties that arise when historically and geographically diverse local materials are forced to submit to inherited forms of emplotment. Narrative tension—and thus also interest and innovation—arises wherever these local materials in all their complexity and diversity resist assimilation to predetermined narrative schemata. The meeting of local content and abstract form, of empirical detail and aesthetic totality, thus results not in the subordination of one to the other ("the content of the *Bildungsroman* becomes the forming-of-content") but rather in a "metastable" third term that unites characteristics of both. The results are "garrulous, erratic, and rudderless" narrators: a description that could apply to a good

---

57. Franco Moretti, "Conjectures on World Literature," *New Left Review* 1 (2000): 65 (emphasis in original).

many nineteenth-century texts, including Stendhal's ironic authorial presence or the world-weary first-person report in *Green Henry*.

Moretti's conjectures provide a broad theoretical framework that helps explain the inadequacy of traditional approaches to the *Bildungsroman*, which define the genre through its teleological movement toward a revealed form. At the same time, they also explain why efforts to equate this revealed form with the bounded totality of the nation-state repeatedly fall flat when applied to actual texts. Indeed, literary innovation always happens as a "compromise" between national and transnational elements, between cultural forces that are rooted in particular environments and those that sweep across the globe ("trees" and "waves" in Moretti's parlance). The interplay between these two elements raises interesting questions for diachronic genre studies, questions that will also serve as a fitting conclusion to my exploration of the vexed relationship between critical traditions that take the "nation" and the "world" as their respective objects and arenas.

The *Genus* of Genre

A curious feature of many monographs on the history of the *Bildungsroman* is that their titles allude more or less openly to kinship structures among the texts they examine. Thus two classic studies of the genre are named *Wilhelm Meister and His English Kinsmen* and *Wilhelm Meister and His Brothers*. The latter has recently been joined by a long overdue study entitled *Wilhelm Meister's Sisters*. In a slightly different register, Jeffrey Sammons chooses not to italicize the name of Goethe's protagonist in the subtitle of his article "The Mystery of the Missing *Bildungsroman*, or: What Happened to Wilhelm Meister's Legacy?", thus suggesting that the metaphorical "legacy" he is talking about not only circulates among novels, but also passes from one fictional character to another. Michael Minden's *The German Bildungsroman: Incest and Inheritance*, finally, derives its subtitle from the two dynamics that Minden finds at work within the works he examines. Given Minden's blunt assertion that his book presents a "study of the German *Bildungsroman* as a series of variations on Goethe's *Wilhelm Meisters Lehrjahre*," however, it is hard not to conclude that "incest" and "inheritance" point to intertextual in addition to intratextual dynamics.[58] It is perhaps natural that authors who have spent years examining the features of individual lives in a series of novels would eventually come to regard the relationship between their case studies as that between members of an extended family. Nevertheless, I would like to suggest that this nomenclatorial eccentricity highlights an interesting feature of diachronic genre studies more generally, namely

---

58. Susanne Howe, *Wilhelm Meister and His English Kinsmen: Apprentices to Life* (New York: Columbia University Press, 1930); Anja May, *Wilhelm Meisters Schwestern: Bildungsromane von Frauen im ausgehenden 18. Jahrhundert* (Königstein im Taunus: Helmer, 2006). For the works by Jacobs and Sammons, see note 29 above. For the study by Minden, see note 35.

that their organizing metaphor frequently is that of genealogy. It is worth remembering in this context that the words "genre" and "genealogy" have common etymological roots in the Latin word *genus*, meaning not only "class" or "kind," but also "family" or "descent."

Genealogy, a subtype of the chronicle whose first appearance in Western historiography coincides with the rise of aristocratic lineages in France in the twelfth century, differs from modern historical narrative in a number of ways. Perhaps most important among these is that genealogies display an accretive structure, whereas modern historical narrative possesses an inductive one. Genealogies, in other words, create a larger sense of "history" out of the accumulation of individual events. Modern historians, by contrast, treat events as manifestations of larger causal structures. The surveys of the *Bildungsroman* that I have quoted above are "genealogical" in this sense because they attempt to write the history of a genre (or in Sammons's case, the history of the absence of such a genre) out of a cumulative series of case studies. Historicist genre surveys, on the other hand, read individual texts inductively as examples of broader trends, as Todd Kontje does in *Private Lives in the Public Sphere*, his study of the rise of the modern public sphere out of changes in bourgeois reading habits.

Explanatory structures based on the accretion of individual events are not the only characteristics of genealogical historiography, however. According to Gabrielle M. Spiegel, "There are two principal ways in which genealogy as a conceptual metaphor affected historical literature in thirteenth-century France: first, as form, by supplying a model for the disposition of narrative material . . .; second, as meaning, by reinterpreting historical events in accordance with the model of filiation suggested by genealogy."[59] Diachronic genre studies employ this conceptual metaphor in a similar fashion. On the level of form, genealogy allows literary historians to link texts by indexing a comparatively small number of common traits. Scholars group texts into genres in much the same way that a person invited to the wedding of a distant friend might try to make sense of a tangled network of family relationships: they look for telltale similarities, always cognizant that not all identifying characteristics might be present in every member of an extended clan, that recessive genes can surface in unexpected fashions, and that even the most tight-knit family will, over time, change almost beyond recognition as a result of exogamic marriages. On the level of meaning, genre studies rely on genealogical metaphors whenever they portray literary texts as though they were linked to one another through a chain of agnatic filiation. This chain is agnatic rather than enatic, paternal rather than maternal, because the study of literal influence is rarely an issue in modern literary scholarship. Few experts on the *Bildungsroman*, for instance, waste much ink on the question of whether Dickens or Flaubert had actually read

---

59. Gabrielle M. Spiegel, "Genealogy: Form and Function in Medieval Historical Narrative," *History and Theory* 22:1 (1983): 48.

Wilhelm Meister's Apprenticeship when they wrote their own novels of development, nor would the demonstrated absence of such a direct link between two texts count for very much. Instead, great texts are assumed to exert a palpable force on the literary field even in cases where their direct workings may be invisible—the influence is taken to exist even in cases where it cannot be traced by means of biographical research and genetic criticism. Harold Bloom's *The Anxiety of Influence* is by far the most famous example of the theory of agnatic filiation in literary studies.[60] The power of the genealogical metaphor, however, is felt even in those works that rebel directly against it. Sandra M. Gilbert and Susan Gubar, for instance, attack the perniciousness of the "metaphor of literary paternity" in their seminal book *The Madwoman in the Attic*.[61] Yet their title testifies to a lingering allegiance to the genealogical model of literary history; they write not to smash it altogether, but rather in an attempt to enrich it, to draw attention to those members of the family who, like Charlotte Brontë's Antoinette Mason, had hitherto been hidden from public scrutiny.

Historicist genre studies, by contrast, reject the notion of an organic formal relationship between individual texts, a fact that is illustrated by Fredric Jameson's dismissal of the *Bildungsroman* as a "'natural' form" in *The Political Unconscious*. Instead of promoting organic or genealogical metaphors, Jameson argues, genre criticism should aim to "[open] up a new space for the creative construction of experimental entities" and to "project . . . 'diachronic constructs' only the more surely to return to the synchronic historical situation in which such novels can be read as symbolic acts."[62] On the level of meaning, historicist genre studies similarly break with the metaphor of agnatic filiation, grouping texts not into kinship structures, but rather into what might be called "generic syndromes"—meaningful arrangements of individual examples that collectively point to an underlying dynamic. The strength of this syndromatic approach is its flexibility and (from the comparatist's perspective) its ability to transcend national boundaries. There is, of course, nothing that would inherently disqualify the genealogical model from traveling in this fashion, but just as kinship structures become more difficult to trace if they stray beyond borders, so the heuristic force of agnatic influence rapidly decreases in globalized cultural economies. It is one thing to claim that a certain nineteenth-century German poet was influenced by Goethe, and yet another to make that same argument for her British or French contemporary, or for contemporary postcolonial

---

60. Harold Bloom, *The Anxiety of Influence: A Theory of Poetry* (New York: Oxford University Press, 1973).

61. Sandra M. Gilbert and Susan Gubar, *The Madwoman in the Attic: The Woman Writer and the Nineteenth-Century Literary Imagination* (New Haven, CT: Yale University Press, 1979). See especially their opening chapter, "The Queen's Looking Glass: Female Creativity, Male Images of Women, and the Metaphor of Literary Paternity" (3–44).

62. Fredric Jameson, *The Political Unconscious: Narrative as a Socially Symbolic Act* (Ithaca, NY: Cornell University Press, 1981), 145.

writers. Even if such authors can be proven to have studied *Wilhelm Meister*, does such evidence really amount to much? Or do the cultural differences inevitably outweigh any similarities? Historicist genre studies are at an advantage here, or at least they are if they are written with broad enough brushstrokes. Precisely this is also their biggest danger, however, for they perennially open themselves to the charge of treating poetic works instrumentally, as mere symptoms of extraliterary dynamics.

I have dwelt on this comparison between two different models of genre studies at some length because it can be contrasted with a different and, I think, more productive model of the relationship between genealogy and history. I borrow this model from Arjun Appadurai, who defines the two terms in the following fashion:

> History leads you outward, to link patterns of changes to increasingly larger universes of interaction; genealogy leads you inward, toward cultural dispositions and styles that might be stubbornly embedded both in local institutions and in the history of the local habitus. Thus, the history of Mahatma Gandhi's ascetical relationship to the world of goods might lead outward to John Ruskin, Henry David Thoreau, and others in the West who articulated a pastoral, anti-industrial vision. But the genealogy of Gandhi's hostility to goods and possessive individualism generally leads inward, to a long-standing Indic discomfort with attachment to sensory experience at large.[63]

The appeal of Appadurai's approach is that he refuses to treat history and genealogy as dichotomous metaphors, as opposite ways of configuring the relationship between events and their historical "ground." Instead, the two become intertwined with one another, until every instance of cultural consumption (or, in our case, of literary production) comes to be understood in both local and global, genealogical and historical, contexts. In this, he offers an obvious parallel to Franco Moretti, whose "Conjectures on World Literature" postulates a similar fusion.

The three comparative studies that form the heart of this book were written as a direct response to the methodological challenges posed by Appadurai and Moretti. They focus on three German *Bildungsromane* chosen for the genealogical chains that connect them. First, each of these novels was written with obvious knowledge of, and to some extent as a response to, Goethe's *Wilhelm Meister's Apprenticeship*. Second, all of them comment consciously and explicitly on a developing national identity in Germany. At the same time, however, each of the chapters reaches synchronically outward, to other linguistic and cultural traditions. In this way, I hope to show how historical transformations on so vast a scale that they sweep through

---

63. Arjun Appadurai, *Modernity at Large: Cultural Dimensions of Globalization* (Minneapolis: University of Minnesota Press, 1996), 74.

all of Western Europe more or less simultaneously lead to new kinds of plots, new ways of conceptualizing "development," and how these new strategies, when they collide with the local materials provided by national traditions, result in profound changes to the performative work done by the *Bildungsroman*. The novel of formation, as I have claimed all along, strives to create a national form, and to involve the reader in a meaningful shared journey through historical time. The strategies used to create such national form, however, are, to use Franco Moretti's term, "metastable": they combine elements inherited from literary forebears with other elements invented as a response to contemporary transnational influences. The *Bildungsroman* thus inevitably also has a cosmopolitan character.

These three central studies are bookended by two further chapters that each focus on an individual novel in which the relationships between narrative and history, nationalism and cosmopolitanism, are submitted to explicit literary scrutiny. The first of these novels is *Wilhelm Meister* itself, and it is with Goethe's masterpiece that any revisionist reading of the *Bildungsroman* must begin, not in order to sketch out a new tradition of literary paternity, but in order to submit it more rigorously to the demands of history.

2

Apprenticeship of the Novel:
Goethe and the Invention of History

At the end of the seventh book of *Wilhelm Meister's Apprenticeship*, Goethe's protagonist, Wilhelm, finally gains access to the inner sanctuary of the Tower Society, the mysterious organization that has been clandestinely guiding his development. Inside the tower's padded walls, he discovers a complex bureaucratic surveillance apparatus: a vast collection of scrolls recording the story of his own life as well as that of many of the other characters whom he has encountered over the course of the novel. Biographies that meet the society's approval are matched with a second scroll containing a *Lehrbrief* (certificate of apprenticeship). The discovery of this archival repository sheds a new light on the almost manic impulse toward *auto*biographical writing that so clearly marks Goethe's characters. The numerous letters, confessions, and late-night conversations through which Wilhelm and his companions expose their lives to one another's scrutiny are revealed as an indirect product of the society's disciplining influence. In both outward appearance and function, the tower thus emerges as a perfect mirror of the Benthamite Panopticon, the structure that Michel Foucault identified as an architectural metaphor for the creation of modern subjectivity through the internalization of discursive power.[1]

---

1. See Michel Foucault, *Discipline & Punish: The Birth of the Prison* (New York: Vintage, 1977), 195–230.

But an important organizational difference distinguishes the Tower Society's archive from the way in which the autobiographical reminiscences are arranged throughout the rest of Goethe's novel. The relationship between Wilhelm's *Bildung* and the numerous autobiographical insets that interrupt it can perhaps best be described as one of narrative hypotaxis: the insets are subordinated in both form and content to the overriding imperative of the protagonist's socialization and self-discovery. Even the "Confessions of a Beautiful Soul"—a functionally complete novella embedded within the novel—serves the ultimate purpose of advancing Wilhelm's development. The Tower archive, on the other hand, reorganizes these narratives into a paratactic system: "To his amazement [Wilhelm] found there Lothario's apprenticeship, Jarno's apprenticeship, and his own, in amongst many others with names unknown to him."[2] Previously subordinate characters are thus given scrolls of their own in the society library and possess *Lehrjahre* that are outwardly indistinguishable from his. The very barrenness of the initiation chamber already indicates its multifunctionality. Other characters have previously passed through it, and yet others will follow after Wilhelm.

The induction ceremony stages the creation of an imagined community of fellow travelers through time in the most dramatic way possible. Wilhelm enters into the tower as a self-centered individual; he leaves it with the recognition that there are many other people just like him, each grasping toward their own sense of personal fulfillment in a confusing and overwhelming world. And yet he also recognizes (by means of his certificate of apprenticeship as well as by the sudden revelation of the numerous interventions that the society undertook in his earlier life) that all of these people are united by a common providential power, and that they do not stagger through the mists of time at random.

Closely aligned with this emerging communal allegory is an important structural change in Goethe's novel. Much of *Wilhelm Meister* is written in a style that is typical for the eighteenth-century novel: its many inset stories fill in crucial details that have previously been occluded (such as Barbara's revelation that Mariane remained faithful to Wilhelm), or provide models that can either inspire (Therese's biography) or repulse the protagonist (Werner's encomia to the life of a merchant). Goethe even includes a lengthy theoretical excursus (the Hamlet discussion in the fifth book), in which he demonstrates how foreign biographies might productively be exploited for life lessons. The organizational structure of the Tower archive, on the other hand, suggests that individual stories should be approached not as allegorical depictions of specific virtues and vices, but as so many different reactions to general tendencies that express themselves in every single life. Wilhelm's entry

---

2. Johann Wolfgang von Goethe, *Collected Works*, ed. Victor Lange, Eric A. Blackall, and Cyrus Hamlin, vol. 9, *Wilhelm Meister's Apprenticeship*, ed. and trans. Eric A. Blackall in cooperation with Victor Lange (New York: Suhrkamp, 1989), 217. Further references to this edition will appear in parentheses in the text.

into the tower might thus be said to signal the end not only of his own apprenticeship, but also of that of the novel: a rite of passage by which the novel assumes the mature form that will characterize it throughout the nineteenth and for much of the twentieth century.[3] This process (only hinted at in *Wilhelm Meister*) by which a character leaves behind the merely structural functions that he or she performs in one narrative and acquires an independent existence as the protagonist of another would later find its fullest expression in Honoré de Balzac's *Human Comedy*—that vast repository of stories through which, as Oscar Wilde once quipped, the nineteenth century was invented.[4]

In the following pages, I will argue that this structural change from a hypotactic to a paratactic organizing principle in Goethe's narrative is an expression of the logic of historicism that gained ground in Germany during the outgoing eighteenth century. Historicism, in turn, would have a crucial influence not only on the form of the *Bildungsroman* tradition, but also on the national imagination, and indeed *Wilhelm Meister's Apprenticeship* can be read as a first tentative expression of the national dynamic. At the same time, however, there are elements within Goethe's text that resist assimilation toward either historicism or nationalism. The induction ceremony itself already offers an example of such an element. The performative elements that the Tower Society employs therein are of such an overtly spectacular character that the attentive reader will immediately be reminded of the novel's earlier rejection of theatrical illusion (*Schein*) for authentic being (*Sein*). There is a touch of irony and of Blochian "non-synchronicity" in this attempt by a supposedly progressive and enlightened organization to win converts by means of a spectacle that would have pleased the most retrograde of Goethe's characters, the Count.

In connecting *Wilhelm Meister's Apprenticeship* to the rise of historicism (and thus to an intellectual revolution that began in the mid-eighteenth century) I explicitly intend to weaken the influence that German idealism has exerted on *Bildungsroman* theory throughout the last century. It is true that classical historicism embraced the notions of perfectibility and continuity-through-change that would become central also to the later flowering of idealism. But conceptually prior to this was the revolutionary vision of a world in flux, populated by individuals and by cultures that all respond in unique ways to a universal dynamic of historical transformation. In acknowledging the tower chamber as an archive, a place concerned with the simultaneous development of multiple protagonists, rather than

---

3. In *Discipline & Punish*, Foucault already draws attention to the fact that the transition from punitive to disciplinary societies will inevitably produce new literary forms: "If from the early Middle Ages to the present day the 'adventure' is an account of individuality, the passage from the epic to the novel, from the noble deed to the secret singularity, from long exiles to the internal search for childhood, from combats to phantasies, it is also inscribed in the formation of disciplinary societies" (193).

4. Oscar Wilde, *The Artist as Critic: Critical Writings of Oscar Wilde*, ed. Richard Ellmann (Chicago: University of Chicago Press, 1969), 309.

with that of Wilhelm alone, we can come to appreciate Goethe's novel as an attempt to bestow narrative order on the chaotic implications of such a vision. No longer merely an objective analogy to the internal laws that have structured Wilhelm's development, the Tower Society now emerges as an ongoing attempt to record and transcribe the conditions of a collective historical existence.

Bildung, Historicism, and the Age of Herder

The German term *Bildung* is notoriously difficult to translate into other languages. Like the English word *education*, it can refer both to a dynamic process and to the static outcome of that process. Unlike *education*, however, which derives from the Latin verb *educare* (to bring up), a word that in turn is related to *educere* (to lead forth), *Bildung* does not imply any outside guidance or sculpting influence. For reasons to which I will return shortly, *Bildung* instead refers to a formative development governed by an inner law; the term is thus often contrasted with *Erziehung*, and German genre criticism has sometimes drawn a distinction between the *Bildungsroman* (novel of formation) and the *Erziehungsroman* (novel of education). The verbal form of *Bildung, bilden,* can be used reflexively with an idiomatic ease that is entirely lacking in English equivalents such as "to cultivate oneself" or "to develop one's faculties." Like many other German words, furthermore, both *Bildung* and *bilden* can combine with a number of prefixes to form new terms whose meaning subtly extends that of the lexical stem. *Abbilden, ausbilden, einbilden,* even *durchbilden,* are all philosophically charged words whose meaning would be impossible to render into English with a similar set of etymologically related terms. In light of all these distinguishing features, it is perhaps not surprising that *Bildung* became a major anchoring point of a specifically German national identity over the course of the nineteenth century. To this day, upper-middle-class Germans will self-define their status not only in economic, but also in cultural terms by claiming membership in the *Bildungsbürgertum*, while government subsidies for public television stations are justified with the claim that an emphasis on cultural programming, political news, and the national soccer team will benefit the *Bildung* of a wide audience.[5]

---

5. The German literature on the conceptual history of the terms *bilden* and *Bildung* is vast. Ernst Ludwig Stahl's *Die religiöse und die humanitätsphilosophische Bildungsidee und die Entstehung des deutschen Bildungsromans im 18. Jahrhundert* (Bern: Paul Haupt, 1934) is especially good on the religious context. Georg Bollenbeck's *Bildung und Kultur: Glanz und Elend eines deutschen Deutungsmusters* (Frankfurt am Main: Insel Verlag, 1994) offers a comprehensive overview of the subject. Other useful works include Ilse Schaarschmidt, "Der Bedeutungswandel der Begriffe 'Bildung' und 'bilden' in der Literaturepoche von Gottsched bis Herder," in *Beiträge zur Geschichte des Bildungsbegriffs,* ed. Franz Rauhut and Ilse Schaarschmidt (Weinheim: Verlag Julius Belz, 1965), 28–36; Ernst Liechtenstein, *Zur Entwicklung des Bildungsbegriffs von Meister Eckhart bis Hegel* (Heidelberg: Quelle & Meyer, 1966); and the entry on *Bildung* in Otto Brunner, Werner Conze, and Reinhart Koselleck, eds., *Geschichtliche Grundbegriffe: Historisches Lexikon zur politisch-sozialen Sprache in Deutschland* (Stuttgart: E. Klett, 1994). In English, the

Given the strong resonance of the term in contemporary German, and given the close association that literary studies have always drawn between *Bildung* and the "age of Goethe," it comes as a surprise to learn that Moses Mendelssohn, as late as 1784, could begin his essay "What Does It Mean to Enlighten?" with the confident assertion that *Bildung*, like the related terms "enlightenment" (*Aufklärung*) and "culture" (*Kultur*), represented "a new arrival in our language." These three terms, Mendelssohn continues, "evidently belong to the written language only. The common mob (*der gemeine Haufen*) does not understand them."[6] Mendelssohn's claim needs to be taken with a grain of salt, since *Bildung*, far from being a recent linguistic arrival, in fact has etymological roots in Middle High German. Nevertheless, this quotation illustrates that the rise of the term to the status of a central marker of German cultural identity began at a specific point in time (the second half of the eighteenth century), and within a specific intellectual context (the philosophical discourse of the Enlightenment). Before about 1750, *Bildung* and its lexical relatives occurred primarily in theological contexts. For the medieval mystic Meister Eckhart, for instance, it signified the process by which the soul comes to approximate the divine. And in the Pietist tradition, which exerted such a profound impact on German Enlightenment thought, the term referred to the shaping of the passive Christian soul through the active intervention of God. Common to all these uses is the Neoplatonic understanding of *Bildung* as a true act of "formation," that is, as an imitation of an externally given "form."

Sometime around the middle of the eighteenth century, however, the term *Bildung* began to spread in usage and to simultaneously undergo a semantic shift. Documentary proof for this can be found in the most important dictionary of the period, Johann Christoph Adelung's *Grammatico-Critical Dictionary of the High German Dialect* of 1774. Adelung lists the following as the principal definitions of *bilden*: "(1) to give a body its external shape . . . , (2) to imitate the shape of a thing, to model it" ([1] Einem Körper seine äußere Gestalt geben . . . [2] Die Gestalt einer Sache nachahmen, abbilden). Adelung's somewhat tautological use of the cognate *abbilden* in this definition, which highlights his conception of *Bildung* as a formation "away" or "down from" (*ab-*) a privileged original model, clearly documents his debt to the older conceptual tradition. Under "figural uses," however, he also lists "to give the proper direction to the abilities of the spirit and the will" (den Fähigkeiten des Geistes und Willens die gehörige Richtung geben), a

---

best short introduction to the subject remains Susan Cocalis, "The Transformation of *Bildung* from an Image to an Ideal," *Monatshefte* 70 (1978): 399–414. A more extensive overview is provided by W. H. Bruford in *The German Tradition of Self-Cultivation: 'Bildung' from Humboldt to Thomas Mann* (Cambridge: Cambridge University Press, 1975).

6. Moses Mendelssohn, "Ueber die Frage: Was heißt aufklären?" in *Gesammelte Schriften: Jubiläumsausgabe*, ed. Alexander Altmann and Eva J. Engel (repr., Stuttgart: Friedrich Frommann Verlag, 1971), 6.1:113. Mendelssohn submitted this text as an entry in the same essay competition that also inspired Kant's better-known essay "What Is Enlightenment?"

phrasing that leaves open the question of how this "proper" direction might be defined.[7]

In adding this figurative definition of the term, Adelung was in all probability alluding to the writings of Shaftesbury, which had started appearing in German translation over the prior three decades. Translators such as Georg Vensky and Johann Joachim Spalding used the words *bilden* and *Bildung* to render Shaftesbury's "to form" and "formation," and thereby made a crucial interpretive decision, since *gestalten* and *Gestaltung* would have provided more idiomatic alternatives. Significantly, they also translated Shaftesbury's "inner form" as *innere Bildung*.[8] Through the German reception of Shaftesbury, *Bildung* thus moved from its original mystical-Pietist context into a moral and aesthetic one; put differently, it was pried loose from the grasp of theology and rescued for philosophy, the new "queen of the sciences" during the Enlightenment. At the same time, *Bildung* lost its associations with passive receptivity and moved into the realm of active striving, as the process through which the soul grappled for its proper form. The importance of this process of secularization, which was carried out more or less accidentally, cannot be overestimated, because it allowed the term *Bildung* to gain a previously unprecedented level of conceptual depth. As Georg Bollenbeck explains, "Words become concepts as soon as they begin to resist their naming and signifying function and take on a communicative weight of their own; that is, when they no longer primarily refer to a communicative content but instead become such content themselves."[9] Its reception in the fertile field of eighteenth-century philosophy allowed *Bildung* to undergo just such a transformation. As Moses Mendelssohn's text makes clear, late eighteenth-century thinkers eagerly debated the scope and relevance of the new term. As was the case with *Aufklärung*, *Kultur*, and a few other words, *Bildung* no longer merely signified but also began to accumulate a discursive context of its own. Essays were written and letters sent back and forth to debate the relevance of the term to contemporary life. As such, *Bildung* mutated from an ancillary term in theology into an anchoring point of a new philosophical worldview.

This new worldview, perhaps the most important German contribution to the intellectual culture of the eighteenth century, would much later come to be known as "historicism."[10] Its development was set into motion during the 1760s, starting with a group of thinkers that included Friedrich Gottlieb Klopstock, Christoph Martin

---

7. Johann Christoph Adelung, *Grammatisch-kritisches Wörterbuch der hochdeutschen Mundart*, 3rd ed. (Leipzig, 1811), Münchener DigitalisierungsZentrum der Bayerischen Staatsbibliothek, http://lexika.digitale-sammlungen.de/adelung/online/angebot.

8. On the importance of Shaftesbury, see Bollenbeck, *Bildung und Kultur*, 114–16; Schaarschmidt, "Der Bedeutungswandel," 48–51; and Cocalis, "The Transformation of *Bildung*," 402–4.

9. Bollenbeck, *Bildung und Kultur*, 16.

10. Friedrich Meinecke, in his classic study *Historism: The Rise of a New Historical Outlook* (New York: Herder and Herder, 1972), liv, traces the origin of the term back to Karl Werner's 1879 study, *G. B. Vico als Philosoph und gelehrter Forscher*.

Wieland, and Johann Friedrich Blumenbach. It found its foremost expression, however, in the work of Johann Gottfried Herder. In these authors, *Bildung* emerged as a prime indicator of the great transformative process that historian Reinhart Koselleck has evocatively named the "temporalization of history" (*Verzeitlichung der Geschichte*)—a paradigm shift in late Enlightenment thought in which rationalism and abstract systematizing in historical philosophy gave way to a greater awareness of flux and dynamic exchange. Koselleck argues that the process of temporalization left an indelible imprint on the conceptual vocabulary of the modern social sciences, and that many terms, such as "progress," "development," and, indeed, "history" itself, only achieved their present-day meaning during the period from 1770 to 1820.[11]

Klopstock was one of the earliest writers to both popularize and secularize the term *Bildung*. In his epic poem *The Messiah* (the first complete version of which was published in 1773), the word occurs a half dozen times, even if the context here is still religious and closely tied to the much more frequent *Bild* (image), signifying an imitation of God. Nevertheless, Klopstock's exuberant exhortation in the first canto to "let us create the image of God in every human being anew!" contains as much of the creative as it does of the imitative.[12] For Klopstock, every individual being is like a creative cell that strives toward perfection of its own accord. In his shorter poems, he further translated this notion of *Bildung* as a cultivation of individual faculties into a secular humanist context. In the ode "To My Friends" ("Auf meine Freunde"), for instance, he apostrophizes the poet Johann Adolf Schlegel (the father of Friedrich and August Wilhelm) with the words "And there were songs—and I saw them develop into human shapes that he created by breathing into them spirit and life." (da wurden ihm Lieder!—die sah ich menschliche Bildungen annehmen! Ihnen haucht' er, schaffend, Leben und Geist ein.)[13] *Bildung* here not only has a human shape, but also a human creator. Perhaps most importantly, it appears in the plural, no longer tied to the slavish imitation of a singular Platonic ideal.

Wieland, heavily influenced by both Shaftesbury and Klopstock, also exerted a profound influence on the conceptual development of *Bildung*. As a young man, he published an essay called "Plan for an Academy for the Cultivation of the Heart and Mind of Young People" (1758), which played an important part in introducing the Greek term *kalokagathia* to the philosophical vocabulary of the day. Originally derived from Plato, *kalokagathia* refers to a process of development toward a timeless conception of nobility and goodness of character.[14] As Wieland's title already

---

11. On Koselleck's notion of a "temporalization of history," see his *Futures Past: On the Semantics of Historical Time*, trans. Keith Tribe (New York: Columbia University Press, 2004), 11–17.
12. Friedrich Gottlieb Klopstock, *Ausgewählte Werke*, ed. Karl August Schleiden (Munich: Carl Hanser Verlag, 1962), 199.
13. Klopstock, *Ausgewählte Werke*, 20.
14. On the conceptual history of *kalokagathia* in the late Enlightenment, see Robert E. Norton, *The Beautiful Soul: Aesthetic Morality in the Eighteenth Century* (Ithaca, NY: Cornell University Press, 1995), 100–136, to whom I also owe the Wieland reference.

makes clear, at this stage of Enlightenment discourse the term closely approximated contemporary uses of *Bildung*, although without any of the religious overtones that adhered to it in the context of Pietism. As an older man, however, Wieland began to embrace aesthetics that were inspired by the historical turn of his day and provided a theoretical foundation for the ascendant middle classes. He now equated *Bildung* with the cultivation of good taste, by which he meant the imitation of suitable models from literature and philosophy. *Bildung*, in other words, was something to be gained through mental labor and as such was a process that would actively create identity rather than merely reveal it. Through the literary and pedagogical influence of Klopstock and Wieland, *Bildung* was thus freed from its original theological associations and placed at the center of a nascent bourgeois ideology that defined itself through public exchange and the formation of common aesthetic principles, rather than through secrecy and exclusivity, as had been the case with the Masonic lodges and Pietist conventicles of the eighteenth century.

Another important impulse affecting the conceptual development of *Bildung* came from the philosophy of biology, especially from the work of Johann Friedrich Blumenbach. In his principal work, *On the Formative Drive* (*Über den Bildungstrieb*, 1781), Blumenbach tackled the question of how biological organisms develop from a germinal state into fully mature entities. According to the then-dominant theories of biological preformation (or "evolution," in the language of the day), each seed or embryo contains within it the latent form of the organism in its entirety; the developmental process thus consists of a mere "unfolding" or "unrolling" (the original meaning of the Latin verb *evolvere*) of what is already there. Blumenbach noted that theories of preformation could not possibly account for observable species variations and mutations, and instead postulated the existence of a dynamic developmental force, a *Bildungstrieb*, which he saw operative in every single organism, and considered coextensive with life itself.[15] Eighteenth-century philosophy had certainly toyed with the idea of a "life force" before. But Blumenbach's formative drive, unlike, say, Christian Wolff's *vis essentialis*, was more than just a spiritual current animating dead matter: it was a dynamic power that coursed through all organisms, forcing them to constantly change and develop. In the second edition of his *De generis humani* (1781), furthermore, Blumenbach made his *Bildungstrieb* the centerpiece of a new theory of natural history, when he proposed that external forces, such as climate and nutrition, could deflect the formative drive into different directions and therefore introduce species variations.

---

15. Blumenbach's work is a foremost example of the "epigenicist" movement in the philosophy of biology, which began to compete with evolutionism in the late eighteenth century. For more on the quarrel between the two camps, see Robert J. Richards, *The Romantic Conception of Life: Science and Philosophy in the Age of Goethe* (Chicago: University of Chicago Press, 2002), 211–16. On the relationship between epigenesis and *Bildung*, see Stahl, *Die religiöse und humanitätsphilosophische Bildungsidee*, 84–94.

Klopstock's humanist poetry, Wieland's campaign on behalf of bourgeois culture, and Blumenbach's struggle to turn eighteenth-century biology into a dynamic science all contributed to the rise of historicism. The greatest exponent of this new movement, however, was Johann Gottfried Herder, in whose work these early influences underwent a kind of catalytic conversion, until they erupted with explosive force in a series of works that would alter the course of European cultural history forever. Herder was precociously well-read and already as a young clergyman in provincial Riga could boast of an encyclopedic mastery of the most advanced currents of thought of his day. One of the texts that particularly roused his attention was "Plan for an Academy," the essay in which Wieland examined the Greek concept of *kalokagathia*. Herder took issue with Wieland's explications and in a review suggested that the Greek word might, in fact, have meant different things to different people at different points in time: "In every language all of the words that express the actual character of the age are subject to change, and, it seems to me, this is precisely the case with [*kalokagathia*]."[16]

Herder's true intellectual breakthrough came on his journey home from Riga, however, and was intimately tied to his grand resolution to "write the universal history of the *Bildung* of the world."[17] In a move that would become constitutive of historicism as such, Herder explicitly connected the concept of *Bildung* with an understanding of history as a universal and transformative current, a force that affects all of reality simultaneously and sweeps people, nations, and even the world entire into an unknown future. Blumenbach's "formative drive" was a natural force that affected plants and animals no differently than human beings; Herder, however, took the far more radical step of applying the notion of an inner force to the products of human culture. His *Leaflets on German Art and Letters* (*Von deutscher Art und Kunst: Einige fliegende Blätter*) thus contains the almost Faustian lament that "the human race is damned to a progression of scenes, of formative stages [*Stufen der Bildung*], of customs: woe to the man who dislikes the scene in which he has been destined to act and to live out his life!"[18] The notion of historical progress was, of course, a cliché in the eighteenth century, and one of the most important points in which the rationalist philosophers differentiated themselves from less enlightened ages that had approached human history as an uninterrupted plateau stretching from biblical times toward the Revelation. But progress, in the eighteenth century, implied an essentially linear progression toward ever more perfect realizations of a rationally comprehensible ideal. The *querelle des Anciens et des Modernes*

---

16. Johann Gottfried Herder, *Ueber die neuere deutsche Litteratur*, in *Sämmtliche Werke*, ed. Bernhard Suphan (Berlin: Weidmannsche Buchhandlung: 1877–1913), 1:303. I here adopt the translation of Robert E. Norton, who has more to say about Herder's review of Wieland's essay on pages 119–21 of *The Beautiful Soul*.
17. Herder, *Sämmtliche Werke*, 4:353.
18. Herder, *Sämmtliche Werke*, 5:168.

may have been won by the moderns, but the victorious faction would never have denied that the ideals of beauty and the good that Plato strove for were the same goals for which they also aimed. Herder, by contrast, argued that different cultures and different ages admired conflicting ideals, because the inner trajectories of their developments—their entelechies—pointed them in different directions.

For this reason, Herder has sometimes been interpreted (most influentially by Isaiah Berlin) as a romantic or even postmodern irrationalist *avant la lettre*, as a thinker who rejected all universals and believed that the individual will creates its own values and reality.[19] This is a clear exaggeration. Not for nothing did Herder describe his dream as that of a *universal* history of the *Bildung* of the world. But neither did he dream simply of an all-encompassing narrative of the development of the world; the Enlightenment ambition to confine all that there was to know between the leather covers of an encyclopedia was fundamentally alien to him. The intermediate term *Bildung* is crucial to an understanding of Herder: it is *Bildung* that is universal; the individual expressions that it may take, on the other hand, are almost infinitely varied. *Bildung*, for Herder, is a panentheistic force that suffuses all matter and causes it to partake in an ideal to a greater or lesser extent, as a passage from the *Treatise on the Origins of Language* makes clear: "The so-called divine language, the Hebrew language, is entirely imprinted with [metaphors]. Only, let this spirit of metaphor please not, though, be called 'Asiatic,' as if it were not to be found anywhere else! It lives in all savage languages—only, to be sure, in each one in proportion to the nation's *Bildung* and in accordance with the peculiar character of the nation's manner of thought."[20] For Herder, metaphor is an attribute of divine language; the fact that Hebrew is penetrated so deeply by this trope moves it closest of all human languages to the divine. This does not mean that Hebrew is entirely metaphorical, however, nor that all other languages are entirely without metaphor. Instead, the metaphorical spirit inhabits each language to a different degree and finds in each an expression that is at once unique and perfectly appropriate to the nation to which it belongs.

With Herder, then, the idea of *Bildung* is not only put into the service of a dynamic sense of history, it is also connected to a newly emergent sense of collective identity focused on the idea of the nation. When Karl Morgenstern praised *Wilhelm Meister* as an exemplary expression of "German life, German thought and the morals of our time" he was therefore expressing an idea that by 1819, sixteen years after Herder's death, had long entered into the mainstream of European thought: the idea that individual lives could participate in a collective destiny, and that this destiny, in turn, was different from that experienced by other peoples in other parts

---

19. See, for instance, Isaiah Berlin, *The Roots of Romanticism* (Princeton, NJ: Princeton University Press, 2001), 60–67.

20. Johann Gottfried Herder, *Philosophical Writings*, trans. Michael N. Forster (Cambridge: Cambridge University Press, 2002), 114.

of the world. This was the fundamental assumption of German historicism, which in turn paved the way for the nineteenth-century idea of nationalism. The rise of the novel of formation as well can be tied to the eighteenth-century transformations in the understanding of *Bildung* and the development of the historicist outlook—an outlook in whose birth many novelists of the day were actively involved.

The Rise of History and the Rise of the Novel

In the spring of 1773, Wieland, then already well on his way to becoming the most influential German novelist of his day, wrote a new preface to the forthcoming second edition of his greatest success, *The History of Agathon*. Entitled "On the Historical in *Agathon*," this little essay offers an illuminating glimpse of a decisive moment in the development of the modern European novel. Wieland's intention was to anchor his work amid the crosscurrents of two very different literary traditions that were flowing into one another in the 1770s: on the one hand, the ancient novel, whose origins stretched back to Xenophon; on the other, the more recent "realist" style of writing, best represented by Fielding. Somewhat surprisingly to the present-day reader, Wieland differentiates between these two traditions not according to such criteria as believability, verisimilitude, and social elevation of the subject matter, but rather according to how they prioritize the relationship between poetry and history. For Wieland, the work of Xenophon is distinguished by the fact that its author "wove poetry into historical truth," while Fielding instead "weaves the historically true into poetry."[21] For the ancients, in other words, poetry was the starting point to which they then gave a historically appropriate form, while the moderns start from historical observation and then adapt it to the purposes of their narrative.

Wieland acknowledges that a casual reader might well be tempted to classify *The History of Agathon* alongside Xenophon's *Cyropedia* on account of its Hellenistic subject matter. After all, only a few months earlier Wieland had published a didactic novel entitled *The Golden Mirror*, which openly borrowed from Xenophon's novel as well as from more recent works in a similar style, such as Fénelon's *The Adventures of Telemachus*. Wieland had other things in mind, however, as he goes on to specify in a pivotal passage of his essay:

> However, it has not been the intention of the author of *The History of Agathon* to draw up an image [*Bild*] of moral perfection, but rather to describe how a man of Agathon's disposition would have actually lived given the circumstances. With this in

---

21. Christoph Martin Wieland, "Über das Historische im Agathon," in *Werke*, ed. Gonthier-Luis Fink, Manfred Fuhrmann, et al., vol. 3, *Geschichte des Agathon*, ed. Klaus Manger (Frankfurt am Main: Deutscher Klassiker Verlag, 1986), 573. Further references to this work will appear in parentheses in the text.

mind, he has chosen the Horatian verse, *quid virtus et quid sapientia possit* [what virtue and wisdom might be able to accomplish] as his motto: not because he wanted to use Agathon as an example to show what wisdom and virtue are *as such*, but rather to illustrate how far a mortal might advance in both by the forces of nature, how much external circumstances contribute to our way of thinking and to our actions. . . . It is for all these reasons that the author hopes to persuade those among his readers who know human nature that his book (even though in a sense it belongs to the products of the imagination) is nevertheless not unworthy to *be called a history*. (573–74, emphasis in original)

Wieland's allusion to the title of his novel is a transparent ploy to reap for his *Agathon* some of the prestige associated with the English novels of social realism that were then taking the German-speaking countries by storm, and of which Fielding's *The History of Tom Jones* and Richardson's *Clarissa, or the History of a Young Lady* are merely the best-known examples. At the same time, however, Wieland draws a clear connection between his aspirations to have his novel classified as a "history," and an entirely new kind of spiritual development that he purports to represent. His protagonist, he asserts, does not advance toward some abstract and timeless ideal of "wisdom and virtue *as such*" (i.e., toward *kalokagathia*), but rather toward contingent expressions of such ideals that have previously been shaped by "external circumstances" and by historical contexts.

The publishing history of Wieland's *The History of Agathon* thus illustrates the changing understanding of personal development in the second half of the eighteenth century. When the first version of the novel appeared in 1766, timeless models of formation, such as the Pietist understanding of *Bildung* or the Platonic notion of *kalokagathia*, still dominated the intellectual landscape. By the early 1770s, however, history had already been set into motion, and the publication, in 1771, of a German translation of *Tom Jones* called on the novel to respond in kind. Wieland's new preface suggests that he rewrote his successful book at least in part out of consideration for these changes.

The vogue to title or subtitle novels as "histories" would quickly fade during the late eighteenth century, however. Almost a third of the German novels published in the year 1790 were explicitly labeled as *Geschichten*; by 1800, this percentage was reached only among gothic novels, which frequently carried intentionally archaic titles.[22] A quick reflection on the content of the best-known European novels of this period highlights the transition far better than any statistic could, however. Titles such as *The History of Tom Jones, a Foundling, Evelina, or the History of a*

---

22. I derive these numbers from the bibliographical appendices to, respectively, Michael Hadley, *The German Novel in 1790: A Descriptive Account and Critical Bibliography* (Bern: Herbert Lang, 1973), and Manfred W. Heiderich, *The German Novel of 1800: A Study of Popular Prose Fiction* (Bern: Peter Lang, 1982).

Young Lady's Entrance into the World, and *The History of Agathon* perfectly capture the distance between narrator and protagonist that is a general characteristic of eighteenth-century fiction. But how utterly inappropriate would those same epithets be if they were suddenly applied to the work of, for instance, Jane Austen, and thereby created a title such as *Emma, or the History of a Young Lady's Entrance into the World*! Austen's Emma radiates an outward force and possesses a textual presence that spills beyond any attempt to contain her as the mere hero of a "history."

This change in novelistic nomenclature doesn't merely reflect the rise of romantic sensibility, however (a category, at any rate, that would ill fit Jane Austen's creations). Even more important was a fundamental shift in the understanding of what was meant by "history" itself, for an important grammatical fact differentiates the literary term "history" as it is used by Fielding, Burney, or Richardson from the principal use that we now have for this term: there can be many *literary* "histories," but we nowadays think of "history" as a solidly singular phenomenon. Indeed, to this day, the German noun *die Geschichte* and its plural form *die Geschichten* can be used to indicate "stories," while the singular alone refers to the modern conception of "history."

As Reinhart Koselleck has shown, the emergence of the term *die Geschichte* as a collective singular noun unifying many *Geschichten* is another consequence of the "temporalization of history" that occurred during the last three decades of the eighteenth century. Before that time, *Geschichte* was in fact almost exclusively used as a plural noun collecting (but not imposing any order on) individual stories. Thus Johann Theodor Jablonski could write in his *General Encyclopedia of the Arts and Sciences* of 1748: "History are [sic] a mirror for virtues and vices in which one can learn through assumed experience what is to be done or left undone; they are a monument to evil as well as praiseworthy deeds." (Die geschichte sind ein spiegel der tugend und laster, darinnen man durch fremde erfahrung lernen kann, was zu tun oder zu lassen; sie sind ein denkmal der bösen sowohl als der löblichen taten.)[23] Missing from this early modern definition is a notion of emplotment, a sense that history is itself a dynamic narrative system and thus something that progresses over time.

Jablonski viewed the book of history as an almanac, a collection of instructive tales related to one another through a common morality rather than through causal chains. In the Christian worldview that dominated European thought from late antiquity to the Enlightenment, after all, human history was conceived as an essentially uniform sequence of events filling the interim between man's original sin and the eventual final redemption. As Karl Löwith describes it, "This 'interim,' i.e. the whole of history, is neither an empty period in which nothing happens nor a busy period in which everything may happen, but the decisive time of probation

---

23. Quoted in Koselleck, *Futures Past*, 33.

and final discrimination between the wheat and the tares. Its constant content are [*sic*] variations of one single theme: God's call and man's response to it."[24] Early modern altarpieces and historical paintings consequently depict events from antiquity in the garb of the present, since their creators did not conceive of secular history as having developed in any meaningful way since the time of the church fathers.

There were certainly models of historiography that broke with this Christian worldview, most central among them that of Vico. But Vico, although his understanding of historical time is undoubtedly dynamic, still lacks any notion of Walter Benjamin's "homogeneous, empty time" through which history *progresses* and undergoes significant changes. In Friedrich Meinecke's view, Vico "introduced the proposition that the universally valid forms for determining the changes in human nature were recurrent and basically unchanging. He put a dynamic content into a static vessel, thus furnishing one of the greatest examples of the continuity of development in the history of thought, by virtue of which the defeated cause somehow or other lives on in the cause that triumphs."[25] The notion of a progressive and variable history was, instead, the distinctive accomplishment of the historicist movement.

If Jablonski still saw the book of history as an almanac, German philosophers toward the end of the eighteenth century approached it as though it were a novel with a clearly discernible plot, which they made it their duty to track down and summarize. This is especially clear from an offhand remark made by Immanuel Kant in his "An Idea Towards a Universal History in a Cosmopolitan Sense," in which the philosopher from Königsberg admits:: "It may seem, at first sight, a strange and even absurd proposal to suggest the composition of a History according to the idea of how the course of the world is to proceed, if it is to be conformable to certain rational laws. It may well appear that only a novel could be produced from such an intention."[26] Kant did not hesitate to put such qualms behind him in his pursuit to put the "story" into "history," but his remark locates a legitimate concern. Indeed, in the attempt to give a narrative shape to a formless procession of present moments, the historical philosophers mainly copied the laws of plotting that had originally been developed for narratives shaped by human intentionality. And these laws were comparatively primitive in nature, having survived in unmodified form since the time of Aristotle, according to whose famous dictum all well-constructed plots must have a beginning, middle, and an end.[27] Consequently,

---

24. Karl Löwith, *Meaning in History: The Theological Implications of the Philosophy of History* (Chicago: University of Chicago Press, 1949), 184.

25. Meinecke, *Historism*, 49.

26. Immanuel Kant, "An Idea Towards a Universal History in a Cosmopolitan Sense," in *Theories of History*, ed. Patrick Gardiner (New York: Free Press, 1959), 32.

27. See Aristotle, *Poetics*, trans. Richard Janko (Indianapolis: Hackett Publishing Company, 1987), 1450b25–1451a15.

the classical historical philosophies always include a moment—known under such manifold names as "cosmopolitan peace," "the absolute manifestation of spirit," and "the classless society"—in which the forward momentum of history is negated, and the "plot" comes to an end.

Kant's notion that history itself might take the form of a *novel* is in many ways the exact inverse of the impulse that drove Fielding, Richardson, and Wieland to label their literary works *histories*. Of course these authors weren't producing factual historical accounts in the literal sense. Following the Aristotelian tradition, however, they believed that fiction could contain a higher degree of historical truth than factual narratives, because fiction is beholden to the laws of the probable, rather than merely to what actually happened.[28] In Wieland's own words from the *Agathon* essay, they made it their mission to "weave the historically true into poetry." Denis Diderot similarly proclaimed in his 1762 essay "In Praise of Richardson": "I would venture to say that history often is merely a bad novel, and that a novel of the kind that you have made is a good history."[29] There is thus a conceptual correlation between the notion of history as an "almanac," or collection of loosely bundled instructive tales, and the eighteenth-century fad for producing "histories" in novel form. By entitling their novels in this manner, Fielding, Richardson, and Burney underlined the representativeness of their literary creations, and even Wieland, whose *Agathon* plays rough and loose with the actual chronology of Hellenistic Greece, could argue that his work nevertheless presents a "true" picture of antiquity.

By the early nineteenth century, however, the conventions of both historiography and novelistic writing had changed considerably, due in no small part to the resounding victory of historicism. "History" was now regarded as a dynamic, forward-moving and "emplotted" process, the laws of which thinkers such as Hegel and Marx set out to codify. Similarly, novels now had to contend with what Georg Lukács termed the "transcendental homelessness" of the modern individual: the ways, in other words, in which human beings try to claim a place for themselves amid the tumultuous flow of history. Accounts of private lives in general no longer claimed to possess a universal moral relevance; instead, they aimed to depict recognizable people solving problems in recognizable historical settings. The historical novel offers one clear example of this transition, for unlike the eighteenth-century "histories," it derives its appeal precisely from its promise of a truthful account of what the world was like at an earlier stage of history that differs from the present in essential regards. As Walter Scott puts it in his famous postscript to *Waverley*, "The gradual influx of wealth and the extension of commerce have since united to render the present people of Scotland a class of beings as different from

---

28. See Aristotle, *Poetics*, 1451b and 1459a.
29. Translation adapted from Denis Diderot, "In Praise of Richardson," in *Selected Writings on Art and Literature*, trans. Geoffrey Bremner (London: Penguin Classics, 1994), 90.

their grandfathers, as the existing English are from those of Queen Elizabeth's time."[30] The plot of *Waverley* may be fictional, as well as shaped by the conventions of romance, but it pretends to be faithful to life during the Jacobite Rebellion, and it is factually detailed as well as informed by historical research.

An obvious structural homology links this new understanding of history to the Herderian notion of *Bildung*: both history and *Bildung* are universal forces that nevertheless manifest differently in different times and different places. It should therefore not surprise that the *Bildungsroman* stands at the very center of the change in novelistic self-understanding, a fact that was immediately recognized by the most cognizant critics of the day. In 1774, for instance, Friedrich von Blanckenburg, in his *Essay on the Novel* (a work devoted in no small part to the explication of Wieland), still described the novelist as the "creator and historian alike of his characters," a phrase that echoes the descriptions of Diderot and other exponents of Enlightenment aesthetics.[31] The publication of *Wilhelm Meister*, on the other hand, was accompanied by the advent of a new and prophetic critical voice: that of Friedrich Schlegel. Schlegel's most famous critical utterance on *Wilhelm Meister* consists of exactly one sentence, in which he declares that the new novel, along with the French Revolution and Fichte's *Science of Knowledge*, "represent[s] the greatest tendencies of the age."[32] The break with Blanckenburg could not be clearer: instead of a verbose treatise masquerading as an "essay," Schlegel offers an intentionally ambiguous statement that nevertheless lights up the literary landscape like a flare shot up into the midnight sky. For Schlegel, clearly, novel and history are no longer interchangeable, as they were for Diderot or, for that matter, Blanckenburg. Nor is history for Schlegel an almanac of instructive tales: the fragment goes on to attack "our shabby histories of civilization, which usually resemble a collection of variants accompanied by a running commentary for which the original text has been lost." For Schlegel, history instead possesses a narrative dynamic of its own, an energy that a single novel can capture only imperfectly, as a "tendency." History is alive, full of energy, and, most importantly, it transcends the horizon of any individual *story*, which necessarily remains caught up in contingent subject matter, in particulars that could have been otherwise.

German romantic literary theory as it constituted itself during the two decades following the publication of *Wilhelm Meister* remained obsessed with this notion of the novel as an expression of a historical tendency, that is, with its capacity to illuminate the macroscopic laws of emplotment that also govern historical events as a whole. Friedrich Schelling declared in 1802 that the novel should be "a general mirror of the course of human events," while Novalis saw the novel as constituting

---

30. Walter Scott, *Waverley* (London: Penguin, 1980), 492.
31. Friedrich von Blanckenburg, *Versuch über den Roman* (Stuttgart: Metzler, 1965), 308–9.
32. Friedrich Schlegel, *Philosophical Fragments*, trans. Peter Firchow (Minneapolis: University of Minnesota Press, 1991), 46.

a "mythology of history." Hegel spoke of the "totality" of historical experience that is captured in the "particular events" portrayed in the novel. The most illuminating critic, however, remained Schlegel himself, who declared that the task of the novel should be to "become the embodiment of the *Bildung* of an age" and to serve as a "universal science of *Bildung*" for a given epoch.[33] The subtle difference between these two phrasings is important: for Schlegel, the novel quite clearly is a metahistorical instrument whose twin task it is to register the formative character of an era (its *Zeitbildung*) and to then develop universal laws that might explain this character (the *Bildungslehre*).

It is in the context of this close coupling between novel theory and historiography that Karl Morgenstern (who, however, took a rather dim view of Schlegel) invented the term *Bildungsroman*. The final lines of Morgenstern's lecture read:

> How much has changed in Germany and in the rest of Europe during the twenty-five years that have passed since the publication of the *Apprenticeship*; how much has already changed its shape and how much strives toward new forms that in some cases have been foreseen, but in others come completely unexpected! . . . [Considering all the recent transformations] we may expect many happy achievements from the current and from future generations. For the same reason, many other marvelous trees with beautiful flowers and ripe fruits shall flourish in the infinitely large garden of novel writing![34]

In this outburst of unadulterated romanticism, the *Bildungsroman* is clearly defined as an infinitely varied instrument by which the equally multiform achievements of future generations might be measured. Just as the form-giving character (the *Bildung*) of historical periods and of nations will differ, so will the novels of formation that spring from them. In each case, however, the literary work offers a poetic expression of the single indomitable course of history that pulses through all these empirical manifestations.

The rise of historicism in the eighteenth century thus provides a fertile starting point for a new and revisionist interpretation of the *Bildungsroman* that differs from established schemata based in the legacy of German idealism. Idealist interpretations of the *Bildungsroman* tend to privilege finality, and focus on the perfected form revealed at the end of the protagonist's development. Eighteenth-century theories of *Bildung*, on the other hand, are concerned with process rather than finality or, as I have previously called it, with "performance" rather than "form." For

---

33. These references are cited in Eberhard Lämmert, "Zum Wandel der Geschichtserfahrung im Reflex der Romantheorie," in *Geschichte: Ereignis und Erzählung*, ed. Reinhart Koselleck and Wolf-Dieter Stempel (Munich: Wilhelm Fink Verlag, 1973), 503–15.

34. Karl Morgenstern, "On the Nature of the *Bildungsroman*," trans. Tobias Boes, *PMLA* 124 (2009): 652.

Blumenbach or Herder, there is no objective correlative, no overarching norm that legitimates individual development, as there is for Humboldt or Hegel. Instead, each person and each culture strives to find its own individual response to a universal formative drive. Viewed through this new interpretive lens, the ultimate question confronted by every *Bildungsroman* is not how the protagonist might actualize some hidden ideal, but rather how a multiplicity of individual developments might be combined into a meaningful whole—how a number of diverse stories might yield to the imperative of a singular "History" writ large. For a romantic critic like Karl Morgenstern, the answer to this question clearly lay in nationalism, but as a closer examination of actual novels makes clear, the matter is rarely this simple.

Goethe, Historicism, Nationalism

When Morgenstern referred to the quarter century that had passed since the publication of *Wilhelm Meister's Apprenticeship* as a period of change and striving, he was looking back at some of the most tumultuous years of modern European history: a time span that had seen the rise and fall of Napoleon Bonaparte, the dissolution of the Holy Roman Empire, the German Wars of Liberation, and the Congress of Vienna. The hope that German political life might find a new collective form had only recently been dampened with the publication of the Carlsbad Decrees, which dissolved the nationalist student fraternities and imposed unprecedented levels of state censorship. Indeed, Morgenstern himself, sitting as he was in faraway Dorpat, was most likely not fully conscious of the extent to which the ancien régime had begun to clamp down on political freedoms. Morgenstern's choice of Goethe's novel—rather than, for instance, Wieland's *Agathon*—as the paradigmatic *Bildungsroman* therefore undoubtedly has political in addition to aesthetic motivations: it wasn't just that *Wilhelm Meister* captured the current of history in a way that *Agathon* did not, but also that the ways in which it did so still seemed to speak to Morgenstern's own era.

There can be little question that Goethe, in addition to all the other things he accomplished in *Wilhelm Meister*, also attempted to formulate a new understanding of collective political life. The classic focus for readings in this vein is the fifth book, devoted in large parts to a discussion and subsequent staging of *Hamlet*, Shakespeare's meditation on the consequences of regicide. *Hamlet* is a play that dramatizes the tensions between personal and public identity, between private emotional commitments and public imperatives for action. In one of the best readings of the fifth book of *Wilhelm Meister*, Joseph Vogl argues that a crucial transformation in Wilhelm's self-understanding occurs at the moment when the Ghost appears on stage during the opening-night performance.[35] The Ghost's voice, which sounds

---

35. See Joseph Vogl, *Kalkül und Leidenschaft: Poetik des ökonomischen Menschen* (Munich: Sequenzia Verlag, 2002), 19–20.

eerily similar to that of Wilhelm's own father, completely unnerves Goethe's protagonist, and he "changed position so often during [his] long narration, he seemed so uncertain of himself and ill at ease, so attentive but at the same time so distracted that his performance aroused the admiration of all" (195). Ironically, Wilhelm's success as an actor is thus linked to his very failure at acting: he gives a believable performance because his Oedipal anxiety is quite real. This disqualifies him for professional life in the theater but opens up a new understanding of himself as an actor in the public sphere. In taking on the part of another, Wilhelm comes to think of himself as a public personality, yet this new understanding remains intimately rooted in his private identity. He neither dissolves in an anonymous mass nor submits his actions to an external ideology; instead, he emerges from his theatrical adventure as an emancipated political subject.

In the final book of *Wilhelm Meister*, this political logic is connected to the workings of the Tower Society, when Wilhelm reads the biography that is on file for him in the inner sanctuary:

> The account of his life was related in every detail and with great incisiveness. His attention was not distracted by the report of individual events or momentary emotions, sympathetic comments enlightened him without embarrassing him, and he saw a picture of himself, not like a second self in a mirror, but a different self, one outside of him, as in a painting. One never approves of everything in a portrait, but one is always glad that a thoughtful mind has seen us thus and a superior talent enjoyed portraying us in such a way that a picture survives of what we were, and will survive longer than we will. (309)

Wilhelm, of course, has heard and read many biographical narratives already and has eagerly incorporated them into his own development. But the society scroll forces him to look at his own life as through the eyes of a stranger, and to therefore think of himself as being essentially like all the others around him. Tellingly, the first thing he does upon finishing his dossier is "to compose in his mind his story for Therese, feeling almost ashamed at having nothing to match her own fine qualities, nothing that testified to any active purpose in his life" (309). Suddenly, it is Therese who becomes the person who must be impressed through evocative biographical detail, and Therese rather than Wilhelm who emerges as the privileged interlocutor.

Through this dynamic, which I have earlier characterized as a transformation of narrative hypotaxis (or subordination to Wilhelm's overarching formative plot) into parataxis (a system in which each character could, theoretically, emerge as a center of attention), Goethe's novel creates a sense of an imagined community. The Tower archive serves as an architectural metaphor for this community, for it collects the individual biographies of all the characters in a giant contiguous arrangement of externally identical scrolls. The promise of this archive is that the biographies will all be fundamentally similar, that they will outline a common struggle to define their subjects' true selves and in so doing also define a larger, collective identity.

The production of subjectivity in *Wilhelm Meister* undeniably takes place in the concrete reality of historical time rather than in the abstract realm of political idealism. In a manner reminiscent of Fichte's *Science of Knowledge*, the work to which Schlegel compared Goethe's novel, Wilhelm recognizes himself as another in his society protocol, but this recognition does not occur through the instantaneous positing of a "not-I," as in Fichte's work, but rather through the slow and deliberate development of a textual identity. And the model of time that is sketched out in *Wilhelm Meister's Apprenticeship* is thoroughly "re-volutionary" in nature, in the sense given to this term throughout much of the eighteenth century. That is to say, rather than positing a temporality of rupture in which new identities can be instantaneously created through an act of sociopolitical upheaval (a "revolution" in the modern sense of the term), Goethe conceives of historical time as a broad expanse structured by periodic returns to the same point, in the way in which we speak of planets as "revolving" around the sun.[36]

Goethe's usage of re-volutionary temporality at once alludes to and improves on the ways in which the eighteenth-century novel treated the narrative foundations of human communities. That this is so is perhaps best demonstrated by comparing this *Bildungsroman* with one of the earliest works of literary realism, to which its plot bears a passing resemblance. Both *Wilhelm Meister* and Daniel Defoe's *Robinson Crusoe* (1719) tell the story of a protagonist who sets out from home toward parts unknown out of dissatisfaction with the life that his parents have planned for him. Both novels, furthermore, chronicle how these protagonists eventually discover what it is that they really want, and triumphantly reenter the society into which they were born. In *Robinson Crusoe*, however, this society is essentially static: when Crusoe finally returns to Europe after twenty-eight long years on his island, the world is basically as he left it, and his financial possessions have ripened into a small fortune according to the dependable logic of annual interest payments. Cyclical repetition also governs Crusoe's life as an outcast—in fact, the entire plot of the novel consists of an extended description of the heroic efforts by which he manages to transform a procession of days into increasingly complex experiential cycles. The early notches in a tree are followed by more and more ambitious ventures into agriculture and animal husbandry, all of which depend for their success on meticulous attention to repetitive actions. When Crusoe

---

36. On Goethe's relationship to the temporality of revolutions, see Dennis Mahoney, "The French Revolution and the *Bildungsroman*," in *The French Revolution and the Age of Goethe*, ed. Gerhart Hoffmeister (Hildesheim: Georg Holms AG, 1989), 127. The larger conceptual history of revolutionary temporality is outlined by Mona Ozouf in her article "Revolution," in *A Critical Dictionary of the French Revolution*, ed. François Furet and Mona Ozouf and trans. Arthur Goldhammer (Cambridge, MA: Harvard University Press, 1989), 806–17.

finally gains a companion, he chooses to turn him from a "savage" into a human being by bestowing a name on him that similarly emphasizes a cyclical relationship to time. Narrative realism in Defoe, in other words, quite literally functions as an attempt to domesticate the unknown—not merely spatially, in the sense that Crusoe turns his savage island into an increasingly livable space, but also temporally, in the sense that the endless expanse of "island time" is mediated into recognizable and controllable patterns.

In *Wilhelm Meister*, by contrast, experiential cycles do not neatly mirror one another but rather accumulate additional significance with each repetition. Goethe's novel is set into motion by Wilhelm's realization that the experiential patterns that his background makes available to him—patterns that revolve around the family business with its secure source of income and guaranteed inheritance, as well as his occasional amorous trysts with Mariane—no longer satisfy him. A force is moving within him that longs for a different expression than that which is available to him in these surroundings. And unlike Robinson Crusoe, who leaves home under similar circumstances but then ends up reproducing precisely the same social patterns of English middle-class life from which he was ostensibly trying to flee, Wilhelm actively experiments with different ways of shaping his life during his travels.

Wilhelm's successive attempts as a theatrical director during his childhood with the puppet theater, with Melina's traveling troupe, and at Serlo's well-established theater thus represent a widening gyre rather than a closed circle: the protagonist grows with each repetition, and the portion of the external world that is subsumed by his experiences increases in kind. In this manner, both the story of the protagonist and that of the world at large *progresses*, and Goethe's novel participates in the larger "temporalization of history" that I have sketched out in the two previous sections. The *Hamlet* performance represents another example of such a widening gyre, for in it the Oedipal anxieties that can already be detected in Wilhelm's behavior during the earlier parts of the novel resurface and are transformed from a purely private preoccupation into a public one. As Goethe's famous theoretical writings regarding the possibilities of a national theater demonstrate, he also hoped that some of the affective energies that turn his young protagonist into such a convincing prince of Denmark might transfer to the audience and thereby instill in it the sense of an imagined community.

Goethe, to be sure, was not a "nationalist" in the commonsensical way in which we nowadays understand the term. Karl Morgenstern lauded *Wilhelm Meister* for its representation of "German life," but this description reveals as much about the critic as it does about the work he was praising. There is nothing essentially "German" about Goethe's novel, at least not if we define "German" in cultural, ethnic, linguistic, or religious terms, to name just four of the criteria that are commonly used to demarcate national boundaries in our postromantic times. In fact, a good deal of literary sleuthing is required to establish that the bulk of *Wilhelm Meister* takes place somewhere in central Germany, most likely in or around the year 1792.[37] As scholars such as Benedict Anderson and Homi Bhabha have shown, however, nationalism, long before it becomes linked to a specific ideological content, is first of all a *narrative* response to modernity. It stems from the observation (made possible by what Anderson calls the rise of "print-capitalism") that large masses of people share the same everyday reality and routinely interact with the same social institutions. This "horizontal" way of conceiving human communities as entities that exist inside historical time gradually yet steadily comes to replace the older "vertical" ways of thinking about social structure, in which the different estates (clergymen, nobility, commoners) were divided from one another by essential barriers that existed outside of historical time.

Wilhelm Meister, which focuses on gradual developments effected within the repetitive structures of everyday life, lends a narrative form to this important conceptual transformation. Here, it is once again useful to look at Wilhelm's relationship to the autobiographical narratives that structure his development. In their original hypotactic arrangement, these stories represent a series of increasingly complex life lessons, in which Therese's story, for instance, appears as a more mature (or at least a more evenly tempered) response to the demands of the world than that of the Beautiful Soul, who in turn appears more mature than Aurelia. The autobiographical insets thus appear clearly subordinate to the overriding narrative preoccupation with Wilhelm's development, his *Bildung*. Within the Tower sanctuary, however, this hierarchy is overthrown, and the individual life stories are reinterpreted as so many contradictory attempts to resolve the problems of the times: competing biographies rather than increasingly finely structured exempla. Through this process, collective experience is shot through with a shared temporal reality; the result is a living vernacular identity. This identity, furthermore, dissolves class boundaries. The Tower sanctuary contains biographies drawn from all three estates (i.e., those of the Abbé, of Jarno, and of Wilhelm), but these differences are of no inherent importance anymore.

Goethe's novel, then, manages to be at once circular and progressive: it gives a narrative shape to the emergence of its protagonist while at the same time insisting that true change can spring only from the contemplative return to an original position. Furthermore, *Wilhelm Meister* also aspires to apply this re-volutionary logic to a social totality, by showing that individual biographies, different as they may otherwise appear to be, in reality form parallel responses to common historical problems. Wilhelm himself expresses his recognition of the new social contract based on parallel experiences and imagined similarities when he exclaims during his initiation into the society: "How strange! . . . Can there be some pattern in chance events? And is what we call 'fate' really only chance?" (302). The dual movement of

---

37. On dating the action of *Wilhelm Meister*, see Mahoney, "The French Revolution and the Bildungsroman," 129–30.

this passage, in which the early modern belief in "fate" gives way to a vision of radical contingency that is nevertheless recognized to obey certain formal structures neatly parallels Schlegel's encomium to the "tendencies" of the age.

There is one further way in which *Wilhelm Meister* stages the creation of a modern, protonational, and "imagined" community. Lynn Hunt, in her classic study of the French Revolution, has described how the violent transition from the ancien régime to a republican form of government in France took the form of a "family romance," in which a metaphor of the state as a family governed by a king as the head of the household was replaced by a different metaphor structured around a presumptive fraternity existing among citizens with equal rights.[38] *Wilhelm Meister* too contains elements of a family romance. Thus, in the ninth chapter of the third book, Goethe for the first time invokes the word "family" to describe the odd grouping of protégés (Mignon, Friedrich, and later also Felix) whom Wilhelm has gathered around himself and whom he "for some time [has] considered his own" (109). Two books later, in the chapter following the successful conclusion of the *Hamlet* performance, Goethe applies the same term to the troupe as a whole, ironically pointing out that the actors' postproduction dinner, which they consume while still in costume, "seemed as if a family of regal spirits had assembled" (196). In both of these instances, the "family" emerges as a metaphorical rather than natural form of association in which membership is earned by one's contributions to a shared destiny rather than through the privilege of nativity.

Cosmopolitanism and the Limits of Nationhood in *Wilhelm Meister*

Interestingly, the last two books of *Wilhelm Meister* revert on this family romance by progressively replacing most of the voluntary associations that Goethe so painstakingly constructed with relationships based on blood. This process begins at the end of the initiation ceremony, when Wilhelm, having been granted the right to ask the Abbé a question, demands to know whether Felix is his biological son, and is answered in the affirmative. Soon after, Mignon, whose own narrative fortune seems inversely correlated to that of Felix, passes away and in death finally acquires biological relatives of her own. Friedrich, for a short while the third member of Wilhelm's imagined family, has meanwhile been unmasked as the brother of Lothario, Natalie, and the Countess, all of whom are also nephews and nieces of the Beautiful Soul. And finally, as if these connections by themselves were not enough to utterly strain credulity, it also turns out that the Abbé has a twin brother, who has taken a part in guiding Wilhelm on his way toward the Tower Society. In addition to these "natural" relationships, Goethe also includes a number that are voluntary

---

38. Lynn Hunt, *The Family Romance of the French Revolution* (Berkeley: University of California Press, 1992).

yet still exclusive, in a way that the earlier metaphorical family units were not. Foremost among these is Wilhelm's impending marriage to Natalie, which is in turn supplemented by Lothario's upcoming marriage to Therese, Jarno's upcoming marriage to Lydie, and Friedrich's proposal to Philine.

The result of all these liaisons is that the characters of Goethe's novel end up connected to one another through more than merely spatiotemporal accidents and shared experiences: blood relations fill a lack left unfulfilled by historical contiguity. At the same time, Wilhelm's own formative trajectory is given a biological subtext, because the endpoint of his development reveals not only personal freedom, but also an obligation to a son who can quite literally be seen as a continuation of his own destiny. While Felix thus epitomizes the "re-volutionary" temporality of *Wilhelm Meister*, in which formative processes advance by way of an ever-widening gyre, the conclusion of the novel associates this temporality with nature rather than with human history: the ultimate destiny of Goethe's protagonist is to have recognized himself as a father, not as an agent of historical change. In political terms, this shift from voluntary to natural forms of affiliation implies a regression from an Enlightened social contract based on the notion of universal brotherhood to an early modern one based on blood relationships. In book 8, chapter 10, Jarno alludes to this fact when he describes the Tower Society with the words "You will find the whole nobility here: Marchese, Marquises, Mylords and Barons. All we lacked was a Count" (366). Much like the aristocracy of the ancien régime, most of the Tower initiates turn out to be related to one another by either descent or marriage.

The final book of *Wilhelm Meister* contains other surprises as well, however. Shortly after Wilhelm's initiation, Jarno confides in him: "Everything you saw in the tower was the relics of a youthful enterprise that most initiates first took very seriously but will probably now just smile at" (335). As Jarno also reveals, his organization is about to undergo a radical structural transformation: "From our ancient Tower a Society shall emerge, which will extend into every corner of the globe, and people from all over the world will be allowed to join it. We will cooperate in safeguarding our means of existence, in case some political revolution should displace one of our members from the land he owns" (345). This sketch has reminded many modern-day readers of a global insurance corporation, and this comparison accurately identifies the two features that are most remarkable about the reformed society: first, its openness to "people from all over the world," and second, the fact that money, rather than autobiographical confession, is presented as the principal criterion for membership.

The conclusion of *Wilhelm Meister's Apprenticeship* thus seems to undo much of what Goethe had previously accomplished, much of what makes this novel such a landmark text in the history of European narrative. In their original form, the Tower Society and its secret repository of biographical narratives represent a potent metaphor for a new historical consciousness. By revealing his characters to be relatives rather than fellow travelers down the currents of history, however, Goethe unexpectedly reaffirms the conventions not only of eighteenth-century narrative, in which such implausible revelations commonly occur even in the most "realist" texts, but also of eighteenth-century politics. Conversely, Jarno's project for a reformed Tower Society seems a leap forward into a nineteenth- or even twentieth-century world of hypermodernity, in which people are no longer the subjects of narratives, but only the variables in a complex risk management calculation.

Before submitting to this interpretation, however, it is useful to consider the case of the one character in *Wilhelm Meister* who seemingly has no place in the Tower Society, the one person for whom it is impossible to even imagine a biographical scroll. This character, of course, is Mignon. Alone among all of Goethe's creations, Mignon does not appear to develop, appearing preformed from the very beginning. Also alone among all the other characters, she never speaks about herself and indeed seems incapable of grasping the narrative conventions that would be required to formulate a lengthy autobiographical narrative. She instead communicates through poetry and dance. The causes of Mignon's special status are evident from the very beginning, for she is a creature of the south, and thus, according to the inner logic of historicist thinking, the product of an entirely different lifeworld. History, so to speak, has not yet begun for her.

If one conceives of *Wilhelm Meister's Apprenticeship* only as the story of Wilhelm's circuitous journey toward self-discovery in the Tower archive, then there simply is no room for a character like Mignon by novel's end. She quite rightly dies. But in departing from the internal logic that structured the earlier sections of the novel, the eighth book of *Wilhelm Meister* opens new spaces for this memorable character. Gazing on the little girl's corpse, the Marchese recognizes her as his own niece, and as the daughter of his brother, the Harper. Suddenly, Mignon acquires not only a family, but also a life's story. This story, however, is told in an idiom unlike any other in the novel: that of the gothic tale, in which inner meaning is predetermined rather than gradually created through a process of development. In terms of tone and content, the "Confessions of a Beautiful Soul" is surely just as different from Wilhelm's own story as is anything that happens to Mignon. But unlike Mignon's tale, the "Confessions" obeys the same formative logic that characterizes all the other autobiographical stories told in the first six books of *Wilhelm Meister*, and it can thus be integrated into the great paratactic system that structures the novel. Mignon's tale remains foreign to this logic. It still demands to be taken seriously, however, drawing within its orbit two other characters and thereby establishing a narrative ordering system that competes with the one of the Tower Society.

The structural reforms promised by Jarno might well be seen as an attempt to deal with this challenge. Indeed, one strange characteristic of the "new" society is that while all of its most important members will be required to travel, nobody is being sent to familiar territory. Lothario remains where he is rather than returning to America, the Abbé goes to Russia instead of venturing to France, the Marchese embarks on a tour of the German principalities rather than being recruited to serve as an emissary to Italy. If the older Tower Society represented a powerful metaphor for the kind of "imagined community" that plays such an important role in nationalist thinking, then this diaspora represents a transnational turn, an attempt to spin a new network of meaning among radically different worlds. Tellingly, the inexperienced Wilhelm is initially chosen to serve as a travel companion to the Marchese, and while Goethe dropped this plot idea in his sequel, *Wilhelm Meister's Wandering Years* (1821; revised version, 1829), the later novel is very much preoccupied with the question of how a number of literary genres that refuse to be subsumed in a common form might be fused into a coherent narrative.

The doubly asynchronous character of the final book—in which the imagined community of the Tower Society yields to an eighteenth-century family romance, on the one hand, and to a hypermodern risk management system, on the other—can thus be read as an attempt to come to terms with cultural diversity through narrative means. In Goethe's historicist worldview, influenced by Herder and Blumenbach among others, all living things are animated by the same developmental drive, but this drive expresses itself differently in different cultures. A character like Mignon, who hails from Italy, and thus from a country that in Goethe's mind had an entirely foreign relationship to historical time, can never become part of the same narrative structures that animate Wilhelm and his other companions. Her presence instead generates a counternarrative in the form of a gothic tale, and the adjustments Goethe made to the final book might be seen as an attempt to create a new narrative vernacular that would subsume both "realist" and "gothic" elements. In *Wilhelm Meister*, cosmopolitanism thus emerges as a kind of supplement to nationalism as it is conceived by Benedict Anderson. If nationalism represents an attempt to convince a large group of strangers of their essential similarity by showing that their lives obey a common narrative structure, then cosmopolitanism is instead defined by the search for a larger literary frame that would unite many different structures of this kind.

The differences between a historicist approach to the *Bildungsroman*, which locates the significance of the genre in its capacity to lend a narrative shape to mute historical forces, and an idealist approach, which sees the novel of formation as an essentially allegorical genre in which a prior meaning is gradually unfolded, should by now have become obvious. Wilhelm's development does not *represent* the historical development of the German nation in any allegorical fashion; it instead presupposes a *performative* relationship between story and history. Writing in 1795, Goethe thus intuitively developed an insight that Fredric Jameson has reiterated as one of his "four maxims of modernity"—namely the idea that modernity isn't a concept, and thus not something that can be represented, but a narrative category, and thus something that needs to be enacted.[39] Wilhelm's life enacts history

---

39. Fredric Jameson, *A Singular Modernity: Essay on the Ontology of the Present* (London: Verso, 2002), 40.

rather than merely representing it because it transforms historical time from an empty succession of present moments into the foundation of human social relations, which possess an intrinsic narrative shape. This shape, however, will vary between different peoples and cultures, in accordance with the inherent variations in their social relationships. The cosmopolitan dispersal that concludes *Wilhelm Meister* documents clearly that Goethe regarded it as his great task to find the literary means to accommodate such a multiplicity of forms. *Wilhelm Meister's Wandering Years* may well have been intended as an answer to this challenge; Goethe's revolutionary pronouncements on world literature certainly were.

As I have already noted at the end of the last chapter, the multiplication of narrative forms brought about by the experience of modernity poses a serious challenge to genre criticism. Genres are traditionally thought of in genealogical terms: as "family trees" that have roots in comparatively few (or, in the case of the *Bildungsroman*, even a single) agnatic texts and extend branches through time and across cultural boundaries. By contrast, historicism challenges us to view the entire world as in the grips of a universal formative drive, and to see rooted traditions merely as the local expressions of a panentheistic force. In the following three chapters, which each compare a German novel to one drawn from related Western European tradition, I will try to do justice to these contradictory positions, and to show how a "national tradition" could emerge from a series of structural transformations that were transnational in nature, and left an imprint on French, English, and Irish works in addition to German ones.

PART II

Comparative Studies

3

Epigonal Consciousness: Stendhal, Immermann, and the "Problem of Generations" around 1830

For any student of the European novel, the 1830s are an especially noteworthy decade. In 1830, Stendhal published *The Red and the Black*; in 1839, he followed it up with *The Charterhouse of Parma*. The same years also marked turning points in the literary development of Honoré de Balzac, who in 1830 bundled his first few novels into a series entitled "Scenes from Private Life," and in 1839 began to refer to a much-expanded selection of his writings as *The Human Comedy*. Charles Dickens, meanwhile, serialized the *Pickwick Papers* from 1836 to 1837, *Oliver Twist* from 1837 to 1839, and *Nicholas Nickleby* from 1838 to 1839. The 1830s, in other words, were the years in which French and English writers first began to apply the "realist" style that had been pioneered by authors like Fielding and Richardson to the depiction of complex social systems. This innovation would prove to be so influential that the very term "literary realism" has nowadays become synonymous with the mode of writing introduced during that decade.

German literature, meanwhile, can boast of no Stendhal, Balzac, or Dickens. Its two best-known writers of the period, Heinrich Heine and Georg Büchner, won their fame with poetry and plays, and even specialists struggle to name more than one or two of their novel-writing contemporaries. The very title of one of the few prose narratives from that period to still attract even modest contemporary interest, Karl Leberecht Immermann's *The Epigones* (1835), seems to serve as a literary program. Self-consciously imitative of Goethe's *Wilhelm Meister's Apprenticeship*, The

Epigones can easily be read as a retreat from the literary challenges brought about by an increasingly complex nineteenth-century bourgeois society. In the words of Wilhelmi, whose very name identifies him as an "epigonal" character,

> Nowadays, many good-for-nothings look upon the circumstances in Germany as they existed during the last quarter of the previous century . . . with contempt. They regard this time as shallow and inadequate, but they are wrong. It is true that people then did not know or do as much as they do now, and the social circles in which they moved were smaller. But one felt at home in these circles, one engaged in activities for their own sake, and, if you will pardon my use of a hackneyed proverb, the cobbler stuck to his last. Nowadays, no cobbler is content with his last anymore, and consequently none of our shoes fit us. We are, in a word, epigones, and we all carry the burden of having been born too late.[1]

Only a slight change in optic is required, however, in order to discover connections between Immermann's work and that of his Western European contemporaries lurking in this very same passage. The narrator's observation that life in contemporary Germany is fundamentally different from (and more dreary than) that in the late eighteenth century resembles Stendhal and Balzac's sociologically more astute observations about post-Restoration France. And Immermann, like Stendhal and Balzac, uses the *Bildungsroman* to document these changes, alighting on the narrative of a young man's development as the perfect literary vehicle through which to render a verdict on the times at large. In this, he sets out into unknown territory, transcending all his hackneyed borrowings from Goethe. *Wilhelm Meister's Apprenticeship* gives a poetic form to the experiences of an individual; *The Epigones*, on the other hand, like *The Red and the Black* or Balzac's *Old Man Goriot* (1835), ultimately aims to speak for those of a generation. The Tower Society includes members of many different age groups; Immermann, Stendhal, and Balzac leave no doubt that their tales are meant to be illustrative of a historical cohort, a fact also grasped by their respective protagonists.

These two competing ways of viewing the novel in the 1830s lead back to the questions about genre studies with which I concluded the opening chapter of this study. In Franco Moretti's words, are genres the products of "trees" or of "waves"? Is literary history determined by the continuity of local traditions or rather by sweeping conceptual innovations that spread quickly across various national literatures? And should the *Bildungsroman* ultimately be defined as a series of variations on Goethe, brought about in a political backwater hostile to literary advances supported by the rest of Europe, or rather as a response to a universal problem, such

---

1. Karl Leberecht Immermann, *Die Epigonen: Familienmemoiren in neun Büchern, 1823–1835*, ed. Peter Hasubek (Munich: Winkler Verlag, 1981), 118. All further references to this edition will appear in parentheses in the text.

as the search for an authentic expression of humanity in modern times? The newly found generational consciousness of the 1830s cuts to the heart of this question, because it forces a revision of the historicist mind-set that enabled the rise of the *Bildungsroman* to begin with. Historicism is premised on the notion that all living things are animated by a formative drive, while the *Bildungsroman* struggles to give this drive a narrative shape in which a community of fellow travelers through time might recognize itself. The advent of historicism furthermore coincided with and directly supported a rising nationalist ideology premised on the notion that the formative drive will express itself differently within different communities. Generational thinking merely represents the next logical step in this development: the recognition that formative variation has a temporal as well as geographic component, and that age groups that view one another across the barriers of historical time may have just as little in common as members of one culture have with another.

A century ago, however, Karl Mannheim, then one of the foremost figures in an attack launched by the rising discipline of sociology against the historicist movement in German letters, pointed out that generational thinking exposes an unresolved paradox within nineteenth-century thought. Taking explicit aim at the historicist notion of a *Zeitgeist*, a "spirit of the age" that might lend it a shape and explain its relation to an overall developmental trajectory, Mannheim wrote:

> The concept of the "spirit of the age" with which one had hitherto principally worked, now turns out to be . . . an accidental chord, an apparent harmony, produced by the vertical coincidence of notes which in fact owe a primary horizontal allegiance to the different parts (i.e. the generation-entelechies) of a fugue. The generation-entelechies thus serve to destroy the purely temporal concepts of an epoch over-emphasized in the past (e.g. Spirit of the age or epoch). The epoch as a unit has no homogeneous driving impulse, no homogeneous principle of form—no entelechy. Its unity consists at most in the related nature of the means which the period makes available for the fulfilment of the different historical tasks of the generations living in it.[2]

What Mannheim here expresses (and indeed identifies as such on the following page) is a variation of the argument for a "synchronicity of the non-synchronous" that Wilhelm Pinder had recently introduced to art history, and that Ernst Bloch would soon turn into an explicit tool with which to attack the historicist bias of Lukácsian Marxism. Epochs as a whole have no entelechy, he argues, because the actors who comprise them are "differently located" depending on when they were born, and are thus inclined to differing perceptions and actions: "The fact of belonging to the same class, and that of belonging to the same generation or age group, have this in common, that both endow the individuals sharing in them with

---

2. Karl Mannheim, "The Problem of Generations," in *Essays on the Sociology of Knowledge* (London: Routledge, 1952), 284.

a common location in the social and historical process, and thereby limit them to a specific range of potential experience."[3]

In discussing examples of events that might produce a "generational location," Mannheim foremost lists the Napoleonic Wars and thus highlights a series of events that played an important role in many of the works that were written during the 1830s, including *The Red and the Black* and *The Epigones*. Generational consciousness thus provides an example of the kind of transnational "wave" in literary history that Moretti was talking about. It transforms the shape of the *Bildungsroman*, not the least because the kind of developmental unity on which the genre was previously premised can now no longer be taken for granted. As the examples of Stendhal and Immermann show, however, the responses to this formal challenge were far from uniform throughout Europe, and the respective solutions pursued by the two authors explain a lot about the diverging roads traveled by the French and German novel over the following decades.

"Duodecimo Novels" and the "Common Effort to Possess the Past"

Among the many comparative studies dealing with the rise of the novel during the nineteenth century, none has been more influential than Erich Auerbach's *Mimesis*. Auerbach provides the canonical argument for a bifurcated path taken by the French realist novel on the one hand, and by the German *Bildungsroman* on the other. Whereas in the former case "contemporary political and social conditions are woven into the action in a manner more detailed and more real than had been exhibited in any earlier novel," in the German example external factors prevented a similarly expansive treatment of contemporary reality:[4]

> Contemporary conditions in Germany did not easily lend themselves to broad realistic treatment. The social picture was heterogeneous; the general life was conducted in the confusing setting of a host of "historical territories," units which had come into existence through dynastic and political contingencies. In each of them the oppressive and at times choking atmosphere was counterbalanced by a certain pious submission and the sense of a historical solidity, all of which was more conducive to speculation, introspection, intellectual cocooning, and the development of local idiosyncrasies than to coming to grips with the practical and the real in a spirit of determination and with an awareness of greater contexts and more extensive territories.[5]

---

3. Mannheim, "The Problem of Generations," 291.
4. Erich Auerbach, *Mimesis: The Representation of Reality in Western Literature*, trans. Willard R. Trask (Princeton, NJ: Princeton University Press, 1968), 457.
5. Auerbach, *Mimesis*, 445.

Although he has sometimes been attacked by specialists in German literature for writing these lines, Auerbach was merely repeating a critical commonplace shared by many of his contemporaries, and one that had first surfaced in no less distinguished a work than Wilhelm Dilthey's *Poetry and Experience* (1906). Here, Dilthey argued that the German *Bildungsroman*, in its early examples following *Wilhelm Meister*, "gave expression to the individualism of a culture whose sphere of interest was limited to private life. The governmental authority of the civil service and the military in the small and middle-sized German states confronted the young generation of writers as alien. But these young people were delighted and enraptured by what poets had discovered about the world of the individual and his self-development."[6] This oppositional account (French social realism on the one hand; German introspection and intellectual cocooning on the other) prevailed for much of the twentieth century and has only recently undergone serious challenge.[7]

Despite these revisions, Auerbach and Dilthey remain interesting as prime examples of the kind of arguments that give rise to the notion of a "national literature" in the first place. One thing that is immediately striking about the two passages that I have quoted is that both employ a twofold spatial metaphor to explain the stunted development of German realism. The fragmented geography of the German principalities, a literal example of spatial constriction, gives rise to a corresponding figurative constriction in the respective phrases "limited sphere of interest" and "intellectual cocooning" (*Sicheinspinnen*). Left on the outside are the "awareness of greater contexts and more extensive territories" that, one infers by chiasmus, were set into motion by the more expansive political geography of France. Similar spatial metaphors can be found in a number of other studies produced throughout the twentieth century. In his 1935 work on German popular literature during the Restoration period, for instance, Ferdinand Joseph Schneider puns that "the literary Biedermeier consists of duodecimo-novels," thereby combining a reference to the miniscule paper format used for the literary works of the period with an allusion to German political geography (the tiny states of the early nineteenth century were known as the *Duodezfürstentümer*).[8] Forty years later, Wolfgang Preisendanz speaks of German poetry's "direct access to the highest court of appeal"

---

6. Wilhelm Dilthey, *Poetry and Experience*, ed. Rudolf A. Makkreel and Frithjof Rodi (Princeton, NJ: Princeton University Press, 1985), 335.
7. Thus Jeffrey L. Sammons has argued that the nineteenth-century German novel was far more diverse than Auerbach suggested, while scholars such as Naomi Schor and Margaret Cohen, working in French departments, have pointed out that realist authors faced serious competition from sentimental and idealist fictions. See Jeffrey L. Sammons, "The Nineteenth-Century German Novel," in *German Literature of the Nineteenth Century*, ed. Clayton Koelb and Eric Downing (Columbia, SC: Camden House, 2005), 184; Naomi Schor, *George Sand and Idealism* (New York: Columbia University Press, 1993); and Margaret Cohen, *The Sentimental Education of the Novel* (Princeton, NJ: Princeton University Press, 1999).
8. Quoted in Elfriede Neubuhr, "Einführung," in *Begriffsbestimmung des literarischen Biedermeier*, ed. Elfriede Neubuhr (Darmstadt: Wissenschaftliche Buchgesellschaft, 1974), 11.

(*Reichsunmittelbarkeit der Poesie*) and thereby expresses the opinion that in the successor states of the Holy Roman Empire, synthetic statements were possible only on a level of abstraction that rivaled that of the famously distant and incompetent imperial court.[9] And in the 1990s, Martin Swales contrasts Western European realism, which focused on big cities like London and Paris that served as synecdoches for the larger world, with German literary production, which frequently centered on smaller "hometowns" in which local customs and traditions were sheltered by a guild economy.[10]

For Auerbach, German literary production is further marked not only by an underlying spatial fragmentation, but also by the country's fealty to tradition, its "sense of a historical solidity." France, on the other hand, emerges as the realm of rapid change and innovation. Writing about Stendhal's invention of realism, Auerbach thus proclaims that "temporal perspective is a factor of which he never loses sight; the concept of incessantly changing forms and manners of life dominates his thought."[11]

In contrast to the German emphasis on spatial fragmentation and temporal continuity, critics of French literature have provided many different accounts of the realist novel's ability to compile social data into a spatially unified model. Peter Brooks, for instance, has compared the novels of Balzac and Dickens to elaborate dollhouses and toy cities: architectural structures that are internally compartmentalized and yet afford their owners with a panoptic stance from which an internally unified parallel world springs into being.[12] These putative differences between French and German novel production can be explained as a consequence of the two countries' very different progression from the ancien régime into the modern period. The French, in the revolutions of 1789 and 1830, replaced hereditary right with popular sovereignty and created an image of themselves as a nation that had wrested control of the future from the clutches of the past: spatial homogeny and temporal heterogeneity. As a result, French realist novels could begin the difficult task of exploring the laws governing a complex but unified social system during times of rapid modernization. The robust public sphere of the July Monarchy, centered in Paris but endowed with the ability to rapidly disseminate information and opinions not only throughout all of France, but also beyond its borders, additionally involved literary realism in a complex network of transnational cultural exchange.[13] The many small states that comprised the Holy Roman Empire, on

---

9. Quoted in Martin Swales, *Studies of German Prose Fiction in the Age of European Realism* (Lampeter, Wales: Edwin Mellen Press, 1995), 8. The English translation is by Swales.
10. Swales, *Studies of German Prose Fiction*, 14.
11. Auerbach, *Mimesis*, 462.
12. Peter Brooks, *Realist Vision* (New Haven, CT: Yale University Press, 2005), 3–5.
13. On transnational exchange and its effect on the rise of the French novel, see Margaret Cohen and Carolyn Dever, eds., *The Literary Channel: The Inter-National Invention of the Novel* (Princeton, NJ: Princeton University Press, 2002).

the other hand, fell only at the hands of an external military power and found a renewed lease on life under Metternich: spatial heterogeneity and temporal homogeny. Faced with external stasis and a fragmented society, German authors withdrew inward to find referential totality and the opportunity for meaningful temporal development in the individual.

Since 1990, however, scholars have begun to advance a very different account, stressing the similarities between various countries during the Restoration period over their dissimilarities. For instance, the literary critic Martina Lauster claims:

> A cosmopolitan spirit characterizes the period from 1815 to 1848, in which as rarely before in European history political developments in one nation were interpreted as internationally significant and trendsetting. European interest in the Greek liberation struggle preceded these two decades, which in turn saw fiery enthusiasm for the July Revolution of 1830 (an event that emboldened constitutionalism all over Europe), international support for Polish independence, and continental interest in British election reforms, Chartism, and the "Irish Question," not to mention the problems of industrialization. . . . The years leading up to 1848 [*Vormärzzeit*] thus rival the Weimar Republic as a period in which cosmopolitan sentiments undermined the authority of national "codes," all the while social modernization reformulated precisely these codes in such a way that national identity would henceforth be defined through the exclusion of everything foreign.[14]

A number of different reasons could be cited to explain this shift in interest from the national to the cosmopolitan, central among them no doubt the resurgence of "world history" in the works of C. A. Bayly, Jürgen Osterhammel, and others. Bayly speaks of the period between 1815 and 1865 as a "New World Order," while Osterhammel refers to an "international state system" (*Weltstaatensystem*).[15] More immediately relevant for the present purposes, however, is the rise of cultural memory studies, which has singled out the first half of the nineteenth century as an era of collective stock-taking of the traumata that attended the "age of revolution" and the Napoleonic Wars. As historian Peter Fritzsche puts it especially forcefully, "While I recognize differences in the particular organization of historical time in Prussia and France and Britain and the United States, I do not find these differences as important as the common endeavor to think historically and to possess the past. This effort was transnational, even as it was constitutive of the idea of the national."[16]

---

14. Martina Lauster, "Einführung," in *Deutschland und der europäische Zeitgeist*, ed. Martina Lauster (Bielefeld: Aisthesis, 1994), 9–10.

15. See C. A. Bayly, *The Birth of the Modern World, 1780–1914: Global Connections and Comparisons* (Oxford: Blackwell, 2003), 134–38; and Jürgen Osterhammel, *Die Verwandlung der Welt: Eine Geschichte des 19. Jahrhunderts* (Munich: C. H. Beck, 2009), 674–81.

16. Peter Fritzsche, *Stranded in the Present: Modern Time and the Melancholy of History* (Cambridge, MA: Harvard University Press, 2004), 10.

On one level, this "common endeavor to think historically and to possess the past" represents nothing else than the culmination of the inexorable process by which the spirit of historicism turns from an obsession of the intellectual few into a preoccupation of the masses. Once the tremors and aftershocks of the French Revolution had passed over Europe, it became impossible even for ordinary peasants to think of their lives as anything other than a product of the contested past. On another level, however, the new obsession with collective memory counteracts the tendency of eighteenth-century historicism to conceptualize temporal flow in terms of national entelechies, precisely because these tremors travel across national boundaries and provide a unifying experience. Here is Fritzsche again, commenting on an 1815 travel narrative:

> Figures such as Napoleon, Talleyrand, Blücher, and red-lettered events such as Tilsit or Pamplona, belonged to the repertory of everyday conversations, but their significance was not self-evident; this was argued out among cobblers and tailors, Jews and farmers, Poles and Italians, who do not hesitate to place their own experiences ("Pamplona '13") into the larger picture. What is striking is not simply all the talk about the revolution and the wars, which is taken up again and again, before dinner, "after dinner," cabin to cabin, but also the exchange of opinion and evidence whereby well-known public events are retold in various personalized versions. The travelers participated in a common historical drama by which they organized and connected the events of their time and through which they told their own stories and found that others were interested in them.[17]

On first sight, two interpretive paradigms that I have just described seem irreconcilable with one another. The first, represented by Auerbach and Dilthey, claims that European culture during the 1830s was firmly divided into national traditions whose internal differences were largely the consequence of sociopolitical factors brought about by the Napoleonic conquests. The second, represented by Lauster and Fritzsche, claims that those very same conquests inaugurated a European-wide cosmopolitan memory culture. In reality, however, there is no inherent obstacle that would prevent *both* of these interpretations from being true simultaneously, as Fritzsche already points out when he describes the new memory culture as "transnational, even as it was constitutive of the idea of the national." Fritzsche's riverboat passengers, who "participated in a common historical drama by which they organized and connected the events of their time," remain Poles and Italians, Germans and Frenchmen, whose individual attempts to possess the past must inevitably be conditioned by the events put at their disposal by their respective national traditions.

---

17. Fritzsche, *Stranded in the Present*, 12.

The novels of Stendhal and Immermann participate in the new cosmopolitan memory culture through their attempts to articulate a post-Napoleonic generational consciousness. Both Stendhal's Julien Sorel and Immermann's Hermann believe themselves to be representatives of a historical cohort, and they try to act accordingly. The organization of intellectual life into generational groupings was a common feature of European society during the Restoration period, and one that Goethe himself already anticipated when he wrote, in his autobiography *Poetry and Truth*: "One may well say [someone] would have been quite a different person if born ten years before or after, as far as his *Bildung* and his effect on others are concerned."[18] These lines were written in 1811, before the Restoration had even begun, but they are nevertheless a world removed from anything he might have said fifteen years earlier, at the time of the publication of *Wilhelm Meister*. Indeed, although the years of Weimar Classicism were a period of considerable change and innovation for the novel, Wieland (born in 1733), Goethe (1749), and Schiller (1759) more often than not provided a united front in aesthetic matters. Jena Romanticism, on the other hand, was very much a generational concern, not just empirically (Novalis, Tieck, and Wilhelm Schlegel were all born within one year of one another) but also ideologically, while the poets and critics of Immermann's own time defined their entire aesthetic project as a struggle between the "Old" and the "Young" Germany.[19]

My own understanding of "generation" is somewhat looser than the one implied in the foregoing quote, however—a fact that will already be clear from my intent to compare a novel by Stendhal, born in 1783, to one by Immermann, born in 1796. What unites Immermann and Stendhal is not their membership in a

---

18. Johann Wolfgang von Goethe, *Collected Works*, ed. Victor Lange, Eric A. Blackall, and Cyrus Hamlin, vol. 4, *Poetry and Truth, Parts One to Three*, trans. Robert R. Heitner and ed. Thomas P. Saine and Jeffrey L. Sammons (New York: Suhrkamp, 1987), 17.

19. In 1824, Leopold von Ranke became the first person to use the concept of the "generation" as a methodological tool of academic historiography in his *History of the Latin and Teutonic Nations from 1494 to 1514*. In France as well, generational struggles were a defining feature of intellectual life in the years following the fall of Napoleon. As Alan Spitzer explains, "It was widely believed during and after the Restoration that the most visible and articulate members of a group whose mean age was twenty-three or twenty-four in 1820 constituted a privileged cohort, set apart by its talents and its coherence from older and younger contemporaries." See Alan B. Spitzer, *The French Generation of 1820* (Princeton, NJ: Princeton University Press, 1987), 4. Spitzer also stresses the transnational dimension of these experiences, drawing explicit parallels to the German context: "The trauma of growing up in an age of transition was scarcely confined to our French cohort even in its own era. The most relevant comparison is probably with the roughly identical age group in the contemporary German youth, notably those who formed the association of the 'Burschenschaften'. They too shared the sense of a world-historical mission for which their elders were inadequate. They too contrasted their stainless lives and selfless idealism with the shopworn and timeserving character of the preceding generation, which had fallen so far short of its own ideals. They felt themselves adrift in a universe without landmarks and yearned for some higher synthesis that would guarantee an indispensable ideological and social coherence. They rejected those skeptical and materialist philosophies that had contributed to the moral void" (267).

common age group, but rather a set of similar experiences the two writers had independently of one another and at different points in historical time.[20] Both writers were young boys when the ancien régime came to a sudden (and as it would turn out temporary) end in their respective countries: Stendhal was six when the French Revolution arrived in Grenoble, while Immermann was ten when he witnessed the demise of the Holy Roman Empire in the battle of Jena and Auerstedt, just a short distance from his native town of Magdeburg. Both authors, furthermore, began their adult life by participating in military campaigns that seemed to foreshadow glorious national futures, only to see these hopes smashed on the rocks of the Restoration. Stendhal was seventeen when he followed Napoleon into Italy, the exact same age at which Immermann, fighting on the opposite side, participated in the "Battle of the Nations" at Leipzig. The importance of these events to the two authors is well documented in Stendhal's *Life of Henri Brulard* (1835–36) and in Immermann's *The Youth of Twenty-Five Years Ago* (1840)—works that undoubtedly rank among the earliest "generational autobiographies" in literary history. In the opening lines of his text, Immermann declares his intention to describe the experiences of all those Germans who "were at least ten and at most sixteen years old in October of 1806, and who were thus between seventeen and twenty-three on February 3 of 1813."[21]

Stendhal and Immermann were born thirteen years apart, but their novels confront the same question, namely how to bestow a narrative shape on European culture at a time (the 1820s) in which both France and Germany found themselves torn apart by a historically unprecedented clash of generations. Older men who had come into power and fortune during the ancien régime confronted a rising tide of younger people whose formative experiences had coincided with the Napoleonic Wars. This clash entailed much more than a collision of values and opinions about such subjects as political emancipation and property distribution. Also at stake was a fundamental disagreement about historical narrative, about the ways in which the past should be connected to the present. For obvious reasons, the *Bildungsroman* is an ideal vehicle with which to meditate on this question; Stendhal and Immermann embraced it eagerly, taking the novel in directions that Goethe could never have anticipated. But although they respond to a common problem, *The Red and the Black* and *The Epigones* could hardly be more different from one another, a fact that points to the continued relevance of national circumstance in literary history.

---

20. As Mannheim puts it, "The fact people are born at the same time, or that their youth, adulthood, and old age coincide, does not itself involve similarity of location; what does create a similar location is that they are in a position to experience the same events and data, etc., and especially that these experiences impinge upon a similarly 'stratified' consciousness" ("The Problem of Generations," 297).

21. Karl Immermann, *Die Jugend vor fünfundzwanzig Jahren*, in *Werke in fünf Bänden*, ed. Benno von Wiese, vol. 4, *Autobiographische Schriften* (Frankfurt am Main: Athenäum, 1973), 361. February 3, 1813, was the date of a general call to arms to the German youth.

The Red, the Black, and the Young

The writings of both Immermann and Stendhal are marked by a certain elegiac tone, a longing for an earlier age in which literary production could still address itself to a unified public. In Stendhal, this elegiac tone is perhaps most pronounced in a note he inscribed in a copy of *The Red and the Black* in 1834, eleven years after giving up his youthful ambition to become a comic playwright in the manner of Molière: "It has become impossible to write theatrical comedy since the Revolution; there are now two publics: the vulgar one and the refined. A young woman cannot be blond and brunette at the same time. . . . Ever since democracy has populated the theaters with vulgar people, incapable of appreciating refined subject matter, I have come to regard the novel as the comedy of the nineteenth century." Two years later, he tempered this blunt attack on "vulgar people" (*gens grossiers*) by offering a more nuanced analysis of the two publics ushered in by the Revolution. A performance of Molière's *The Bourgeois Gentleman* in 1836 would necessarily have to be a failure, Stendhal argued, because one half of the audience would laugh at the bourgeois M. Jourdain while the other would laugh at the disheveled aristocrat Dorante.[22] Stendhal's thesis regarding the impossibility of theatrical comedy in the nineteenth century is, in other words, premised on his recognition that the events of 1789 have wreaked havoc on the historical self-understanding of the French people. A theater in 1830 would, perforce, bring together audience members who regard the post-Napoleonic monarchy as essentially a continuation of the ancien régime, and for whom M. Jourdain is a pretentious upstart, with others who regard the days of the aristocracy as numbered, and for whom Dorante is a mere fossil. In the absence of any interpretive certainty regarding the status of the twenty-five years between 1789 and 1814, it is difficult to know whether to laugh at events that depart from the way things were once supposed to be, or whether to embrace them.

Novels, on the other hand, are consumed in the private setting of a salon or bedchamber. In the act of reading a novel, a fragmented audience can imagine itself as whole again; indeed it can even imagine its fragmentation as the starting point for a more fundamental wholeness. This, at any rate, is the promise that Stendhal holds out in *The Red and the Black*, and which he even seems to inscribe in the novel's enigmatic title. "Red," as many exegetes have pointed out, is the color of the Napoleonic army uniform, and thus a metonym for a worldview that values courage, independent thinking, and resolute action. "Black," on the other hand, stands for the habit of the ultramontanist clergy, and thus for a worldview that privileges obedience over courage, conformity over independence, and stasis over action. The two colors furthermore seem aligned with competing historical interpretations,

---

22. I owe both of these references to Peter Brooks, *The Novel of Worldliness* (Princeton, NJ: Princeton University Press, 1969), 262.

since the "red" seeks guidance for the future from the years between 1799 and 1815, while the "black" attempts to restore French society to the state it found itself in before 1789.

Yet "red" and "black" are also the colors that one can find on a roulette wheel, where they are locked into the same eternal dance around a common center. This roulette metaphor certainly provides an apt description of Stendhal's novel. *The Red and the Black* presents its reader with a panoramic view of French society, moving from a small village to a midsize town in the Franche-Comté and eventually to the capital. Each of these settings is lovingly detailed and possesses a distinctive cast of characters. But there can never be any doubt that Verrières, Besançon, and Paris are part of the same world, or that they follow a parallel path through history. Of course, each of the three settings witnesses its own struggles between revolution and reaction, between "red" and "black," but precisely because the shape of this struggle is everywhere the same (and because the "black" everywhere seems to be winning) the novel appears internally unified. There is no better proof of this than the fact that Julien Sorel is able to pursue an essentially unbroken development through all three stages. He improves on his early achievements in dissimulation and flattery during his subsequent stays in Besançon and Paris, but what he has learned in the household of M. de Rênal essentially carries over into the more rarified setting of the Hôtel de la Mole.

It is only upon closer inspection that a number of cracks begin to appear in the unified front presented by this fictional world. When he wrote *The Red and Black*, Stendhal borrowed heavily from an actual murder case that had taken place in the Dauphiné, but made the strategic decision to relocate the action to the Franche-Comté. This was a significant choice, for unlike the Dauphiné, the Franche-Comté was a rather recent acquisition of the kingdom of France. A medieval fiefdom of the duchy of Burgundy, it became a part of the Holy Roman Empire and thus a vassal state of the Spaniards before it was eventually conquered by Louis XIV in the mid-seventeenth century. Even more significantly, it almost did not return to France after the Napoleonic interlude, for the Prussians laid claim to it during the Congress of Vienna. The Franche-Comté, in other words, is a potent reminder of the fact that the Hexagon is a culturally constructed rather than natural entity, and that the territorial integrity of France was in considerable danger after Napoleon's defeat on the battlefield at Waterloo. Had things gone only a little bit differently, Verrières and Besançon could now find themselves cut off from Paris and the rest of French society.

Stendhal weaves a number of reminders of this contested history into the opening chapters of *The Red and the Black*. The first paragraph of the novel, for instance, explains that "[the] Doubs flows a couple of hundred feet below [Verrières's] fortifications, built long ago by the Spaniards and now fallen into ruins," while M. de Rênal comes from a family that "is Spanish, ancient, and . . . was established in the land long before the conquest of Louis XIV."[23] These references to ancient history are given a more contemporary relevance in one of the most celebrated scenes in the novel, in which a foreign king comes to visit Verrières, where the local gentry attempt to demonstrate the political stability of the Restoration by putting on a magnificent spectacle. One of the highlights of the performance is a salute with "an old Spanish cannon belonging to the town" (85), which in turn is operated by "the cannoneers of Leipzig firing five shots a minute just as if they had the Prussians in their sights" (90). Julien, too, becomes a small cog in the inevitable mechanism by which this carnival progresses to its sublime conclusion when, at the very same time in which he is outwardly trying to cut a dashing figure as one of the king's attendants, he imagines himself as "one of Napoleon's orderlies in the act of charging a battery" (81).

This progression from a reference to Spanish fortifications in the opening pages to Julien's hypocritical performance at the culmination of the Verrières episode encapsulates a dynamic that Stendhal stages again and again over the course of his novel. One of the major themes (indeed, *the* major theme) of *The Red and the Black* is that "history" is a contested narrative construct, that people remember events differently and will draw from them diverging conclusions. But the objective reminders of such alternate realities are hidden beneath the placid surface of the novel, which, despite its stated intention to be a "Chronicle of 1830," references neither class struggle nor genuine intellectual dissent to Restoration culture. Upon their first reading, for instance, very few readers will pick up on the fact that Julien owes his meteoric rise within French society not just to flattery and luck, but also to a prolonged territorial dispute between two Restoration officials, the Abbé Frilair and the Marquis de la Mole. "Twelve years before," we learn in an unmistakable reference to the fall of Napoleon, "Abbé Frilair had arrived in Besançon with a very slender carpetbag [*porte-manteau*], which, as the story went, contained his entire fortune.... In the course of making all this money, he had bought half a property, the other half of which passed by inheritance to M. de la Mole. Hence a great lawsuit between these two figures" (167). Robert M. Adams's ingenious translation identifies the Abbé as what he really is, namely a "carpetbagger," who cunningly enriched himself during the years after 1815 and is now fighting off the restitution claims of M. de la Mole, who spent the Napoleonic interregnum in exile and was thus unable to protect his ancestral property. At stake in the lawsuit, then, is a debate over what kind of historical legitimation claims should determine future property relationships in France. But unlike Balzac or Dickens, for whom such a struggle might present the material for an entire novel, Stendhal shows very little

---

23. Stendhal, *The Red and the Black*, trans. Robert M. Adams and ed. Susanna Lee (New York: Norton, 2008) 8–9. All further references to this edition will appear in parentheses in the text.

interest in the further legal proceedings. He needs them only in order to have a plausible explanation for Julien's move to the Hôtel de la Mole.

Another reference to the contested political reality of Bourbon France occurs in the brief passage in which Stendhal whisks his protagonist from Besançon toward Paris. In his mail coach, Julien overhears a conversation between two total strangers. One of them, a man named Saint-Giraud, is complaining of the poor lot that has befallen him ever since he tried to escape the hubbub of the capital by moving to a farm in the Rhone Valley: "For six months the vicar of the village and the local gentry paid court to me; I fed them dinners; I told them I had left Paris in order never again to hear, or be obliged to talk, about politics.... But this wasn't the vicar's game; and before long I was subjected to a thousand different indiscreet requests and bits of chicanery" (190). Driven to despair by the escalating conflict between the vicar and the local faction of liberals, Saint-Giraud eventually concludes: "I'm going to get my solitude and rural peace in the only place where they can be found in France, a fourth-floor apartment off the Champs-Elysées. And even there, I'm wondering whether I hadn't better begin my political career in the district of Roule by presenting the blessed bread in the parish church" (191).

This is one of the few places in the novel in which we find a reference to "France" in its entirety, and Saint-Giraud's description makes it quite clear that he conceives of the nation as a cesspool of political strife. Like the quarrel between M. de la Mole and the Abbé Frilair, furthermore, these struggles largely concern political geography and future property relations, as Julien immediately grasps when he identifies Saint-Giraud as the victorious party in an earlier intrigue concerning a house that M. de Rênal also coveted. And yet when Julien himself arrives in the "district of Roule" (i.e., the Faubourg Saint-Honoré), his overriding concern is to learn how to ride a horse, and his biggest enemy the heavy traffic that moves down the Champs-Elysées. Once again, all material traces of the legitimation struggle that holds Restoration-era France in its grip are sublimated into an episode in Julien's rise through society.

The historical legitimation struggles that are suppressed on the level of sociopolitical reality instead erupt with a vengeance within Julien's personal narrative, and this explains why he represents so many things to so many different people. In his own mind, he is a Napoleonic hero, a reincarnation of the Corsican artillery lieutenant who seized his own place in life rather than settle for what the world had given him. To Mathilde, he is the rebirth not of Bonaparte, but of Boniface, her sixteenth-century ancestor who died as the condemned lover of Queen Marguerite of Navarre. Everything that Julien does, Mathilde interprets not as a symptom of Napoleonic egomania, but rather as a token of true chivalry. M. de la Mole, finally, lives his life as if he were a royal subject of Louis XVI, rather than of Louis XVIII, yet one who has somehow received warning of, and now desperately tries to avert, the impending revolutionary cataclysm. For him, Julien is initially a fellow royalist conspirator, before he morphs into the threatening figure of a Jacobin. At stake here is far more than a mere conflict between different interpretations of Julien's character: these are also competing historical interpretations, competing narratives about what French society does and should look like. Stendhal, of course, repeatedly pokes fun at these attempts to put the past into the service of the present, most viciously in the episode in which Julien attempts to woo Mme de Fervaques (herself a devoted student of Saint-Simon and thus mentally stuck in the eighteenth century) with copies of love letters by the Russian prince Korasoff: "The Russians copy French customs, but always at a distance of fifty years. They are just now coming into the age of Louis XV" (325). The ultimate irony in this episode is that Korasoff's letters are "so ridiculous that [Julien] began to copy [them] line for line without giving a thought to the sense" (338). Their meaning lies not in what they actually say, but rather in their ability to provide the present with a behavioral matrix that carries the authority of the past.

Julien's peculiar fate in literary history thus is to follow three separate developmental trajectories simultaneously, and to thereby give a literary form to the "problem of generations" as it presented itself around 1830. Julien, Mathilde, and M. de la Mole are, to invoke the language of Karl Mannheim, "differently located," and yet the conclusion of the novel confirms each of them in their own worldview. For Julien, the murder of Mme de Rênal is the equivalent of Napoleon's infamous self-coronation: an act of romantic fiat in which he renounces all social obligations and takes his destiny into his own hands, even if this should lead to his inevitable destruction. For Mathilde, that very same act serves as the conclusion to a gothic love story, in which her lover kills the woman who has made her happiness impossible. Finally, for M. de la Mole, the murder merely confirms his darkest suspicions about what Julien is capable of. Each of these characters imposes his or her preferred narrative conventions on the events of Julien's rise and fall, and each derives vindication.

The beauty of this narrative solution is that it allows Stendhal to depict the internal divisions of his age while preserving the conventions of the *Bildungsroman*. There can be no doubt that Julien Sorel undergoes an internally consistent development, even if the various characters who surround him would debate the underlying logic that animates it. Sandy Petrey, in a powerful interpretation of the novels of Stendhal and Balzac, has argued that French realist fiction is characterized by the struggle between denotative and constative speech acts, between words that merely refer to external reality and those that set out to shape it.[24] *The Red and the Black* fulfills this argument with a vengeance, since this self-effacing attempt to present a "Chronicle of 1830" contains no less than a triply constative speech act. Julien's life and death impose meaning on disorder and chaos, but this meaning is in turn tied to a certain historical perspective, a generational location. In this manner,

---

24. Sandy Petrey, *Realism and Revolution: Balzac, Stendhal, Zola, and the Performances of History* (Ithaca, NY: Cornell University Press, 1988), 1–16.

Stendhal achieves the illusion of a unified world, even while he simultaneously challenges the reader to recognize that there are different ways of interpreting it.

Epigonalism and the Novel

At first sight, no novel could possibly be more different from *The Red and the Black* than Karl Leberecht Immermann's *The Epigones*. Stendhal's story possesses the sociopolitical unity so characteristic of realist fiction; only on closer examination does it become clear that it actually contains three very different interpretations of what is happening, and challenges its readers to stake their full confidence on one of them if they ever want to arrive at a picture of the world "as it actually is." Nobody, by contrast, could ever confuse *The Epigones* with a realist, or even an internally unified, text. More than anything else, it resembles a picaresque tale. It jumps between a large number of different locations, all of which obey their own narrative conventions and only some of which can be located on a map, and it introduces such a dazzling variety of characters that its protagonist at times seems all but forgotten.

Furthermore, *The Red and the Black* ranks as one of the undisputed masterpieces of world literature, while *The Epigones* is now almost forgotten. It has never been translated into English and was last published in German thirty years ago in an imposing critical edition printed on Bible paper—a scholarly godsend, but hardly the kind of format liable to win a larger audience. The hero of Immermann's novel is a young man by the name of Hermann, who believes that he is the son of a senator from Bremen, though he is actually the bastard child of an aristocrat. He is twenty-four years old in 1820, when the novel begins, which would make him an exact contemporary of his author.[25] The opening chapter finds him on his way to see his uncle, a rich industrialist who has acquired ownership rights to the ancestral dominions of a duke who is, however, vigorously contesting these claims with the help of his secretary, Wilhelmi. By chance, Hermann comes across the duke at a local inn, recognizes in him an old friend of his ostensible father, the senator, and renews the acquaintance. Much of the novel is then given to Hermann's attempts to mediate between the duke and his uncle, an endeavor that carries him to diverse localities throughout Germany. Over the course of these travels, Hermann becomes involved with the liberal student movement and with its enemies, mingles in Berlin salon society, stages a revival of a feudal tournament, and has numerous other adventures.

---

25. "Hermann" (Arminius), the name of a Germanic king who defeated the Roman general Varus in 9 CE and stopped the expansion of the Roman Empire at the Rhine, was a popular choice of parents who wished to express their patriotism during the years of the Napoleonic occupation and the Restoration period. Hermann can thus be seen as a kind of German everyman. Immermann's chronology is jumbled, however. The subtitle of the novel, for instance, describes it as a "family memoir in nine books, 1823–1835." There are other inconsistencies among the dates given in the text.

This main plot is surrounded by a number of secondary plotlines, a fact that seems to emphasize the origins of the German *Bildungsroman* in the picaresque genre.[26] Among other things, Hermann embarks on a quest to find a tutor for a young circus-performer named Flämmchen, and he also falls in love with a series of women. The first of these is the duchess herself, who is then followed in quick succession by his uncle's adopted daughter Cornelie, and, finally, by the duke's sister Johanna, with whom Hermann believes he has intercourse in a darkened room one night. The climax of the novel occurs when Hermann discovers the secret of his aristocratic heritage and finds out that he is a blood relative both of the duke and of Johanna. He thus concludes that he has committed an incestuous act and promptly goes mad. Fortunately, everything turns out to have been a misunderstanding, and Flämmchen reveals herself to be the mysterious lover. Since both the uncle and the duke, Hermann's last two adult relatives by adoption and by blood, respectively, have meanwhile passed away, Hermann is left as the sole remaining heir on either side of the legal struggle that had provided the narrative backbone of *The Epigones*.

Immermann's novel was immediately recognized as an important work by its contemporaries but faded into obscurity soon afterward. Besides its cumbersome and often creakingly artificial plot, the primary reason for this change in critical fortune undoubtedly lies in the fact that the book appears to be what its title already promises: an epigonal work that recycles a variety of plot elements from *Wilhelm Meister's Apprenticeship*, but without animating them with Goethe's peculiar literary genius. Flämmchen, for instance, is a transparent copy of Goethe's Mignon, but she lacks Mignon's grace and innocent mystery, rising from the pages of the later novel as a grossly sexualized child-woman. The nighttime encounter with an unknown woman is lifted from Goethe as well but here takes on a rather more sordid aspect. Numerous other correspondences—between Goethe's countess and Immermann's duchess, between the Tower Society and Wilhelmi's Masonic lodge, for instance—could be mentioned, none of which testify in favor of *The Epigones*. Not surprisingly, the brief passage from Immermann's novel that I quoted at the beginning of this chapter, and in which the narrator describes his own generation as hopelessly inferior to that of fifty years ago, has often been read as a thinly veiled summary of the work as a whole.

The elegiac tone of this quotation is, however, flatly contradicted by a second passage that occurs much later in the novel:

> But our present age possesses infinite capacities for healing and regeneration, and I could think of no better way to conclude our epistolary conversation, which (like its subject) has admittedly been somewhat chaotic and has violated the temporal order

---

26. On this relationship, see David H. Miles, "The Picaro's Journey to the Confessional: The Changing Image of the Hero in the German *Bildungsroman*," *PMLA* 89 (1974): 980–92.

of things, than by quoting Lamartine, who said: "I can detect no sign of decay in the human spirit, no symptom of fatigue or senescence. It is true that I see rotten institutions collapse upon themselves, but I also see a rejuvenated race animated by the breath of life push forward in every sense. This race will use an unknown plan to reconstruct the never-ending project whose creation and execution God has entrusted to man: his own fate." (558)

It is difficult to reconcile these two passages, unless one reads either one or both of them as fundamentally ironic. The fact that the first of these speeches is attributed to the pedantic character of Wilhelmi, while the second belongs to the pseudoauthorial "publisher" of the "family memoirs" (thus the subtitle of *The Epigones*), seems to suggest that Immermann's sympathies are with those who would identify contemporary events as indicators of a "rejuvenated race." There is a third possibility, however, namely that Immermann wanted his readers to regard both passages as possessing equal merit, and as documenting between them the internally conflicted self-understanding of the Restoration period.

This third possibility is supported by a quick excursus on the etymology of the term "epigone." In contemporary German and English alike, the term refers to "one of a succeeding generation. Chiefly . . . the less distinguished successors of an illustrious generation" (*Oxford English Dictionary*, s.v., www.oed.com). As Manfred Windfuhr has pointed out, however, the word had a very different meaning during the eighteenth century and in fact possessed a *positive* connotation deriving from its roots in Greek mythology, where the *epigonoi* were the sons of the seven heroes of the war against Thebes, who succeeded in conquering the city to which their fathers had ineffectually laid siege. During the 1830s, the term underwent a semantic transvaluation, and indeed, there is some evidence that Immermann's novel was responsible for the shift.[27] Windfuhr links this development to the newly popular historicist tendency to define the present in terms of the past, and to search for distinctions between one's own time and that which came before it: "The union of a comprehensive humanist education with a historical sense sharpened by academic historiography led to a reinterpretation of the concept of the epigone toward the beginning of the nineteenth century. An era that regarded itself as epigonal discovered an expression of its identity in a previously marginal ancient myth."[28] There is thus a delicious circular reasoning in arguments that would interpret the title of Immermann's novel as uncompromisingly elegiac: the academic establishment of

---

27. Manfred Windfuhr, "Der Epigone: Begriff, Phänomen und Bewußtsein," *Archiv für Begriffsgeschichte* 4 (1959): 182–209.

28. Windfuhr, "Der Epigone," 185. Roughly seventy years earlier, Carl Spitteler had already made essentially the same argument in a highly polemical manner when he described epigonalism as a "disease" that "comes into being when a nation stubbornly thinks and feels backwards" and "confuses literary scholarship [*Literaturwissenschaft*] with literature itself." Quoted in Markus Fauser, *Intertextualität als Poetik des Epigonalen* (Munich: Wilhelm Fink, 1999), 23.

the Restoration period, casting about for a term that would describe its own self-perceived inferiority compared to the age of Weimar Classicism, brought about a semantic transvaluation of the term "epigone." This transvaluation, enshrined in definitions like the one from the *Oxford English Dictionary* but still far from universal in the 1830s, was then used to sanction a particular reading of Immermann's novel, and by extension of German literature as a whole. It is true that Immermann refers to the newer understanding of epigonalism when he describes his own generation as "carrying the burden of having been born too late." But he could also count on his readers to possess knowledge of the earlier definition, and thus to be aware of the semantic ambiguities of the term.[29] Far from reinforcing a particular attitude, in other words, Immermann's title opens up a rich field of conflicting possibilities, pointing both toward impotent belatedness and toward vigorous renewal.

The fact that these two contradictory vectors are espoused and clearly articulated by characters *within* the novel already highlights a basic difference between *The Epigones* and *The Red and the Black*. The legitimation struggles that largely remain beneath the surface of Stendhal's realist narrative, giving his depiction of France a unified exterior, find a much more forceful expression in Immermann, where they contribute to the novel's fragmented and picaresque character. The action of *The Epigones* is set in motion by a lawsuit that combines a dispute over territorial possessions with larger philosophical questions about the nature of historical continuity. At the Congress of Vienna, during the same deliberations that ultimately preserved the territorial integrity of France by refusing the Prussian claims to the Franche-Comté, the victorious powers decided to retain a system of miniscule principalities in Germany. In the process, numerous decisions needed to be made regarding the redistribution of property that the French occupational forces had taken away from their aristocratic owners, and the complexity of these decisions enables the uncle's attacks on the duke's holdings. One of the duke's ancestors, so the uncle argues, had married a commoner, and the rightful claims to his estates should thus have passed to the cadet branch of the family, whose last surviving member, a count, sold them to him. The duke's defense rests on a series of technicalities regarding the way in which the feudal properties in Germany were mediatized, that is, restored to their previous owners after the defeat of Napoleon. Via his secretary Wilhelmi, the duke first tries to claim that the intervening occupation effectively negated all legal claims based on events that took place before the fall of the Holy Roman Empire. After this initial defense is dismissed, Wilhelmi argues that if the duke's claim to his estates is agnatic (i.e., part of aristocratic privilege), then the uncle, as a commoner, could never have legally acquired them. But this defense too is dismissed;

---

29. Early reviews of Immermann's novel, quoted at length in the critical edition prepared by Peter Hasubek, document that contemporary readers were indeed keenly aware of such ambiguities. As one reviewer noted, "[It was] the intention of the author of *The Epigones* to depict all individuals whom he sketched as being without direction and inner unity" (698).

the process of mediatization, it turns out, has been incomplete. Commoners are now allowed to hold feudal property, and the duke thus finds himself caught in a double bind: the aristocratic world into which he was born (and which, like Stendhal's Marquis de la Mole, he carried with him into exile once Napoleon took over) has been restituted just enough to let him regain his property, but not sufficiently to allow him to keep it.

The fragmented political geography of Germany thus emerges as the direct cause of the novel's anxiety about proper procedures of inheritance and about the relationship between generations: in a word, as a direct cause of epigonalism in all its semantic ambiguity. Epigonalism, in turn, gives rise to narrative fragmentation, as Hermann stumbles through a number of disconnected settings, populated by an equally large number of disjointed characters that each express a different strategy to possess the past. Immermann's world is filled with revolutionaries and reactionaries, and it devotes oftentimes painfully extended space to such debates as the one between the educational councilor and his brother, who argue about whether a proper school curriculum should be modeled on the ancients or the moderns.

The best illustration of the link between epigonalism and narrative fragmentation, however, is provided by the two spatial domains that serve as the opposing poles of the novel: the duke's castle and the uncle's industrial park. The duke lives in a wonderful palace, and in one crucial scene of the novel hopes to accentuate his noble lineage by staging a carousel, a faux medieval tournament that was possibly inspired by a widely publicized event that took place during the Congress of Vienna. But the whole endeavor quickly turns into a farce, because none of the noble participants know anything about the customs of such an occasion and at any rate lack the necessary military skills to handle a horse or a sharp-edged weapon. The carousel moves from the farcical to the downright disastrous when a group of bourgeois, unimpressed by feudal privilege, attempts to gate-crash the party and mocks the entire spectacle. "This was the way," the narrator concludes his description, "in which an imitation of the tournament at Ashby de la Zouche failed in the nineteenth century" (252).

The uncle, meanwhile, lives in an environment that strikes the contemporary reader as almost Dickensian in its outward aspect:[30]

> Machines rattled, coal smoke rose from the narrow chimneys and darkened the air, carts and workers moved past [Hermann] and by their number announced the proximity of an industrious enterprise. Portions of the green valley were hidden from the eye by yarns and textiles hung out to bleach, and the river, which propelled several

---

30. Jeffrey L. Sammons has, in fact, argued that the uncle "is the first modern capitalist in German fiction and *Die Epigonen* is the first German novel to describe a capitalist industrial milieu." See Jeffrey L. Sammons, *Six Essays on the Young German Novel* (Chapel Hill: University of North Carolina Press, 1972), 132.

engines, was confined to an enclosure of wooden boards and beams. Amid all these signs of bourgeois industriousness, the battlements of the count's palace could be discerned on the top of the highest hill in the area, while the towers of the monastery rose from the valley. The uncle used both buildings for his business. (399)

The uncle obviously has a very different attitude toward the relics of the feudal past than the duke: he has simply integrated the palace with its medieval battlements, and the monastery with its Gothic towers into his capitalist enterprise. Indeed, the uncle seems intent to similarly repurpose the very landscape itself, for he has constructed a giant machine that is continually pumping water away from the foundations of his buildings, turning inhospitable swampland into a site of industrial activity. And yet this triumph of the modern mind-set turns into tragedy when his son Ferdinand climbs the machine and falls to his death, motivated by foolish credence in the old folk belief (given contemporary currency by the enormous success of Carl Maria von Weber's opera *Der Freischütz* [1821]) that lead acquired at the risk of one's life can be cast into infallible bullets. Precisely at the moment in which he seems to abandon epigonal collage for a powerful realistic depiction of modern life, Immermann thus seizes on yet another romantic cliché. His move is so overt that it seems implausible to regard it as anything other than calculated: an attempt, in other words, to show that the most progressive attitudes of his own time are, in reality, built on rotten foundations, just as the seemingly "modern" nationalism of the liberal student movement required the gothic thrills of Weber's opera as a catalyst.

The respective domains of the duke and of the uncle are so different from one another that their very coexistence in one text denies plausibility. And yet Immermann asks his readers to accept them as part of the same internally discontinuous historical reality. Even more importantly, he carefully maintains what Ernest K. Bramsted has called his "negative neutrality," refusing to take sides in the interpretive struggle that is staged by his novel.[31] Pastoral and industrial landscapes, romantic and realist codes, are treated with equal ironic indifference. Immermann mocks the duke for his attempt to hide in the past, the uncle for his attempt to escape from it. The only character that seems immune to all this mockery is Hermann himself, who marches through the disjointed world of *The Epigones* with stolid determination, ready to respond to each of the new settings with which he is confronted, but willing to commit to none. Over the course of his travels, he encounters a number of different strategies to relate the past to the present, and as their number grows, so does his understanding of himself and of the world around him. But this understanding is entirely negative in nature. Hermann grows wiser because, just like his author, he refuses to commit to any particular interpretation of history and to regard himself as either sadly belated or the first product of a new era.

---

31. Ernest K. Bramsted, *Aristocracy and the Middle-Classes in Germany: Social Types in German Literature, 1830–1900* (Chicago: University of Chicago Press, 1964), 62.

Acting One's Age

For all their internal differences, then, *The Red and the Black* and *The Epigones*, two novels that have often been read merely as the foundational examples of diverging national traditions, can be seen as the common outcome of a collective desire to restore narrative order to history. Conventional approaches to the origins of realism have always focused on the novel's struggle to represent sociological complexity and have assumed the unified nation-state to be a necessary prerequisite for a successful solution to this problem. But just as pressing during this period was the need to relate the present to the past, to figure out whether contemporary events constituted a revolutionary break with history or its continuation by other means. "All at once," writes Peter Fritzsche, "the past was reenlivened with the identification of foreclosed possibilities. Contemporaries came to see what I call 'half lives' in the past and to insist on the possibilities of restoring, however incompletely, neglected itineraries."[32] No longer loyal to the organic entelechy of the Goethean model, the *Bildungsroman* of the 1830s commits itself to tracing such neglected itineraries.

The attempts to stake a claim in the past were at once personal and transnational and thus constitute a perfect illustration of what I have called, following Homi K. Bhabha, a "vernacular cosmopolitanism." They were transnational, because Metternich's restoration was transnational, and because the Congress of Vienna, with its Europe-wide efforts at mediatization, provided a spatial metaphor for temporal strife that both Stendhal and Immermann eagerly seized as their own. They were personal, because consciousness of the struggle was disseminated not through the pedagogic instruments of the state but sprang up spontaneously among a generational cohort: those old enough to remember prerevolutionary Europe, but young enough to have grown up in its aftermath. People who were significantly older than Stendhal or Immermann when the ancien régime collapsed in their respective countries, just like those who had not yet been born, tended to lack the dual perspective that rendered life so complicated for the intermediate generation. As Immermann put it, describing circumstances in Germany, "The young people born before the conquest were political nonentities, the young people of today take a contemplative attitude toward politics (if they haven't fallen victim to fantastical illusions), but the young people of twenty-five years ago suffered and acted for their political convictions."[33]

The notion of a generation at odds with itself provides a common theme for *The Red and the Black* and *The Epigones*. But the ways in which this theme is implemented in these two novels remain very different and thereby testify to the importance of local sociopolitical circumstances in shaping literary history. Restoration-era France presented Stendhal's generation with an almost perfect simulacrum of the

---

32. Fritzsche, *Stranded in the Present*, 7.
33. Immermann, *Die Jugend vor fünfundzwanzig Jahren*, 363–64.

prerevolutionary era, thus fostering the notion that, after twenty-five years of violent turmoil, the nation had finally returned to a collective and peaceful road into the future. Stendhal seized on this delusion and created a fictional world that appears as internally unified as the Bourbon authorities wished it to be. Against this backdrop, however, he placed the story of a typical Restoration personality, a young man bent on advancement in the world, and showed how the same "objective" biographical facts, such as Julien's courtship of Mathilde or his murder of Mme de Rênal, might receive dramatically different interpretations (and be twisted into dramatically different narrative shapes) depending on the historical location of those trying to impose meaning on them. France, so Stendhal suggests, may appear externally united, but in the minds of its inhabitants lurks a multitude of competing realities.

Immermann, on the other hand, found himself in a German state-system more fragmented than it had ever been before, even during the frequently chaotic times of the Holy Roman Empire. This geographic fragmentation lent itself to an entirely different narrative treatment, and the result was a picaresque novel featuring a multitude of different spaces that collectively represent the confusion and general lack of direction that Immermann saw at the heart of the Biedermeier condition. Hermann, like Wilhelm Meister before him, moves in ever-expanding historical circles and is able to compare his life to an ever-increasing number of competing stories. But whereas Wilhelm eventually is led into the Tower Society, where he learns that these competing stories in fact run in parallel, Hermann initially matures only in the extent of his ironic detachment. As a result, Germany appears externally multiple, but internally united, even if the unity is one of chaos and indifference.

At least this is true for much of the novel. But much as was already the case with *Wilhelm Meister*, the conclusion of *The Epigones* departs in a startlingly new direction. Hermann eventually discovers the secret of his aristocratic heritage and realizes that he is the rightful heir not only to the domains of the duke, but also to those of his uncle, who has meanwhile passed away without leaving any male offspring. The legal struggle that has motivated the plot for the past few hundred pages is thus rendered moot. In the final pages of the novel, Wilhelmi sums up Hermann's inheritance with the following words: "From the detonation of the underground mines that aristocratic lust and bourgeois greed drove against one another, . . . from the confusion of laws and rights, there arises a third combination that nobody had hitherto thought of. The legacy of feudalism and of industrialism falls into the lap of one who belongs to both estates and to none" (637). Suddenly, in other words, the novel offers up the possibility of a utopian solution.

This conclusion could not possibly be more different from that of *The Red and the Black*, where Julien ends his once so promising career on the guillotine. Immediately before this, he has become doubly fatherless, having first renounced his actual father, the sawmill proprietor Sorel, in order to take on the fake identity of a "Chevalier de la Vernaye," and then lost his symbolic father, the Marquis de la Mole, to the treachery (or honesty, depending on one's viewpoint) of Mme de Rênal. His fate is thus, in a sense, the exact inverse of Hermann's, whose happiness is founded on the realization that he has two fathers, the first an aristocrat, the other a commoner. Nor does Julien's fate do anything to resolve the fundamental contradiction between the various strategies of historical emplotment that have been presented in the novel. Julien's death can be just as convincingly interpreted as a recapitulation of Napoleon Bonaparte's supposed murder through poison in 1821, of Robespierre's execution in 1794, or of Boniface de la Mole's punishment in 1574. The final lines of the book, in which Mathilde de la Mole cradles the severed head of her lover in imitation of Queen Marguerite of Navarre, while Fouqué looks on in shock and disgust, stage a contrast between two different epochs and two different modes of behavior that is the exact inverse of the conciliatory tone struck at the end of *The Epigones*.

The obvious differences between these two endings can be explained through the rather different ways in which Immermann and Stendhal relate the concept of the generation to the regulative structures of family life. In *Wilhelm Meister's Apprenticeship*, Goethe used family bonds as a cosmopolitan bridge between individuals who otherwise lacked shared experiences, and thereby restored shades of the eighteenth-century notion of *le monde* to a novel that in other respects foreshadows the rise of the imagined national community. Immermann's novel picks up on this solution but turns it against itself. Instead of expressing a cosmopolitan dimension, family relationships in *The Epigones* establish a "national" unity that the internally conflicted memory culture can no longer create for itself. In the absence of any consensus regarding what the future should look like and how one might get to it, filial pieties have to plaster over existential anxieties. In his "Youth of Twenty-Five Years Ago," Immermann would write: "I believe that only in Germany has family life attained its highest degree of perfection. And it would be sad if this weren't the case, since for a long time the family was the only thing that our nation possessed, and even now, it is the only thing that approaches a fully rounded form [*Bildung*], while everything else is caught up in a process of becoming."[34] Amid the confusion of modernity, then, the family can still provide the organic ideal that historicism postulated as the driving force behind all individual development.

Indeed, the final chapters of *The Epigones* can be read as a single sustained attempt to drive home the novel's central point: we are all one family, and by recognizing this fact we can redeem the misery of our conflicted epoch. This is true not only of Wilhelmi's description of Hermann's inheritance, but also of the scene that ends the novel, which summons the entire arsenal of Biedermeier kitsch in order to reunite the protagonist with his long-suffering betrothed: "'It is I, my brother,

---

34. Immermann, *Die Jugend vor fünfundzwanzig Jahren*, 409–10.

and I have come to bring you your bride!' cried Johanna in the full bloom of her bliss. Speechless, [Hermann] fell first into the open arms of Cornelie, and then into the bosom of his exalted sister. He allowed himself to rest between the two of them, whom he loved from the bottom of his heart. Tenderly they held him. Wilhelmi gazed on the group with folded hands. The general, meanwhile, supported himself with his sword and fought down his emotions. With this tableau, bathed in the red light of the setting sun, we want to say good-bye to our friend."[35] Cornelie is the uncle's adopted daughter, while Johanna is the duke's younger sister. The hug that concludes the novel thus fuses not only the warring social classes, but also the competing generations.

Once one recognizes the importance of the family dynamic to Immermann's ideological project of restoring unity to a conflicted age, it is easy to find many other examples throughout the book. In book 3, chapter 10, for instance, the Spanish refugee is revealed to be the son of the educational councilor in whose house Hermann has taken temporary lodgings, while in book 3, chapter 14, Hermann recognizes as his own aunt a sick woman whom he had previously nursed. In each of these cases, a possible conflict is averted by the timely recognition of intergenerational relationships. Immermann's use of this topos differs from Goethe's because so much more is at stake in the former's novel. The connections between Goethe's characters might be seen as a poetic legacy of eighteenth-century thought, which still understood political, social, and cultural communities as finite networks rather than as an indeterminate "public sphere." Immermann, however, premises his entire literary project on the notion of an "epigonal" generation whose individual members are connected to one another only through the accidents of their birth. His proposal to resolve the conflicts of his day through an intergenerational inheritance thus not only strains credulity but also robs his novel of its analytical edge. The fundamental messiness of Mannheim's "problem of generations," expressed by Immermann as the feeling of having been born at once too late and too early, is resolved into a tidy generational sequence.

In *The Red and the Black*, things work out quite differently. The crucial distinction here is that Stendhal never falls victim to the illusion that blood relationships between people can adequately suture the social rifts opened up by the experience of modernity. As the novel steers toward its conclusion, Julien too seems poised to make a fateful inheritance. This inheritance, however, is predicated on a series of clever stratagems. Central among these is his romantic conquest of Mathilde de la Mole, whose heart the brooding provincial wins by catering to her melancholic attachment to a lost chivalric era. But the fear of Napoleonic upstarts is so great in French society that even this conquest, together with the resulting pregnancy,

---

35. Michael Minden, who has written several perceptive articles on *The Epigones*, rightly condemns this scene as "genuinely awful." See his "Problems of Realism in Immermann's *Die Epigonen*," *Oxford German Studies* 16 (1985): 78.

might not have been enough to win over Mathilde's father had it not been for another series of deceptions by which Julien has, in effect, already turned himself into a nobleman, the "Chevalier de la Vernaye." Julien's transformation thus results from a deliberate falsehood told about the past, much as the legitimacy of the Bourbon dynasty depends on a lie told about an uninterrupted dynastic succession that would link Louis XVIII to his nephew, who had died in 1795.

The contrast between Stendhal's acid pen and Immermann's sugary conclusion to *The Epigones* is all too obvious but should not distract attention from the fact that both authors respond to a common poetic problem. This problem is how to give aesthetic closure to a generational experience that they themselves defined as internally contradictory and directionless. Immermann's solution consists of reducing social strife to family troubles—no real "solution" at all from the modern perspective, though at least it has the benefit of invoking a Goethean precedent. Stendhal's solution is far more radical: he acknowledges that in postrevolutionary France, social bonds require performative assertion, and takes the ultimate step of declaring the family itself to be an "imagined community."

As a thought experiment, one might conceive an ending to *The Red and the Black* in which Julien marries Mathilde, and their child lives to inherit both Julien's title of "Chevalier" and his grandfather's estates in Languedoc. Such an ending would be deeply cynical, but it *would* offer a successful resolution to the crisis of historical interpretation that plagues France in the 1820s. It would, in other words, successfully answer the question, "How should one live as the member of a generation that has known both Napoleon and the Bourbon kings?" The answer would be "by finding a mutually agreeable lie and living by it, until this lie becomes the truth." Mathilde de la Mole grasps as much when she describes to her father the consequences that would await not only him, but French society in general should he withhold his blessing from their marriage: "With [Julien], I have no fear of obscurity. If there is a revolution, I am sure he will have a leading role in it" (357). To insist too much on the truth would mean to court disaster. But by turning the private fantasy of the "Chevalier de la Vernaye" into a public one, Napoleonic ambition and Bourbon desire to preserve the status quo can find a mutually agreeable middle ground that is based on a shared misreading of the past.

The fact that *The Red and the Black* does not end in this fashion can surely be read as a sign of Stendhal's fundamentally revolutionary temper. The final chapters of the novel are among its most accomplished because they depict the interpretive chaos that erupts in the absence of the shared narrative that a successful marriage would have brought into being. In the light of this catastrophe, Julien, Mathilde, and Mme de Rênal turn to competing literary codes for guidance, all of which also invoke the authority of the past. Julien goes to the scaffold with the resolve characteristic of heroic romance and thereby pays a final tribute to the *Mémorial de Sainte-Hélène*. Mathilde enacts a bizarre gothic ritual that for her is the only way to reach back to the sixteenth century and the story of her ancestor Boniface. Mme de Rênal, finally, attempts to stay faithful to the sentimental fiction of the old regime even as her heart breaks under the contradiction of her hypocritical behavior.

It is tempting to add to this list of literary codes and the behaviors that they inspire Fouqué's more neutral attitude as an example of the nascent realism to which Stendhal himself aspires. But Fouqué is a provincial lumber merchant; what does he truly know about French society? In the July Revolution of 1830, which took place just as Stendhal was writing his novel and which he nevertheless carefully excised from his story, backdating the action to 1827, the French people opted for the kind of compromise that Julien almost pulled off in *The Red and the Black*. Louis Philippe, the "citizen king," would come to serve, at least for a little while, as a screen on which the bourgeoisie could project its dreams of social mobility even as the principle of aristocratic succession was effectively left intact. It is within the society created by this mutually acceptable compromise that French realist fiction would advance to its next great flowering in the works of Balzac.

Stendhal's greatest achievement in *The Red and the Black* was thus not that he found a convincing way to represent sociological complexity, or that he gave a unified shape to a multitude of Frenchmen. His greatest achievement was that he correctly understood the role of myth in the modern world. In an age in which even ordinary people had come to understand that "history" is a dynamic system whose narrative shape is subject to endless negotiations, myth has lost its totalizing function. It can at best be a compromise formation that conflicting social groups might equally claim as their own. Louis Philippe, at once "citizen" and "king," would become one example of such a modern myth; the American "founding fathers," who mean so many different things to so many different people, provide another. In turning himself into the Chevalier de la Vernaye, Julien aspires to the status of a modern myth as well—at once "red" and "black," a self-made man in the footsteps of Bonaparte who nevertheless renders obedient service to Restoration culture. The very failure of his enterprise only underscores its potency as it strips bare how many different things he means to different people.

Immermann's failure to rise to the same level of achievement as his French contemporary should be located not in the picaresque structure of his plots, nor in his inability to transform hackneyed motifs into a realistic picture of his times, but rather in his basic incomprehension of the meaning of modern myth. In a metaliterary gloss on his own craft that he inserted into the eighth book of *The Epigones*, Immermann compares world history to a flood that covers all details of the physical landscape and leaves behind a uniform expanse of water. To describe this expanse is the work of the historian; as a novelist, Immermann finds himself inadequate to the task, for "only the contemplation of great men can unlock the sense of an entire epoch. We, however, do not possess such great men" (500). Convinced that the "sense" of an epoch can still be found externally, in the actual deeds of living people, Immermann fails to realize that the best that modern men can hope for is what Mannheim called an "accidental harmony" created from the "vertical coincidence" of different generational entelechies. Immermann instead declares his intention to ascend to the mountain ranges from which all tributaries to the great flood of history spring. Individual characters will represent individual tendencies of his age, and only when they are all brought together will the true nature of an epoch be revealed: the cloying embrace that concludes *The Epigones* is an attempt at precisely such a fusion.

The contrasting political geographies of Germany and France during the 1830s are thus only partially to blame for the decisive differences between Immermann's and Stendhal's fiction. Just as crucial are the authors' diverging responses to the transnational memory culture that engulfed their countries during that time. And Stendhal, by offering a frayed ending in which multiple efforts to possess the past stand in jarring contrast to one another, says much more about his age than Immermann, who insists on harmony and conciliation. The shocking end of *The Red and the Black* destroys the illusion of a spiritual unity on which both classical *Bildungsroman* theory and academic historicism are founded: the eighteenth-century understanding, according to which both nations and individual characters are the products of an organic self-realization gives way to Mannheim's model of polyphonically contrasted "generation-entelechies." *The Red and the Black* draws attention to the profound historical anxieties that ran across national borders during the Restoration period and provided this era with a cosmopolitan unity. Immermann's novel provides another example of this dynamic but fails to find an adequate poetic expression for it. The ultimate fate that befell this text in literary history is thus not without irony. In detaching the term "epigone" from its semantic bearings, Immermann found a fitting expression for the historical consciousness of his age, but he also tied the meaning of his work to that of his more illustrious forebear. The German *Bildungsroman* tradition has had to pay a heavy price for this decision, and the stigma of the epigonal clings to it still.

4

Long-Distance Fantasies: Freytag, Eliot, and National Literature in the Age of Empire

In the previous chapter, I examined two works that seem to epitomize the diverging French and German novel traditions in the early nineteenth century, and yet can both be read as evidence of a continent-spanning effort to "possess the past" in the wake of the Napoleonic interregnum. Viewed in this latter fashion, both Restoration-era France and Biedermeier Germany emerge as the battlegrounds of hostile generational cohorts, a fact that puts significant strains on the ability of the *Bildungsroman* to endow these nations with a developmental unity. The present chapter pursues a similarly bifurcated approach while focusing on geographical and ethnic sources of internal discord, rather than on temporal ones.

Like *The Red and the Black* and *The Epigones* before them, the two novels that I will examine in this chapter seem to represent oppositional paths in literary history. George Eliot's *Daniel Deronda* (1876) is acclaimed for its depiction of the struggles confronted by women hoping to maintain their autonomy in a patriarchal society, its subtle critique of British imperialism, and its philo-Semitism. If Stendhal's name, like that of Balzac or Dickens, has become synonymous with sociological complexity in the novel, Eliot's, like that of Austen or James, vouches for literature's ability to ask innovative questions about the human bonds that create civil societies. Gustav Freytag's *Debit and Credit* (1855), on the other hand, seems the very epitome of a novel that remains ensconced in smug self-certainty. It is a chauvinistic and misogynistic work, as well as a blatantly anti-Semitic one. Yet despite these obvious ideological deficiencies, *Debit and Credit* proved to be hugely popular in Germany, outselling all other German novels save Thomas Mann's *Buddenbrooks* during the ninety years between its publication and the end of the Second World War.[1] Once again, in other words, it appears as though literary differences can be mapped onto national ones, and that Freytag's anti-Semitism and refusal to critically investigate the structures of society are indicative of a separate German path into modernity.[2]

There is much that connects *Debit and Credit* to *Daniel Deronda*, however. For instance, both Freytag and Eliot were firm believers in the doctrines of liberal nationalism and wrote their novels in the wake of traumatic blows against the liberal imagination in their respective countries.[3] In Freytag's case, this blow came with the failed 1848 revolution, which signaled a temporary end to the emancipatory ambitions of the middle classes and the resurgence in power of the ancien régime. For George Eliot, a similarly decisive event came with the 1865 Morant Bay rebellion, in which starving black farmers on the island of Jamaica rose against their white neighbors, answering long-standing systemic oppression with individual actions of overwhelming brutality. At first sight, these two historical occasions have little in common with one another, but in fact their lasting impact on political discussions in Germany and England can be linked to the rise of modern imperialism throughout the second half of the nineteenth century.

Imperialism poses a serious conceptual challenge to liberal nationalism (defined, for the present moment, as the belief that national communities are held together by the rights and duties that are the product of a collective history) in that it aims to bring together members of multiple ethnicities or cultural communities within the administrative confines of a single state. The Morant Bay rebellion shed a revealing light on the illiberal foundations of the British Empire and on the extent to which, even thirty years after the nominal abolition of slavery, racial identity largely determined destiny. The connection between imperialism and the 1848 revolution is less direct, but there can be little doubt that the failure of a liberal revolution on

---

1. Peter Heinz Hubrich, *Gustav Freytags "Deutsche Ideologie" in "Soll und Haben"* (Kronberg im Taunus: Scriptor, 1974), 43–45.

2. Needless to say, I am here sketching out a reductively schematic picture in order to summarize what I take to be a dominant view concerning the differences between the English and German novel traditions in the middle of the nineteenth century. In fact, the putative virtues of *Daniel Deronda* have been at the center of much debate in the scholarly literature. Susan Meyer, for instance, in her *Imperialism at Home: Race and Victorian Women's Fiction* (Ithaca, NY: Cornell University Press, 1996), argues that "the final suppression of feminist impulses in *Daniel Deronda* is accompanied by, and also metaphorically enacted through, an *increase* in imperialist sentiment and an endorsement, by way of proto-Zionism, of racial separatism" (160).

3. On Freytag and Eliot as proponents of liberalism, see Larry L. Ping, *Gustav Freytag and the Prussian Gospel: Novels, Liberalism, and History* (Frankfurt am Main: Peter Lang, 2006), as well as Nancy Henry, "George Eliot and Politics," in *The Cambridge Companion to George Eliot*, ed. George Levine (Cambridge: Cambridge University Press, 2001), 138–58.

German soil was at least partially caused by the inability of political leaders to reach a consensus regarding what actually constituted "Germany" after more than sixty years of settler colonialism in Eastern Europe on the part of both Prussia and the Habsburg Empire. Of course, both the British claims to Jamaica and the German claims to territories in Silesia, Pomerania, and elsewhere were the results of early modern forms of colonial domination that had their origins in the seventeenth and eighteenth centuries. Nevertheless, the treatment of these claims in the novels by Freytag and Eliot has an undeniably modern countenance, in that it involves an intensive engagement with new affective and intellectual formations that attended the imperial scramble of the Victorian era.

As was the case with the two novels considered in the previous chapter, both *Debit and Credit* and *Daniel Deronda* can be read in two contradictory ways: either as characteristic examples of diverging national traditions or as complementary responses to a new form of historical emplotment that swept across Europe in a response to sociopolitical changes on a transnational scale. In the case of the post-Napoleonic effort to possess the past, the resulting changes to the *Bildungsroman* took a temporal form, in that they added a generational location to the formative trajectory of the protagonist. The transformations wrought by imperialism and its accompanying rhetoric have a different shape, in that they force the novel of formation to engage with ethnic and geographical difference. The struggle to find a developmental unity for characters who may share no immediate cultural context throws the cosmopolitan dimensions of the *Bildungsroman* into sharp relief and provides a possible explanation for yet another similarity between Freytag and Eliot, namely their decision to write dual-plot *Bildungsromane* that intertwine the fate of a "rooted" Gentile protagonist with that of a more mercurial Jewish counterpart.

The Politics of Collective Consumption

Although the action of *Debit and Credit* is set entirely during the early 1840s, the failed revolution of 1848 provided both the original inspiration and an underlying theme for Freytag's novel. This is a work written for demonstration purposes, a conscious literary realization of an aesthetic program that was drafted by Freytag's friend and collaborator Julian Schmidt in response to a crisis of liberalism. Since political emancipation seemed temporarily out of the question, Schmidt, who coedited the literary journal *The Border Herald* (*Die Grenzboten*) with Freytag, counseled the German middle classes to focus their attention on economic activity and turn financial power into political influence. This social agenda required corresponding aesthetic adjustments, including a narrative focus on the life of the bourgeoisie and a new programmatic optimism. As Schmidt put it in a phrase that Freytag chose as an epigraph for *Debit and Credit*, "The novel should seek out the German people where they are to be found in all their virtuous proficiency, namely at work."[4] "Work," in the ideology of *The Border Herald*, always refers to merchant capitalism, never to industrial production, and *Debit and Credit*, as its title already indicates, is a novel of formation set entirely in a mercantile environment. By thus departing from the traditional structure of the *Bildungsroman* and siding with Werner rather than Wilhelm, Freytag makes clear that he intended his work to serve as the conscious adaptation of a classical form to a new stage in German social life.

Freytag's preoccupation with merchant capitalism as a cultural good has attracted a substantial body of critical literature, most of which focuses on the first half of *Debit and Credit*. This first half is devoted to the apprentice years of Anton Wohlfart, the son of a minor bureaucrat in the small town of Ostrau in Prussian Silesia (now Ostrava in the Czech Republic), who embarks on a promising career as an employee of the merchant T. O. Schröter in the nearby provincial capital of Breslau (now Wrocław in Poland). During his time in the company office, Wohlfart earns the enmity of the novel's second major protagonist, his former classmate Veitel Itzig, who is now completing an apprenticeship of his own with the Jewish financier Hirsch Ehrenthal. At the same time, he wins the friendship of two young aristocrats: the dashing globetrotter Friedrich (Fritz) von Fink, who dreams of owning a hacienda in the New World but is meanwhile stuck in an internship at the Schröter company, and the beautiful if stubborn Lenore von Rothsattel, who serves as the novel's main love interest.

In presenting this summary, I have emphasized the geographical particulars of Freytag's plot because a second major theme of the novel, and one that has received considerably less attention, concerns the cultural consequences of the Prussian occupation of Poland.[5] And yet this second theme is closely related to the first, both in the sense that Freytag connects colonialism to merchant capitalism, and in the sense that his reflections on territorial occupation have plausible roots in the same intellectual crisis that triggered the narrative turn to mercantile activity in the first place. The German revolution of 1848 was aided in its rapid descent into farce by the bitter debates over which territories and cultural communities should be included in the new German state. Besides the principal clash over whether German-speaking Austria should be admitted to the union, a smaller but nevertheless

---

4. Gustav Freytag, *Soll und Haben: Roman in sechs Büchern* (Waltrop: Manuscriptum, 2002), 4. No unabridged version of Freytag's novel exists in English, and the most complete available translation, L. C. Cummings's effort of 1857, leaves out the epigraph as well many other crucial passages. In this chapter, I will therefore correct and amend Cummings with my own translations and, for the benefit of the English-speaking reader, follow each quotation with two parenthetical references. The first page number refers to the German original, while the second refers to Gustav Freytag, *Debit and Credit*, trans. L. C. Cummings (repr., New York: Howard Fertig, Inc., 1990), and indicates the spot where the passage in question would be located in the context of the available abridged version.

5. For a discussion of this lacuna and an attempt to fill it, see Kristin Kopp, "Ich stehe jetzt hier als einer von den Eroberern: *Soll und Haben* als Kolonialroman," in *150 Jahre "Soll und Haben": Studien zu Gustav Freytags kontroversem Roman*, ed. Florian Krobb (Würzburg: Königshausen & Neumann, 2005), 225–38.

important quarrel focused on those territories of the Habsburg Empire in which ethnic Germans represented only a minority. Inclusion of these territories would have threatened the cultural integrity of the new nation. Their exclusion, however, would have meant the partition of the empire and thus a significant loss of power.

My principal argument in the following pages will be that Freytag's turn toward merchant capitalism is not just a symptom of narrative retrenchment in the face of political impotence but instead expresses an attempt to solve the problems that Germany and Austria's colonial possessions in Eastern Europe posed for liberal nationalism during the 1850s. Put succinctly, *Debit and Credit* endeavors to show that commodities can build an affective bridge between far-flung human communities and thereby help them maintain a developmental unity under conditions of imperialism. This claim was unprecedented within the context of the German novel and points toward an important shift in the self-understanding of empires in general, which over the course of the nineteenth century transitioned from primarily mercantilist systems of global domination to modern capitalist ones. Within the earlier systems, the rhetoric of "development" and "improvement" had operated largely independently from the economic exploitation that accompanied it: the white man's "civilizing mission" was largely left to clergy and doctors and functioned principally as ideological varnish to cover up the real work of empire, which was carried out by planters, company agents, and compradors. Within modern capitalist systems, however, the logic of development becomes inextricably entwined with economic activity, and exploitation is justified with the supposed benefits that the unfettered global exchange of goods will bestow on all its participants. Modern imperialism, to put it differently, is among other things a form of historical emplotment, and one to which Freytag hopes to respond in his *Bildungsroman* set at the Prussian colonial frontier.

It is important to differentiate between contemporary neoliberal apologies of globalization, however, which tend to also be deterritorializing and suspicious of national sovereignty, and Freytag's considerably more limited project, which hopes to ultimately vindicate the nation-state.[6] Freytag's trust in the affective dimension

---

6. There have been several attempts by German critics to link Freytag's novel to various discourses of globality. Patrick Ramponi, for instance, invokes Edward Said's concept of "worldliness" to argue: "Literature derives its global dimension not necessarily from a direct thematization of transcultural phenomena in world-encompassing plots. A poetic approach that centers on locality and the formation of identity, on regionalism and provinciality—in short, of the kind that undoubtedly characterizes German realism in the second half of the nineteenth century— . . . can also claim world literary status." See Patrick Ramponi, "Orte des Globalen: Zur Poetik der Globalisierung in der Literatur des deutschsprachigen Realismus (Freytag, Raabe, Fontane)," in *Poetische Ordnungen: Zur Erzählprosa des deutschen Realismus*, ed. Ulrich Kittstein and Stefani Kugler (Würzburg: Königshausen & Neumann, 2007), 20. I find this argument unconvincing, not the least because *Debit and Credit* seems to me to lack the principal characteristic of "worldliness" as Said defines it, namely a reciprocal relationship between world and text in which the text's "status as an event having sensuous particularity as well as historical contingency" becomes "an infrangible part of [its] capacity for conveying and producing meaning." See Edward Said, *The World, the Text, and the Critic* (Cambridge, MA: Harvard University Press, 1983), 39.

of global commodities is best illustrated by an early passage in the novel, in which Anton enters T. O. Schröter's richly stocked storerooms for the first time:

> Nearly all the countries of the earth and all the races of humanity had labored and gathered in order to pile up useful and valuable objects before the eyes of our hero.... A Hindu woman had woven this matting, and an industrious Chinese had painted red and black hieroglyphs on that chest. A negro from the Congo in the service of a Virginia planter had looped those canes over the cotton bales, this log of tropical wood had been rolled over Mexican beaches, and that square block of zebra or jacaranda wood had grown in the primeval forests of Brazil, where monkeys and brightly hued parrots had sat among its branches....
>
> Anton remained in this ancient hall for hours after his instructor's lessons had ended, absorbed in wonder and interest; the arches and pillars seemed to transform themselves into broad-leafed palm trees, the noise of the street resembled the roar of the sea, which he only knew from his dreams, and he imagined that he heard the waves of the ocean drum a steady beat on the coast on which he stood so securely. (60–61/52–53)

This youthful epiphany is given a stronger and more systematic expression at a later point, when Freytag's protagonist is driven to defend his profession in front of Hirsch Ehrenthal's invalid son, Bernhard. In the context of this conversation, Anton enthuses:

> I know nothing that is quite as interesting as business. We live amidst a many-colored web of countless threads that stretch from one person to the next, across land and sea, from one part of the world to another. These threads connect everyone to everybody else. All that we wear on our bodies, and all that surrounds us reminds us of the strange customs of other countries and of all human activity, and this renders everything attractive. And since I have the feeling that I too do my part to ensure a continuous connection between each and every human being, I am quite satisfied with my occupation. When I place a sack of coffee on the scales, I am weaving an invisible thread between the colonist's daughter in Brazil, who plucked the beans, and the young farmer's son who drinks it for breakfast; and when I take up a stick of cinnamon, I seem to see on one side the squatting Malay who has prepared and packed it, and on the other the old woman from my home town who grates it over her rice pudding. (239–40/125)

The striking thing about both of these passages is the way in which they first open Freytag's novel out onto the world, only to then pull back and conclude with a closer examination of Anton Wohlfart's feelings. Anton talks about "invisible threads" that connect him with such faraway places as Brazil, Mexico, and Malaysia, but Freytag is clearly not interested in moving beyond the narrow provincial focus of his tale in any extended fashion. He aims not to pay tribute to a cosmopolitan capitalist community but rather to document the sense of self-worth and purpose that Anton wins from contemplating these foreign commodities.

Anton's storeroom epiphany can usefully be compared to a quite different lesson about commodities learned at around the same time by Veitel Itzig, Anton's shadowy double. Unlike Anton, Itzig (who is an anti-Semitic cliché through and through: even his name alludes to the adjectives *eitel* [vain] and *hitzig* [rash]) is from the very beginning superbly attuned to the ways of the business world. He also differs from Anton in that he lacks any capacity to appreciate the affective life of commodities, seeing an emotional investment in goods only as a weakness from which to derive material gain. While spying on his landlord, the innkeeper Pinkus, who derives a lucrative secondary income as a fence and smuggler, Itzig thus experiences an epiphany of his own that in every regard is the opposite of the one experienced by Freytag's Gentile protagonist: "Suddenly it dawned on Veitel: these goods were destined for the East; they would be smuggled across the border and brought deep into the Russian Empire, right up to the border with Asia, where an ambitious nomad would wear out the shirts and overcoats that a German tailor had made. All according to the principle that the Russians inherit those things that the Germans no longer want" (104–5/73). What Itzig learns in this scene is that profits can be derived from the affective estrangement that often characterizes international trade carried out over great distances: Pinkus's Russian clients simply do not care where the clothes that they buy come from, why their previous owners discarded them, or whether they perhaps have been stolen. Hirsch Ehrenthal banks on exactly this kind of affective estrangement when he convinces Baron von Rothsattel to buy a large quantity of wood from a desperate anonymous seller who is offering them far below market value. A little later, the two Jews also convince the baron to invest in a mortgage on an insolvent estate in nearby Poznań, again to be had far below market value. In both of these cases, Rothsattel expresses some initial reluctance because his chivalric conception of honor forbids him to turn the misfortunes of others into a source of profit. But the realization that he will never have to meet any of the victims of his speculation soon puts his qualms to rest, especially once Ehrenthal comforts him with the casuistic remark that the sellers could always have chosen not to part with their property.

This contrast between Anton and Itzig highlights one axiom that underlies *Debit and Credit*, namely that commercial activity driven merely by the lust for profit and without any emotional investment is inherently evil and ultimately corrodes the social bonds that tie together human communities. A second axiom can be drawn out by comparing the bourgeois Anton to his second major antagonist, the aristocrat Baron Anton von Rothsattel. Anton briefly flirts with aristocratic values when he falls in love with Rothsattel's daughter Lenore and gains access to her social circle through a clever ruse of his friend Fritz von Fink. This ruse also combines capitalism with global imaginative projection, though in a manner quite different from Anton's storehouse epiphany. Fink happens to be the owner of a worthless piece of property on Long Island, which he makes over to Anton without the hapless protagonist's knowledge. He then uses the notarized deed to sow rumors that Anton is the bastard son of a nobleman and stands to inherit millions. The gullible high society of Breslau promptly falls for the ruse, and for a few brief weeks, Anton experiences the rather vapid social life of the hereditary upper classes, complete with excursions on horseback, quadrilles, and romantic intrigues. Though Anton withdraws from the Rothsattel salon in disgust as soon as he learns of the lie by which Fink has rendered him socially acceptable, his brief time there allows Freytag to draw a basic distinction between bourgeois and aristocratic cosmopolitanism: the former has a material basis in actual commodities; the latter is based entirely on social appearances.

Taken together, these two axioms phrase the simple message of *Debit and Credit*, namely that human relationships require some kind of material basis in order to become real, especially when conducted over great distances, and that the main purpose of commercial activity is to supply such a basis, rather than make money. The first half of Freytag's novel never strays beyond the immediate surroundings of Breslau and certainly never aspires to take in the entire world, as was hinted at in the storehouse epiphany, but is nevertheless full of examples that illustrate how commodities draw people closer together. An especially powerful example of this can be found in the opening pages, which explain the origins of Anton's apprenticeship. Anton's father, it turns out, years earlier found a misplaced document in the town archives that helped Schröter win a protracted lawsuit. Henceforth, the grateful merchant sent a box containing "a loaf of the finest sugar and a packet of the best coffee" (6/26) to the Wohlfarts every Christmas and, as the narrator stresses, "the bond that connected the accountant's household with the busy activity of the world at large was light and inconspicuous, yet it became the guiding thread for Anton's entire further life" (8/27).

Although the narrator emphasizes a connection between the Wohlfart household and the "world at large," in reality the affective bond created by the gift stretches no further than to the provincial capital. The loaf of cane sugar and the packet of coffee promise what Germans call the "smell of the wide world," but in reality unfold their power as bourgeois comestibles, not as indices of faraway places. They arrive on the Wohlfart doorstep as imported trade goods (loaves, packets) but are immediately converted for domestic consumption. The sugar is smashed into pieces, the coffee is roasted, and in the subsequent atmosphere of bourgeois *Gemütlichkeit*, Anton's father luxuriates in a worldliness that has no relationship to any actual foreign elements: "[The father's] happiness wasn't caused by pounds of sugar or the coffee from Cuba, but rather by the poetry of this comfortable relationship to a completely unfamiliar human life" (7/26).

The early idyll in the Wohlfart household sets a tone for many others that follow it. The operative logic of these scenes always remains the same: men (and less often women) assemble to drink punch, smoke cigars, or share coffee and pies and in the process use goods imported from afar to strengthen emotional connections that reach only to those who are near. Despite Anton's opening claim that his trade has brought him closer to Brazilian planters and Chinese furniture-makers, *Debit and Credit* remains firmly grounded in the concrete reality of domestic communities. A particularly powerful example of this dynamic occurs when the Schröter employees assemble to celebrate the twenty-fifth anniversary of their principal's entry into business. The whole firm goes on an outing that concludes at a local inn, where Schröter's sister Sabine serves everyone "a brown concoction that the associates drank with the silent superiority of people who know what good coffee is" (262/134). Sabine's ministrations mingle with the associates' smug satisfaction to construct an image of bourgeois domesticity that Freytag clearly differentiates from several other forms of social belonging over the course of his novel. Schröter's employees are, at least in theory, men whose everyday dealings involve transactions with foreign countries and require experience with one of the world's most expensive commodities. But Freytag shows no larger interest in this special kind of cosmopolitan knowledge; he cares only about the effects that it has on domestic sociability.

Long-Distance Nationalism and the Journeyman Years of German Capitalism

By the end of the first half of *Debit and Credit*, then, Freytag has made a powerful case for the affective life of commodities but has yet to supply an explanation for how the collective consumption of colonial goods might bridge the rift between far-flung middle-class communities under conditions of empire. The quotidian rituals that the narrator illustrates with such loving detail require proximity and a shared cultural heritage. When it comes to the distant regions of the earth—the regions that can be said to be part of a common cosmos, but not of a common nation—the only alternatives seem to be Veitel Itzig's exploitative embrace of capitalism and Baron von Rothsattel's worship of hereditary titles and family names.

The second half of the novel proposes to resolve this problem. Required for this is a sudden shift not only in setting but also in narrative direction, a shift that is set into motion by the abortive revolution of 1846, in which the citizens of the nearby Republic of Cracow (nominally independent, but actually an Austrian puppet state) sought to establish an independent Poland only to be brutally crushed by combined Prussian, Austrian, and Russian forces. Freytag's narrator describes these events in a characteristically apolitical vocabulary, in keeping with *Debit and Credit*'s ultimate intention to deemphasize the institutions of the state in the self-understanding of the German nation: "A bad year came upon the country and the sudden sounds of war alarmed the German border countries, including our province. The terrible consequences of a national panic were soon perceptible. Trade stood still, the price of goods fell, everybody tried to save what was his and withdraw from business. Large sums of capital were in danger, and nobody had the heart for new ventures. Hundreds of bonds, woven out of mutual interest over the span of many years, were cut at once" (322/167). For Anton Wohlfart, the Cracow insurrection of 1846 represents an opportunity to examine at first hand the commercial bonds that connect his office in Breslau with the far corners of the earth. When one of Schröter's trade caravans goes missing, the merchant takes his apprentice with him in order to retrieve it. Anton's journeyman years have begun.

During their joint journey eastward, Schröter delivers a speech that is crucial to the programmatic message of *Debit and Credit*:

> There is no race so little qualified to make progress and to gain humanity and civilization [*Menschlichkeit und Bildung*] by spending its capital as the Slavic one. Everything that the people over there in their idleness have acquired through oppressing the ignorant masses they now waste in foolish diversion. With us, only a few privileged classes act thus, and the nation can bear it. But over there, the privileged classes claim to represent the people. As if nobles and their bondsmen alone could form a state! ...
>
> "They have no middle class [*Bürgerstand*]," Anton interjected eagerly.
>
> "And that means they do not have culture," the merchant continued. (332/173)

The problem with the Cracow uprising, in other words, is not just that its political violence interferes with trade and thus with the true road to bourgeois happiness. This charge, after all, could also have been leveled against the 1848 revolution in Germany. The problem is, rather, that the present insurrection represents the wrong kind of revolution carried out by the wrong kind of people. The Polish middle class, this is Schröter's argument, is constitutionally incapable of converting its accumulation of capital into a collective social form of development, a *Bildung*. Instead, national fate lies entirely in the hands of nobles and their bondsmen, and thus with classes that possess no formative trajectory of their own.

Anton initially puts up a timid fight against Schröter's blanket condemnation of all Slavs, asking: "But what about Conrad Günther in the rebellious city, and what about the three Hildebrandts in Galicia?" "They are all worthy people" is the reply that he receives, "but they are all merely immigrants" (332/173). The last names of the partners leave no question as to where they immigrated from, and this in turn highlights the political project that Freytag will pursue over the second half of the novel. In linking political worth and sobriety in difficult times to ethnic heritage, *Debit and Credit* establishes a first tentative link between the bourgeois politics of collective consumption and settler colonialism. Freytag's position here appears to be roughly midway between the older mercantilist justifications of empire and the newer capitalist ones. He does not believe, in other words, that cultural improvement and economic development are separate issues, or that one can be carried out without the other. Neither, however, does he imply that the two are entirely coextensive, and that an exchange of goods between imperial center and periphery will inevitably lead to both economic and cultural improvement. Instead, settler colonialism in Freytag is a process by which a certain attitude toward commodities is exported into regions of the world that would otherwise be incapable of steering their own economic development.

Colonialism in *Debit and Credit* is, in other words, always a cultural issue, a slow and accretive process that leads to the creation of a transnational bourgeois community. Freytag consistently contrasts it with purely administrative and interventionist forms of imperial control. Thus Schröter's journey to Cracow proceeds in tandem with, yet strictly separate from, the Prussian military mobilization. The old merchant and his assistant even carry with them a leather cigar case, which "the whole office viewed as a kind of war flag that was only displayed on remarkable occasions, and which was taken along on the wagons when the main force of the company embarked on a special expedition" (328/170). Near the border crossing into the Republic of Cracow, a troop of hussars under the command of Lenore's brother Eugen von Rothsattel shows up to escort the traders the final stretch of the way but has to stand back while the Prussian high command consults with its imperial neighbors about how to best respond to the crisis. Schröter and Anton, meanwhile, cross the invisible border with perfect ease and quickly recover the company's stolen assets. The Prussian inability to act and Schröter's self-made success illustrate once again Freytag's deep mistrust of established political powers, which are linked in the imaginative work done by this novel to the ancien régime and to aristocratic solidarity. To drive home this point, Freytag makes Eugen von Rothsattel an especially disagreeable character, a general good-for-nothing with a gambling addiction who will contribute significantly to his father's eventual financial ruin.

Niels Werber, in an analysis of the "geopolitics" of Freytag's novel, has used the Cracow interlude to develop a reading of *Debit and Credit* that is based on Michael Hardt and Antonio Negri's notion of "Empire." "Empire," in contrast to "imperialism," describes a sociohistorical dynamic that is opposed to the centralizing demands of state power and is instead closely linked to the development of modern transnational capitalism. As Werber puts it, "World trade requires the state as a guarantor of peace, security and order, as a keeper of contracts and property, and yet nevertheless the capitalist exposes the limits of state power, because he does not respect territorial borders and demands that all trade be global in nature."[7] Indeed, Werber's definition of capitalism recalls that of Marx and Engels, who wrote their *Communist Manifesto* in great temporal proximity to (though at even greater ideological distance from) *Debit and Credit*: "The bourgeoisie has through its

---

7. Niels Werber, *Die Geopolitik der Literatur: Eine Vermessung der medialen Weltraumordnung* (Munich: Carl Hanser Verlag, 2007), 155.

exploitation of the world market given a cosmopolitan character to production and consumption in every country. To the great chagrin of Reactionists, it has drawn from under the feet of industry the national ground on which it stood."[8]

What Werber misses, however, is that Freytag's ultimate point of reference always remains the nation, never the kind of global unbounded space so beloved of postmodern capitalism. For instance, Hardt and Negri claim that Empire is premised on the "construction of a new order that envelops the entire space of what it considers civilization" and "exhausts historical time, suspends history, and summons the past and future within its own ethical order."[9] Such an exhaustion of historical time would represent a direct challenge to the historicist logic of the classical *Bildungsroman* but is nowhere borne out by the actual structure of Freytag's novel. Schröter's leather cigar case already makes this clear: modern multinational corporations such as BP and Halliburton hoist flags of convenience on their tankers and move entire operative divisions into offshore tax shelters, while Freytag's merchant proudly stresses his rootedness in tradition and bourgeois solidity. As I will show later, *Debit and Credit* in fact concludes with its own explicit commentary on the ethical order of history that thoroughly contradicts Hardt and Negri's demands.

Anton's Cracow expedition is only the first step in a larger narrative transformation that turns *Debit and Credit* into a very different novel from what a reader of the first few hundred pages might have anticipated. His self-confidence strengthened by the revolutionary adventure, Freytag's protagonist quits his employment at T. O. Schröter's to come to the aid of Lenore's family, which has meanwhile been bled dry by Itzig's treachery. After being forced to sell their ancestral estate in Silesia, the Rothsattels are left only with the nearly worthless farm near Rosmin (Rościmin) in Poznań that they once bought, thinking they would never have to inspect it personally. Though technically a part of the country that was given to Prussia during the second partition of Poland, Poznań had since 1815 formed a semiautonomous grand duchy, and Freytag consequently depicts Rosmin as a kind of Wild West community inhabited by only a few German settlers encircled by semibarbaric Slavs. Anton agrees to serve as a farm overseer for the blind and increasingly cantankerous Rothsattel, and the last third or so of *Debit and Credit* turns into a Polish "cowboys and Indians" narrative, complete with bloodthirsty natives who lay siege to the Rothsattel farm before they are driven off at the last moment by the arrival of Fritz von Fink and an expeditionary force of German workers. The novel concludes when Fink, rather than Anton, marries Lenore, while Anton returns to Schröter's company, marries the principal's sister, and takes over the accounts. Meanwhile, Itzig's betrayals catch up to him, and he dies an ignominious death in the sewers of Breslau.

---

8. Karl Marx and Friedrich Engels, *The Communist Manifesto* (London: Penguin, 1967), 283.
9. Michael Hardt and Antonio Negri, *Empire* (Cambridge, MA: Harvard University Press, 2000), 11.

Much as Anton's apprenticeship as Schröter's bookkeeper began with a lengthy paean to international trade, so his service to the Rothsattels commences with an encomium to agricultural labor and industry: "Happy the foot that can roam over a wide expanse of property—happy the head that knows how to subject the forces of ever-fresh nature to an intelligent human will" (400/228). Over the course of three more pages, the narrator paints an increasingly ecstatic picture of the ways in which wild nature is domesticated by the labors of several generations and eventually yields to a primitive export industry. The description culminates in the assertion that the successful farmer "is linked by many threads to men of other callings; strangers rejoice to hold out their hands to him, and unite their efforts with his" (401/229). By contrast, the landowner who "precipitously invokes the black art of steam to settle on his land, in order to educe from it energies which it does not possess" (403/230), as Baron Rothsattel does when, at the urging of Veitel Itzig, he builds a ruinous factory on his Silesian estate, "is swept away in a vortex of complicated business, claims surge in upon him wave upon wave, and he, in his desperate struggle, drowning man that he is, has no choice but to cling to whatever comes within his grasp" (404/230).

In this passage, the ultimate outcome of sedentary agricultural labor is imagined in terms that are almost identical to those that earlier characterized trade. An affective network connecting strangers by myriad threads on the one hand is contrasted with an inchoate vortex of complicated claims on the other, and the successful farmer stands in the same relationship to the talentless one as the successful German merchant stands to the Jewish finance capitalist. Despite its digressive plot, in other words, the second half of *Debit and Credit* can productively be read as a supplement to the first. Having already demonstrated the vital function that colonial commodities perform in binding together domestic communities, Freytag now turns his gaze abroad to show how the producers, too, participate in the transnational network created by trade and collective consumption. In this context it is surely significant that the primary cash crop planted by Rothsattel and others on their eastern estates is the sugar beet, chosen in an attempt to compete with the cane sugar dumped on the European market by Great Britain with its Caribbean plantations. This domestic substitution, in turn, shows how far away from Anton's initial storehouse fantasy the novel has moved. Far from presenting a euphoric celebration of globalization, *Debit and Credit* actually reinscribes what is a traditionally "national" form of communal self-understanding on a transnational scale.

In this regard, Freytag's novel differs from the narratives of American settler colonialism with which it otherwise has so much in common. In the stereotypical American frontier narrative, the gaze is firmly westward, toward the manifest destiny of an as yet unfounded community that will redeem the sins of established life back east. In *Debit and Credit*, on the other hand, the ultimate frame of reference remains Germany, and the novel quite logically concludes with Anton's return to his former life back in Breslau. In other words, it illustrates what Benedict Anderson has usefully called the structures of "long-distance nationalism": a nationalism of exiles and émigrés, who longingly look back at the metropole from which they originated.[10]

Freytag gives a powerful expression to such long-distance nationalism when he argues: "[Whosoever] finds himself suddenly thrown among strangers, where law can but imperfectly protect him, and where he must assert by daily struggles his right to exist, will soon recognize for the first time the full blessing of the holy circle woven around each individual by thousands of other people: by his family, his companions in labor, his race, his country. . . . Only in foreign parts do we come to appreciate the dialects of home, and only when surrounded by strangers do we recognize our fatherland" (515/314). The initial metaphor of trade as an open "web" spanning the globe has here been replaced with that of a closed circle of like-minded people—a circle, however, whose presence is felt only in a foreign country. Freytag's assertion that we come "to appreciate the dialects of home" only when we have been transported to foreign soils bears a vivid resemblance to Anderson's specimen study of Mary Rowlandson, who also came to think of herself as English only after she had been abducted by a Native American war party. In Freytag, of course, such sentiments have less violent origins and arise instead from the productive powers of global communication and commodity exchange. In successful colonies, "country lanes turn into tree-lined roads, while muddy ditches are transformed into canals. Caravans of covered wagons pass between cornfields, and the red roofs of new houses spring up in formerly deserted spots. The postman, who formerly came just twice a week, appears daily now, his bag heavy with letters and newspapers, and whenever he stops at a new house to deliver a letter from home to some young wife who has newly settled there, he gratefully accepts the glass of milk she offers him at the door" (402/229). Laboring on the colonial frontier, Anton thus not only learns to cultivate the soil and create a functioning homestead but also comes to understand himself as part of a transnational community whose unifying characteristics he internalized during his apprenticeship in Schröter's company.

It is thus perfectly logical that Anton, as soon as he has proven his mettle as an administrator and steward of property by putting down the Polish uprising, returns to his bourgeois life in the Silesian capital. The Rosmin episode serves a purely didactic function in *Debit and Credit*; it remains a device through which Freytag can estrange and thereby highlight German values. The threat that imperialism poses for liberal democracy by bringing together multiple nations and incompatible recognition claims under one sovereign umbrella is neutralized by Freytag's presentation of Poznań as a "wild" or "unclaimed" space. There are no previously existing communities there. The Polish peasants and the scattered aristocrats who

---

10. Benedict Anderson, "Long-Distance Nationalism," in *The Spectre of Comparisons: Nationalism, Southeast Asia, and the World* (London: Verso, 1998), 58–76.

rule over them are depicted as little more than savages, and the lands that they so insufficiently develop are available for cultivation at the hands of the German settlers. And this cultivation happens, it is important to note, without any kind of state intervention. Poznań appears in the novel as a lawless region, without local gendarmes or nearby Prussian military; the final rescue of the besieged Rothsattels is carried out precisely *not* by some kind of equivalent of the U.S. cavalry, but rather by a private relief force of German workers.

That this final rescue operation is by necessity spearheaded by the only other character in the book whom Freytag has endowed with heroic characteristics, namely by the itinerant nobleman Fritz von Fink, points to a gash in the ideological fabric of *Debit and Credit*. At novel's end, Anton finds himself trapped between two aristocrats: his love interest Lenore on the one hand, his best friend Fink on the other. The narrative conventions of frontier romances would dictate that the hero gets his girl and is amicably reunited with his friend. Such an ending, however, would dilute the ideological purity of *Debit and Credit*. After all, it would move the bourgeois protagonist into uncomfortable proximity to the aristocrats whom Freytag spends so much time belittling over the course of his novel. Instead of marrying Lenore von Rothsattel, then, Anton graciously hands her over to Fink and returns to Breslau to marry Schröter's sister Sabine, a woman who is clearly his elder by a number of years. If Hegel's famous observation that the *Bildungsroman* usually ends when the hero "gets his position, marries, and becomes a Philistine like everybody else" was originally meant to be tragic, then Freytag's formulation repeats it as farce.[11]

This ending must have seemed as cruelly unsatisfactory to Freytag's devoted nineteenth-century readership as it does to us now, and in order to make it more palatable, the author applies an extra dose of ideological varnish on the final pages. Anton not only receives Sabine as a wife but also joins the Schröter business as a full partner and is granted access to the company ledger. Referring to this volume, the narrator remarks: "The old book of his life is now over, and [Wohlfart's] further debit and credit . . . shall be recorded in the secret ledger" (851/564). Anton's individual destiny is, in other words, fused with that of the company that employs him, just as the novel of formation, the narrative of an individual development, makes way for the company ledger, the chronicle of a collective one. Rarely has the performative logic of the *Bildungsroman* been as explicitly reaffirmed as here: by going to Rosmin and planting the seeds not only of new crops, but also of middle-class values, Anton widens the imaginative reach of German liberal culture and helps to adapt it to the new age of empire and nascent globalization. In return, the goods

---

11. G. W. F. Hegel, *Aesthetics: Lectures on Fine Art*, trans. T. M. Knox (Oxford: Clarendon Press, 1975), 1:593. Not the least farcical element of this set-up is, of course, that Anton's wandering years literally end in the same way that they usually did in the early modern period: with a marriage into the guild master's family. The lives of Anton's friends Pix and Specht have previously taken a similar course.

he sends home from his colonial outpost not only strengthen domestic communities but also ensure the continued success of men like T. O. Schröter, who rewards Anton's efforts by certifying the official end of his journeyman years and his arrival at a secure position within society.

Evolution and Devolution in *Daniel Deronda*

The performative dimensions of the *Bildungsroman*—the ways, in other words, in which a character's coming-to-consciousness affects the self-understanding of his or her immediate community and, by extension, also that of the readership—take center stage in *Daniel Deronda* as well. Like Freytag, Eliot wrote as a liberal nationalist grappling with the perplexing effects of modern-day imperialism. Unlike Freytag, however, she did so at a time when the British Empire was arguably near the zenith of its power. This meant that she could not afford the luxury of imagining a bourgeois culture that somehow stands anterior to the structures of imperialism. In the Cracovian episode of *Debit and Credit*, Freytag explicitly pits Anton Wohlfart and T. O. Schröter against the instruments of the Prussian state and proposes that transnational merchant capitalism is capable of reaching across barriers that stymie armies and colonial administrators. English life during the mid-1860s (*Daniel Deronda* takes place from October 1864 to October 1866), on the other hand, was shaped by imperial influence in any number of ways. For Eliot, the central question thus had to be how liberalism should respond to a world that has already been remade by cavalry charges and gunboat diplomacy.

Edward Said, in his *Culture and Imperialism*, famously traced how the marriage economy depicted in Jane Austen's *Mansfield Park* (1814) fed on the fruits of colonial labor, specifically the Antiguan plantation of the novel's father figure, Sir Thomas Bertram. Eliot's heroine Gwendolen Harleth derives her inheritance from a similar source, since her grandfather was a planter on Barbados. Roughly fifty years have passed between the events of *Mansfield Park* and those of *Daniel Deronda*, however, and the lost inheritance that sets the plot of the latter novel into motion is motivated not by labor trouble in the Caribbean, but by a rather more modern catastrophe, namely the failure of the industrial interest in which Gwendolen's legal guardian has invested her family's money. In other words, imperialism is depicted as a fully structured economic and cultural system. Instead of deriving their income directly from colonial labor, as was still the case with the Bertrams, Eliot's protagonists profit from it indirectly, through the intermediary of modern capitalist production.[12] Exploitation has become disguised and systemic, as Eliot

---

12. As Nancy Henry summarizes it, "The spectacular loss of [Gwendolen's] income resulting from the failure of Grapnell and Co. is just one of the many ways in which the novel represents the general shift from a land-based economy and social hierarchy to a market-driven capitalist society. In contrast to her other English novels, all of which are set during or before the early 1830s, Deronda (which is set

illustrates in a number of passages. Regarding Gwendolen's relationship to her Anglican religion, for instance, the narrator comments: "The question whether she believed it had not occurred to her, any more than it had occurred to her to inquire into the conditions of colonial property and banking, on which, as she had had many opportunities of knowing, the family fortune was dependent."[13]

Every once in a while, however, the exploitative tensions that build up gradually and quietly in fully formed imperial societies will erupt into full-blown violence, as happened, for instance, during the Morant Bay rebellion that features briefly yet decisively in the novel, and which no doubt helped motivate Eliot's choice to set her novel in the mid-1860s. Roughly halfway through the novel, a number of characters discuss the recent uprising of impoverished black farmers on Jamaica against their exploitative white neighbors:

> Grandcourt held that the Jamaican negro was a beastly sort of Baptist Caliban; Deronda said he had always felt a little with Caliban, who naturally had his own point of view and could sing a good song; [Gwendolen's mother] observed that her father had an estate in Barbadoes, but that she herself had never been to the West Indies; Mrs. Torrington was sure she should never sleep in her bed if she lived among blacks; her husband corrected her by saying that the blacks would be manageable enough if it were not for the half-breeds; and Deronda remarked that the whites had to thank themselves for the half-breeds. (279)

Besides serving as a convenient means of adding some illustrative depth to various characters and reminding the reader of the source of Gwendolen's income, this passage also highlights race as the principal means by which the deleterious effects of imperialism are depicted throughout the novel. One of the animating questions of *Daniel Deronda* is, quite simply, whether liberal democracy can be maintained across racial lines, and it is for this reason, presumably, that Eliot on several occasions also draws attention to the American Civil War, which seemed to answer this question in the negative.

The close relationship between all this political talk and the generic nature of *Daniel Deronda* as a *Bildungsroman* is made clear by one of the more famous of several metaliterary asides over the course of the novel. Eliot's narrator asks: "Could there be a slenderer, more insignificant thread in human history than this consciousness of a girl, busy with her small inferences of the way in which she could make her life pleasant?—in a time, too, when ideas were with fresh vigour making

---

in 1864–6) represents the long-term effect of social and political changes, such as the abolition of the slave trade (1807) and of slavery in the British colonies (1833), on the descendants of West Indian absentee planters." Nancy Henry, *George Eliot and the British Empire* (Cambridge: Cambridge University Press, 2002), 111.

13. George Eliot, *Daniel Deronda* (New York: Oxford World's Classics, 1988), 51. All further references to this edition will appear in parentheses in the text.

armies of themselves" (102). The "slender insignificant thread" to which Eliot is here alluding has, of course, provided not merely the English realist novel, but more specifically the female *Bildungsroman* with one of its prime subject matters.[14] Novels illustrating the consciousness of women, particularly those that dramatize the search for a suitable husband (a plot that throughout the nineteenth century was virtually the only one available to female protagonists), were important tributaries of liberal thought, because they illustrate the need, and indeed the benefit, of civil settlements of personal differences. When Elizabeth is finally united with Darcy, or Jane with Rochester, their respective plots have not only reached a formally satisfying conclusion; they have also served as thought experiments probing what it means to recognize that other people can have differing wishes and opinions from us, and offering a solution for how such disagreements might be amicably negotiated. *Daniel Deronda* takes these thought experiments a step further, asking how racial difference might affect the process of both individual and collective identity formation in liberal societies.

Despite all the talk about Morant Bay and the battlefields in America, however, Eliot's novel does not feature a single black protagonist. Instead, racial difference is here projected exclusively onto Jewish characters—not only by the Gentiles who form various prejudices against them, but also by those characters themselves. The Jewish music teacher Klesmer, for instance, who will go on to marry the Gentile Ms. Arrowcourt, loudly proclaims that he "looks forward to a fusion of races" (206), while the various discussants at the Hand and Banner also argue along explicitly racial lines. And in a development that some readers have found difficult to swallow, Eliot herself shifts the focus of her narrative from Gwendolen Harleth to the Jewish character Daniel Deronda roughly a third of the way into the book, in order to more thoroughly explore the vicissitudes of interracial communication. F. R. Leavis famously fulminated against this move, arguing that the two characters have nothing in common and that the novel best be sliced in half, with the good half to be renamed *Gwendolen Harleth*.[15] Against this suggestion, I wish to argue that Gwendolen and Deronda are, in fact, intertwined doubles of one another and that the Deronda plot allows Eliot to think through certain issues that she cannot adequately resolve through Gwendolen alone.

That Gwendolen and Deronda are meant to some extent to double one another is already made clear in the novel's opening chapters, when their lives briefly touch before going largely separate paths for the next few hundred pages. Deronda observes Gwendolen on the night that she learns of her family's financial ruin, news that causes her to break off her vacation at a spa town in Germany and pawn a

---

14. On the subject of the English female *Bildungsroman*, see Susan Fraiman, *Unbecoming Women: British Women Writers and the Novel of Development* (New York: Columbia University Press, 1993).

15. F. R. Leavis, *The Great Tradition: George Eliot, Henry James, Joseph Conrad* (New York: New York University Press, 1963).

turquoise necklace she inherited from her father in order to return all the more speedily to her mother in England. The family heirloom proves harder to get rid of than Gwendolen thought, however, since Deronda immediately returns it to her. As the reader later learns, Deronda too possesses a piece of jewelry that was left to him by his unknown parents, and while he does not know the story behind the turquoise necklace, he naturally cannot bear to see Gwendolen rid herself of what is obviously one of her most cherished possessions. This brief encounter brings together not only Eliot's doubled protagonists, but also the two dominant narrative codes of the nineteenth-century British novel: the social-realist and the melodramatic. For Gwendolen, the necklace is a material link to a now-vanished fortune; for Deronda, on the other hand, it is a symbol of destiny.

The problem of inheritance thus links Gwendolen's plot to Deronda's, but there are important differences between the two. In keeping with the social-realist code of the novel, the question of inheritance in Gwendolen's case is materialistic, while in the case of Deronda, whose plot obeys a melodramatic code, it is symbolic. Gwendolen, in other words, fears that she may slide into poverty. Deronda's existence, on the other hand, is secure, since he finds himself the ward of the excessively wealthy Sir Hugo Mallinger. He is instead concerned about who he truly is and what hidden factors might have played a role in his conception.

This shift to hidden factors is important because, as critics such as Gillian Beer and Sally Shuttleworth have shown, Eliot's composition of *Daniel Deronda* was haunted by the 1871 publication of Charles Darwin's *The Descent of Man*, in which the British naturalist applied the principles of heredity and evolutionary theory to the human species for the very first time.[16] Evolutionary theory is a general problem for literary realism, because it privileges chance over causal determination, biological destiny over individual choice. More importantly for the present context, Social Darwinism, the vulgar popularization to which evolutionary theory gave rise in the late Victorian period, it is also a problem for liberal nationalism, since the liberal believes, to quote John Stuart Mill's classic dictum, that "the worth of a State, in the long run, is the worth of the individuals composing it."[17] Social Darwinism, on

---

16. In the words of Gillian Beer, "Daniel Deronda is a novel haunted by the future, that purest and most taxing realm of fiction. For the first time in George Eliot's work the dependence of the future on the past is brought into question. Earlier in her career she had found a meta-religious security in the 'great concept of universal sequence,' 'the gradual reduction of all phenomena within the sphere of established law, which carries as a consequence the rejection of the miraculous.' Causal sequence had been the organising principle both of her morality and her practice as a novelist." Gillian Beer, *Darwin's Plots: Evolutionary Narrative in Darwin, George Eliot, and Nineteenth-Century Fiction* (Cambridge: Cambridge University Press, 1983), 169. Beer's choice of the words "meta-religious security" seems to me especially pregnant here. As I will show shortly, in *Daniel Deronda*, Eliot embraces a different kind of religiosity, one grounded not in abstract principles, but in the experience of specific communities. See also Sally Shuttleworth, *George Eliot and Nineteenth-Century Science: The Make-Believe of a Beginning* (Cambridge: Cambridge University Press, 1987).

17. John Stuart Mill, *On Liberty* (London: Penguin, 1974), 187.

the other hand, proclaims that the worth of the state inheres neither in individuals nor even in national communities as the liberal understands them, but rather in races, that is, in pseudoscientific entities constructed on the basis of heredity, rather than of shared culture.[18] But if racial identities are real and unequal, and if the rise and fall of states depend on them, then isn't imperialism justified, and isn't liberal nationalism an outdated mind-set? This is the true challenge that Eliot confronts in her novel. Her interest in the black farmers of Morant Bay or the slaves of the American South expresses not so much pity for the wretched of the earth as it does anxiety over the future of England itself.

Social Darwinism makes a first appearance on the opening pages of *Daniel Deronda*, when Eliot depicts the gamblers in the German casino as a series of ethnological types:

> Those who were taking their pleasure at a higher strength, and were absorbed in play, showed very distant varieties of European type: Livonian and Spanish, Graeco-Italian and miscellaneous German, English aristocratic and English plebeian. Here certainly was a striking admission of human equality. The white bejeweled fingers of an English countess were very near touching a bony, yellow, crab-like hand stretching a bared wrist to clutch a heap of coin—a hand easy to sort with the square, gaunt face, deep-set eyes, grizzled eye-brows, and ill-combed scanty hair which seemed a slight metamorphosis of the vulture. (4)

But it finds its strongest expression in the description of Henleigh Mallinger Grandcourt, Gwendolen's eventual husband. As Marc E. Wohlfarth has documented, Grandcourt is an archetype of hereditary degeneracy: feckless, flaccid, and bored.[19] That he is also Sir Hugo's nephew and presumptive heir adds additional force to Deronda's anxieties about his own ancestry and casts a negative light on England's hereditary ruling class.

Not coincidentally, Jews and aristocrats thus emerge as the twin symptoms of a malaise that is afflicting liberal nationalism in an age of empire, much as they did in Freytag's *Debit and Credit*. I say not coincidentally because Jews and aristocrats are also traditional ciphers of cosmopolitanism, and cosmopolitanism for Eliot represents a danger to national identity not at all unlike that posed by racialism. What at least certain strains of cosmopolitanism share with certain other strains of racial thinking is a rejection of identity formations rooted in sociological "thick description," a move that Eliot treats with a great deal of suspicion throughout *Daniel Deronda*. Klesmer, for instance, not only proudly asserts his "racial" identity; he

---

18. On social Darwinism as a challenge to classical liberalism in England, see Pericles Lewis, *Modernism, Nationalism, and the Novel* (Cambridge: Cambridge University Press, 2000), 89–93.

19. Mark E. Wohlfarth, "Daniel Deronda and the Politics of Nationalism," *Nineteenth-Century Literature* 53:2 (1998): 188–210.

is also a self-confessed cosmopolitan who sees in music a universal language that transcends all national boundaries.[20] Grandcourt's degeneracy too is powerfully reinforced by the fact that he is a cosmopolitan dandy who uses a yachting trip in the Mediterranean as a weapon against Gwendolen, in order to deprive her of her emotional support network back home. Deronda's mother, finally, the Princess Halm-Eberstein, embodies all three points of the triangle that I have just sketched. At once Jewish and aristocratic, she renounces her "racial" identity and substitutes for it an itinerant cosmopolitan existence, even at the terrible cost of abandoning her only son.

While Freytag viewed liberal nationalism and Judaism as entirely antithetical categories, however, Eliot pursues what might be called a dialectical solution in *Debit and Credit*. By novel's end, Deronda emerges as a powerful figurehead for a rejuvenated nationalism, but Eliot's titular protagonist is also an aristocratic, cosmopolitan Jew. The great accomplishment of *Daniel Deronda* is that it shows that none of these terms excludes any of the others.

Cosmopolitan Affections and the Search for a National Center

Eliot begins this endeavor by rehabilitating Judaism as a religion—that is, as a living set of beliefs and a quotidian practice—rather than using it merely as a racial marker. When Deronda begins his search for Mirah Lapidoth's lost brother, he still thinks of Judaism principally as a relationship of blood, and obsesses over the large numbers of "Ezras" and "Cohens" that exist in London, almost as if all Jews were part of the same family. His attitude toward the actual people he encounters, specifically the family of the "false" Ezra Cohen, is detached, and he is initially hobbled by anti-Semitic prejudice. He even counsels Mirah that her name "is inadmissible for a singer," because for him, "just now the name Cohen was equivalent to the ugliest of yellow badges" (401). As his contacts with Judaism increase, however, his attitude changes. Deronda's mealtime interactions with Ezra Cohen's family, his playful banter with little Jacob, who urges him to "shwop" (331) pocketknives, are thus far more than mere stalling tactics by which Eliot increases the narrative tension leading up to the eventual revelation that Mordecai is Mirah's brother. They represent instances of genuine growth and development in Daniel, who now learns that at least some cosmopolitan communities sustain themselves through the same

---

20. Mark E. Wohlfarth again: "What Klesmer lacks is a sense of communal destiny: he holds cosmopolitan convictions that deprive his art of any larger field of application and meaning other than an exercise in various modes of the sublime. Eliot seeks to lay bare and redress this relative vacuity of Klesmer's art by counterposing an aesthetics embedded within nationalist coordinates. For example, Mirah chooses a musical setting of some words from Leopardi's 'Hymn to Italy' for her recital at Offendene; the nationalist implications are impossible to overlook—although, surely enough, Klesmer concentrates on the artistic quality of her rendition, and thus a hyper-attention to style makes him miss the semantic core of Mirah's singing" ("Daniel Deronda and the Politics of Nationalism," 204).

bonds of tradition and quotidian ritual that also animate national communities. The Meyrick sisters, in a comical version of Deronda's own education, similarly come to embrace Mirah once they recognize that "[her] religion was of one fibre with her affections, and had never presented itself to her as a set of propositions" (305)—in other words, that she takes pleasure in Jewish rituals because they recall to her her childhood and lost mother. Amy Meyrick, trying to square her newfound sentiments with her more conservative upbringing, even argues: "[Mirah] says herself she is a very bad Jewess, and does not half know her people's religion.... Perhaps it would gradually melt away from her, and she would pass into Christianity like the rest of the world, if she got to love us very much, and never found her mother. It is so strange to be of the Jews' religion now" (304). In this remarkable statement, it is Christianity that metamorphoses into a featureless cosmopolitan creed, while Judaism emerges as a religion characterized not by diasporic dispersal, but rather by tribal integrity.

Mirah Lapidoth isn't the only Jewish character to be thus rehabilitated, however. Simultaneously with Deronda's quest for the real Ezra Cohen, Gwendolen Harleth, still hoping to avoid the marriage to Grandcourt that seems to provide the only solution to her financial misfortune, consults Klesmer to obtain from him a realistic estimate of her chances of succeeding on the stage. The ensuing conversation crushes her dreams, but it also sheds new light on Klesmer's character. The music teacher is careful to disabuse Gwendolen of her notion of music as a realm of aesthetic free play. He acquaints her instead with the quotidian drudge that musicians worldwide submit to in order to hone and maintain their talents. While Klesmer previously appeared to be a romantic dreamer whose musical devotion seemed of a piece with his utopian longing for a "fusion of races," he now communicates a quite different conception of the artistic life. Musicians, on this new account, are unmasked as members of yet another community, albeit one held together by the obligations of their craft rather than by religion or national belonging. Both in Gwendolen and in Deronda we thus witness a process not just of education, but of genuine spiritual growth that results in a new appreciation for Judaism as a living cultural practice. What started out as a "race" suddenly no longer looks all that different from a national community.

It is at this point in the novel, of course, that Eliot introduces the character of Mordecai and through him the philosophical discussion circle at the Head and Banner that bats around proto-Zionist ideas, thereby explicitly linking Judaism and national identity. Rather than dwell on these well-known passages, however, I wish to point out another, in which Eliot connects religion and nationalism in a specifically English fashion. Shortly after her fateful marriage to Grandcourt, Gwendolen is given a tour of Sir Hugo Mallinger's country estate, "a picturesque architectural outgrowth from an abbey, which had still remnants of the old monastic trunk" (140). This private tour includes the following exchange:

Sir Hugo, by way of changing the subject, said to her, "Is not this a beautiful room? It was part of the refectory of the Abbey. There was a division made by those pillars and the three arches, and afterwards they were built up. Else it was half as large again originally. There used to be rows of Benedictines sitting where we are sitting. Suppose we were suddenly to see the lights burning low and the ghosts of the old monks rising behind all our chairs!"

"Please don't!" said Gwendolen, with a playful shudder. "It is very nice to come after ancestors and monks, but they should know their place and keep underground. I should be rather frightened to go about this house all alone. I suppose the old generations must be angry with us because we have altered things so much."

"Oh, the ghosts must be of all political parties," said Sir Hugo. "And those fellows who wanted to change things while they lived and couldn't do it, must be on our side." (350)

This passage can be read as an early example of a motif that will become a major preoccupation of the modernist novel in the years following *Daniel Deronda*: the unease felt by basically secular visitors who stumble on abandoned or neglected places of worship.[21] Neither Sir Hugo nor Gwendolen would think of themselves as secularists, of course, although it is worthwhile to remember in this context Lord Acton's description of the author who gave life to them as "the emblem of a generation distracted between the intense need of believing and the difficulty of belief."[22] Unlike Mirah Lapidoth, for whom the quotidian rituals of Judaism are a connection not only to her ancestors, but also to the living community of practitioners around her, Sir Hugo and Gwendolen have lost any sense of Anglicanism as a vital force of English culture. They take religion for granted; it is something that they have inherited and that quite literally has only a spectral presence in their lives. When Gwendolen voices her anxiety over the decayed state of religious life with the words "The old generations must be angry with us because we have altered things so much," Sir Hugo tellingly shifts the discussion toward politics, indicating that he views religion as little more than a subsidiary battlefield in the struggle for the future of the British Empire.

Alterations and improvements, of both an architectural and a spiritual kind, are indeed the focus of much discussion over the next few pages. In a spirited exchange about the appearance of the abbey, Sir Hugo reveals himself as an enemy of historical eclecticism ("Additions ought to smack of the time when they are made and carry the stamp of their period. I wouldn't destroy any old bits, but that notion of reproducing the old is a mistake, I think" [356]), while Deronda comes down

---

21. On this theme, see Pericles Lewis, *Religious Experience and the Modernist Novel* (Cambridge: Cambridge University Press, 2010), 1–22.

22. Quoted in Barry Qualls, "George Eliot and Religion," in Levine, *The Cambridge Companion to George Eliot*, 119.

on the side of tradition ("I think that way of arguing against a course because it may be ridden down to an absurdity would soon bring life to a standstill. . . . It is not the logic of human action, but of a roasting-jack"; 357). To the modern reader, Deronda sounds rather priggish here, but Sir Hugo's flippant response to his objection ("I find the rule of the pocket the best guide") shows that Mallinger's motives are pecuniary rather than ethical or aesthetic in nature. Deronda, meanwhile, has a much more considerate justification for his architectural conservatism:

> "Do you want to keep up the old fashions, then, Mr. Deronda?" said Gwendolen, taking advantage of the freedom of grouping to fall back a little, while Sir Hugo and Grandcourt went on.
> "Some of them. I don't see why we should not use our choice there as we do elsewhere—or why either age or novelty by itself is an argument for or against. To delight in doing things because our fathers did them is good if it shuts out nothing better; it enlarges the range of affection—and affection is the broadest basis of good in life."
> "Do you think so?" said Gwendolen, with a little surprise. "I should have thought you cared most about ideas, knowledge, wisdom, and all that."
> "But to care about *them* is a sort of affection," said Deronda, smiling at her sudden *naïveté*. "Call it attachment, interest, willingness to bear a great deal for the sake of being with them and saving them from injury. Of course it makes a difference if the objects of interest are human beings; but generally in all deep affections the objects are a mixture—half persons and half ideas—sentiments and affections flow in together." (357)

Deronda here articulates a vision of the good in life that surely is also Eliot's own, a vision centered on the willingness to cultivate "attachment, interest, willingness to bear a great deal," for other people and ideas. And these "attachments" or "affections" quite deliberately aim beyond the immediately knowable toward regions as yet undiscovered. A few pages later, when Deronda doffs his hat upon entering Sir Hugo's pièce de resistance, a Gothic choir that has been turned into a stable, Grandcourt quips: "Do you take off your hat to the horses?" (360). The attentive reader, however, already knows that Deronda is actually tipping his hat to the people who built and prayed in the formerly sacred location.

The exchange in the abbey casts a revealing light also on Deronda's reading of a Hebrew grammar the previous night. His growing interest in Judaism is evidently motivated neither by a purely personal attraction to Mirah Lapidoth nor by an abstract interest in the Jewish religion as such. It represents instead "affection" in the sense just defined: a twinned desire to understand Mirah (as well as Mordecai, and perhaps even the Cohens) within the context of a cultural and historical tradition that has shaped her character, as well as to understand the larger shape of that tradition through the access provided him by his personal acquaintances.

Deronda is moving away from a racial understanding of "Jewishness" and toward a more sophisticated awareness of Judaism as a form of practice: as a set of beliefs, attitudes, and behaviors that are acted out by real people trying to mediate between the weight of tradition and the circumstances of their present lives. In the process, he is also learning to escape the grip of his inheritance—both the philistinism of his adoptive father and the Jewish self-hatred of his actual mother, the Princess Halm-Eberstein.

Many critics have faulted Eliot's depiction of Judaism for its idealism, arguing that the author projects onto a foreign religion an organic totality that has long ago been lost in modernity.[23] Indeed, a number of scenes in the novel—from the dinner table idylls chez Cohen to Deronda's newfound piety at the abbey—invite parody. But Eliot's vision of Jewish nationalism is more complex than she is sometimes given credit for. During the Hand and Banner debates, for instance, Mordecai's claim that "the effect of our separateness will not be completed and have its highest transformation unless our race takes on again the character of a nationality" (456) posits a dialectical rather than purely negative relationship between diaspora and national unity. Nationhood, in other words, fulfills and redeems a process that begins with cosmopolitan dispersal. While this is in one sense a very traditional idea with roots in the Pentateuch, it is on another level a thoroughly modern claim full of utopian radicalism, something that Mordecai stresses in his climactic recognition scene with Mirah: "'Seest thou, Mirah,' he said once, after a long silence, 'the *Shemah*, wherein we briefly confess the divine Unity, is the chief devotional exercise of the Hebrew; and this made our religion the fundamental religion for the whole world; for the divine Unity embraces as its consequence the ultimate unity of mankind. See, then—the nation which has been scoffed for its separateness, has given a binding theory to the human race'" (628). The Jewish religion, in other words, possesses much more than merely a foundational wholeness that Gentile English have lost in their quest for world domination. It instead heralds a future in which all human beings, no matter where they live, might feel a part of the same community. In Mordecai's formulation, furthermore, all human races have been subsumed into the collective singular "human race," and it is this race that takes its "binding theory" from the Jewish nation. When Deronda thus proclaims that "the idea that I am possessed with is that of restoring a political existence to my people, making them a nation again, giving them a national centre, such as the English have, though they too are scattered over the face of the globe" (688), he is telling only part of the truth. Indeed, the "political existence" that he envisions, the one that might bestow national unity on a dispersed people, does not yet exist and would benefit the English with their empire as much as it would any Jews.

---

23. For an intelligent discussion of this question, see Amanda Anderson, *The Powers of Distance: Cosmopolitanism and the Cultivation of Detachment* (Princeton, NJ: Princeton University Press, 2001), 119.

Daniel Deronda concludes with an act of symbolic inheritance, in much the same way as did Freytag's novel. In all other regards, however, the two endings are as dissimilar as possible. Mordecai's last words in English are "Where thou goest, Daniel, I shall go. Is it not begun? Have I not breathed my soul into you? We shall live together" (695). The almost Mosaic promise of these lines is directed outward and toward an uncertain future, in stark contrast to the summing up of accounts that concludes *Debit and Credit*. Freytag abhors nothing so much as ambiguity, and most of his book is devoted to showing how people, landscapes, and human communities alike can be ordered and improved through economic activity that is given a national character through its identification with German middle-class values. For Eliot, on the other hand, national identity is a flexible construct that can persist through outward multiplicity.

One problem remains, however. For almost as long as there has been a critical tradition devoted to *Daniel Deronda*, readers have singled out as an unresolved problem in the novel the fact that Deronda himself is Jewish. Precisely because he turns out to be Jewish, his sympathy and attraction toward Mirah retroactively seem fated, predetermined by essential characteristics not at all unlike those proclaimed by Social Darwinism. Certainly it now becomes clear why Eliot abandoned her original focus on the development of Gwendolen Harleth and moved to a different protagonist, one who could more readily move between cultures and religious traditions. The question thus becomes whether Gwendolen, as a Gentile Englishwoman, will ever complete a similar formative journey without the benefits of Deronda's biography. If Eliot's ultimate purpose is to demonstrate how English national culture might regain a lost vitality, doesn't everything ultimately depend on her, rather than on Deronda?

The ending of the novel certainly tries to answer these questions in the affirmative. On the morning of his marriage, Deronda receives from Gwendolen a letter in which she avows: "I have remembered your words—that I may live to be one of the best of women, who make others glad that they were born. I do not yet see how that can be, but you know better than I. If it ever comes true, it will be because you helped me" (694–95). Regarding this passage, Nancy Henry has written: "Gwendolen's determination to live and become better is the type of moral redirection needed by the English generally. Deronda's decision to travel to the East is no more important or momentous than Gwendolen's resolution to live differently; it is merely more important-sounding in its 'worldhistoric' implications."[24] Much depends on this claim, and yet Gwendolen's letter remains a strangely conflicted document, intended as an expression of autonomy but couched in the language of subservience. Even more importantly, Eliot never *shows* us the kind of moral improvement that Gwendolen here promises, even though one of the central claims

---

24. Henry, "George Eliot and Politics," 158.

of realist fiction is that complex issues of this kind are best illustrated and adjudicated through a wealth of individual detail.

It is perhaps telling that Gwendolen's formation, too, depends on an act of inheritance, and one that is linked to a central mystery of the novel: is she or isn't she actively complicit in the death of her husband, Grandcourt? Her traumatic experience certainly sets in motion a process of moral awakening, as the narrator points out in a bit of free indirect discourse filtered through Deronda's mind: "But her remorse was the precious sign of a recoverable nature; it was the culmination of that self-disapproval which had been the awakening of a new life within her; it marked her off from the criminals whose only regret is failure in securing their evil wish" (597). But this moral awakening remains materially dependent on the wealth that Grandcourt has accumulated, and some of its taint surely still clings to Gwendolen, even if Mrs. Glasher, Grandcourt's former mistress, is paid off handsomely.

At novel's end, Gwendolen feels herself "dislodged from her supremacy in her own world, and getting a sense that her horizon was but a dipping onward of an existence with which her own was revolving" (689). But for all practical purposes, *Daniel Deronda* ends with its heroine ensconced in supremacy rather than dislodged from it. Gwendolen is about to begin a new life, but it is a life of luxury and ease rather than of hardship and uncertainty, as presumably await Deronda on his travels. Eliot's cosmopolitan project thus ultimately feeds on Jewish subalternity; it cloaks Deronda's awakening in a mantle of exoticism and fails to offer a direct challenge to a Gentile readership. In the last of my three comparative case studies, I will examine how this impasse can be overcome, and how the affective challenges imposed by empire can be brought home into the imperial center.

5

Urban Vernaculars: Joyce, Döblin, and the "Individuating Rhythm" of Modernity

In his review of *Berlin Alexanderplatz*, entitled "Crisis of the Novel," Walter Benjamin became the first critic to link Alfred Döblin's 1929 masterpiece to the novel of formation, declaring it to be the "most extreme and vertiginous, the last and most advanced stage of the old bourgeois *Bildungsroman*."[1] This was a backhanded compliment at best, for as the title of the review already indicates, Benjamin's main purpose was to plumb the depths of a putative crisis confronted by the bourgeois novel, and to show how this established form was forced into a retreat by the inexorable advance of modernist (or, as Benjamin called it, "epic") writing. For Benjamin, Döblin's work combined elements of both of these competing styles, a fact already indicated by its paradoxical title, which reads in its entirety *Berlin Alexanderplatz: The Story of Franz Biberkopf*. Whereas the first two words draw attention to a social space in a constant state of transformation, the subtitle focuses on an individual being whose development from a criminal into a petit bourgeois lends a sense of unity to the otherwise disparate elements that comprise the novel. Benjamin resented this attempt at formal wholeness, which he declared to be "no more than a heroic metamorphosis of bourgeois

---

1. Walter Benjamin, "Crisis of the Novel," in *Selected Writings*, trans. Rodney Livingstone et al. and ed. Michael W. Jennings, Howard Eiland, and Gary Smith, vol. 2, *1927–1930* (Cambridge, MA: Harvard University Press, 1999), 304 (translation modified).

consciousness."[2] For him, the revolutionary genius of *Berlin Alexanderplatz* lay instead in its loving depiction of the human detritus that comprises the metropolis: the whores and petty criminals who collectively form a popular consciousness that stands in opposition to the older bourgeois variety.

The notion that the modern city—cosmopolitan, frenetic, and constantly self-reinventing—resists the organic metaphor of continuous growth on which historicism (and with it traditional *Bildungsroman* theory) was built certainly did not originate with Benjamin. Twenty years earlier, in his influential *Berlin: Destiny of a City* (1910), the art historian Karl Scheffler had already approached urban space itself as a kind of defective *Bildungsroman* protagonist, summarizing his findings with the pithy observation that the German capital was "a city forever condemned to become, and never to be."[3] And many of the most famous films of the Ufa studios, from Fritz Lang's *Metropolis* (1927) and *M* (1931) to Walter Ruttmann's *Berlin: Symphony of a Large City* (1927), sought to describe urban life in filmic rhythms that bore little resemblance to those of the nineteenth-century novel.

Modern approaches to *Berlin Alexanderplatz* have for the most part hewed close to the terms already laid out by Scheffler and Benjamin, frequently diagnosing a tension between two different approaches to the narrative treatment of time in the novel. Marilyn Sibley Fries, for instance, observes:

> Döblin's Berlin image is characterized by the alternating interplay of realistic and dry presentations of factual information with complex metaphorical and symbolic images, of the objective with the subjective. A fundamental premise of his city concept is contained in this interplay; while human beings whose lives are measured and defined by time comprise the city, the visual city image is always momentary, contained precisely in the "*Augen-blick*." The city is thus presented as an interface between the historical or temporal, as embodied in the human and unidentified mass as well as in specific characters, and momentary reality, presented in recurring concrete visual images. In this context the title assumes a new and more profound meaning: *Berlin Alexanderplatz*—the designation of the visual and the immediate—is juxtaposed and united with *Die Geschichte vom Franz Biberkopf*, which implies in the ambiguity of *Geschichte* the historicity of man.[4]

According to this analysis, Döblin's art juxtaposes concepts such as "human time," "*Geschichte*," and "the historicity of man," that is, precisely those elements that are constitutive of traditional *Bildungsroman* theory, with the Nietzschen "*Augenblick*," and thus with a philosophy of truth revealed not through a process of gradual

---

2. Benjamin, "Crisis of the Novel," 303.
3. Karl Scheffler, *Berlin: Ein Stadtschicksal* (Berlin: Fanei & Walz Verlag, 1989), 219. All further references to this edition will appear in parentheses in the text.
4. Marilyn Sibley Fries, "The City as Metaphor for the Human Condition: Alfred Döblin's *Berlin Alexanderplatz* (1929)," *Modern Fiction Studies* 24 (1978): 45.

unfolding, but rather through the superimposition of incommensurate elements, as it is done in Döblin's favorite literary technique, the montage.[5]

Ever since the so-called expressionism debate of the 1930s, there has been an influential strain within Marxist criticism that sees the clash between different forms of temporal emplotment as a defining characteristic not just of select works from the early twentieth century, but of modernism per se. On this account, modernism is that which gives a narrative shape to Ernst Bloch's notion of the "synchronicity of the non-synchronous." According to Fredric Jameson, the most influential contemporary critic to hold such a position, modernism is furthermore linked to the rise of imperialism, for it is in imperialist societies that the "synchronicity of the non-synchronous" is experienced most intensely.[6] Colonies in particular will feel the clash between lingering forms of historicity and the new mechanical temporality that is imposed on them by an exploitative social order. If Jameson's thesis is correct, then the stylistic elements that Fries diagnoses in *Berlin Alexanderplatz* should have found earlier expressions in colonial novels that also try to mediate between the demands of *Bildung* and those of the modern city. Among such novels, James Joyce's *A Portrait of the Artist as a Young Man* (1914) presents an especially powerful example.

A Portrait is of interest to a discussion of *Berlin Alexanderplatz* not only because the former presents an early example of colonial modernism, but also because Döblin drew stylistic inspiration from Joyce's later *Ulysses* (1922). The relationship between the two novels that I plan to compare in the following pages thus differs from those operative in the previous two chapters, where I intentionally chose works that presented unexpected and even shocking juxtapositions. Nevertheless, my basic ambition remains the same: to examine the changes brought about in the literary history of the *Bildungsroman* by the advent of new forms of historical consciousness, to document how these changes interact with established local ways of expressing collective identity, and, finally, to show the previously hidden connections that unite seemingly oppositional national traditions. In the present case, this will entail showing how the new modernist sensibility of an asynchronous reality took root in the very different Irish and German contexts, and how Döblin's version of modernism was directly influenced by the Irish conception of colonial modernity that he assimilated from Joyce.

The approach to modernism pursued in this chapter differs sharply from the fundamentally Lukácsian paradigm pursued by Franco Moretti in the afterword to his revised second edition of *The Way of the World*. For Moretti, modernism is

---

5. More recently, Paul K. Saint-Amour has examined what he calls "an uncanny splitting in the temporality of a certain recurrent symptom" in *Berlin Alexanderplatz*. He points out that Franz Biberkopf's traumatic hallucinations of the city collapsing in upon him not only interrupt and hinder his development into a fully functioning member of society but can actually be interpreted as regressions in which Döblin's protagonist is taken back to his experiences in the trenches at Arras. See Paul K. Saint-Amour, "Airwar Prophecy and Interwar Modernism," *Comparative Literature Studies* 42:2 (2005): 151.

6. Fredric Jameson, "Modernism and Imperialism," in *The Modernist Papers* (London: Verso, 2007), 152–69.

a discrete period in literary history, separated from nineteenth-century realism by the four years of the First World War, and characterized by plots in which episodes are juxtaposed more or less randomly, as opposed to those in which the action develops organically.[7] Moretti refers directly to both *A Portrait* (which he regards as a "late realist" text) and *Ulysses* in an attempt to demonstrate his thesis, and to argue that the *Bildungsroman* effectively meets its end on the battlefields of World War I. He provides no explanation for the fact that *Ulysses* in turn gave rise to *Berlin Alexanderplatz*, a novel that is undeniably both modernist and a *Bildungsroman*. The literary history of modernism thus turns out to be just as complex and internally asynchronous as the texts that are subsumed by it.

James Joyce and the "Individuating Rhythm" of Colonial Modernity

Any serious approach to the formal structure of *Berlin Alexanderplatz* has to begin by considering the crucial influence that Georg Goyert's 1927 German translation of *Ulysses* exerted on Döblin.[8] Briefly put, Döblin came across Goyert's *Ulysses* soon after its publication, at a time when he had completed roughly the first quarter of *Berlin Alexanderplatz*. He immediately began to make heavy revisions to the passages he had already drafted in order to incorporate characteristically Joycean devices, such as the stream of consciousness or montage sequences. The rest of *Berlin Alexanderplatz* was then continued in the new style. *Ulysses* provided Döblin with at least two main sources of inspiration: a sophisticated literary meditation on the nature of twentieth-century cities and, as a direct outgrowth of this, a radically cosmopolitan inquiry into the spatial and temporal construction of modern subjectivity. Combined with one another, these two aspects of *Ulysses* allowed Döblin to craft the formally most innovative *Bildungsroman* of the early twentieth century. To understand precisely what the German writer gleaned from Joyce, however, it is necessary to take a step back and take a look at Joyce's own attempt to write a novel of formation. Döblin was apparently not familiar with *A Portrait of the Artist as a Young Man* (the novel appeared in German translation only in 1926 and was not favorably received by most reviewers). Nevertheless, some of the problems that Joyce's earlier novel articulates found poetic echoes in *Ulysses* and through this intermediary also affected *Berlin Alexanderplatz*.

A Portrait of the Artist as a Young Man concludes with a brief postscript: "Dublin 1904 Trieste 1914."[9] In contrast to the similar phrase that James Joyce would later

---

7. Franco Moretti, *The Way of the World: The Bildungsroman in European Culture*, trans. Albert Sbragia, new ed. (London: Verso, 2000), 233.
8. The unsurpassed study in this regard remains Breon Mitchell, *James Joyce and the German Novel, 1922–1933* (Athens, OH: Ohio University Press, 1976).
9. James Joyce, *A Portrait of the Artist as a Young Man* (London: Penguin, 1993), 276. All further references to this work will appear in parentheses in the text.

append to *Ulysses*, the two terms of this addendum aren't connected by hyphens indicating a spatiotemporal continuity but instead remain discrete entities, as if to indicate that the work had been carried out twice. A more suitable ending to a novel that similarly frustrates the conventions of the well-made plot by its constant vacillation between disjunctive and conjunctive tendencies could hardly be imagined. *A Portrait* refuses to develop smoothly: at times it moves forward by leaps and bounds, skipping from one phase in Stephen's life to another; at others it seems to merely spin around in circles as each new episode takes on a disturbing resemblance to those that preceded it.

The tension between these narrative vectors can also be felt on the level of style. The epiphany and the leitmotif, the two devices that more than any others define Joyce's prose, are essentially opposites of one another. The epiphany is fundamentally disjunctive: by "transmuting the daily bread of experience into the radiant body of everliving life" (240), it necessarily destroys the flow of mundane reality and therefore also the continuity of sensation. As *A Portrait* demonstrates time and time again, the only way to follow up on an epiphany is with a chapter or section break. The leitmotif, on the other hand, is entirely conjunctive: it points out the prosaic underpinnings of lofty emotions and ties each stage in the development of both plot and protagonist back to the ones that preceded it. The endearingly frustrating nature of Joyce's text stems from the fact that epiphany and leitmotif can hardly be separated from one another. Stephen's famous encounter with the bird-girl on Sandymount Beach is at once radically disjunctive, pushing him "on and on and on and on" (186), and completely overdetermined, invoking a network of well-established motifs that includes birds, Mariolatry, eyesight, falling water, and several others.

The ambiguous status that the concept of "development" thus occupies in Joyce's novel is perhaps best demonstrated by the inevitable contradictions one encounters in the canonical attempts to classify *A Portrait* as a *Bildungsroman*. In order to reconcile Joyce's work to the tradition, Jerome Hamilton Buckley, for example, is forced to dismiss great chunks of the novel as "unnecessarily long-winded" and to remind Joyce's readers that "indecision and inconclusiveness" have always characterized the endings of classical novels of formation.[10] On the other hand, Franco Moretti celebrates precisely the indecision of the final chapter as Joyce's ultimate vindication. By asserting prosaic reality over poetic meaning, leitmotif over epiphany, and (in Moretti's own terms) Flaubert over Rimbaud, Joyce has earned for himself the status as a modernist writer: "the merit of *Portrait* lies in its being an unmistakable failure" as a novel of formation.[11]

The opposition between conjunctive and disjunctive tendencies in Joyce's *A Portrait* parallels, though it does not exactly mirror, that between human historicity

---

10. Jerome Hamilton Buckley, *Season of Youth: The Bildungsroman from Dickens to Golding* (Cambridge, MA: Harvard University Press, 1974), 238, 246.

11. Franco Moretti, *The Way of the World*, 243.

and the simultaneity of the big city that Fries noted in *Berlin Alexanderplatz*. And indeed, it is just a short step from Moretti's condemnation of *A Portrait* to his celebration of *Ulysses* and the modernist urban novel. But there is something else going on here. Joyce's postscript puts into conjunction with one another two cities that otherwise would seem to have little in common except for their sad colonial legacy: Dublin on the shores of the Irish, and Trieste on the coast of the Adriatic Sea. This imaginary conjunction remains somewhat underdeveloped in *A Portrait*, although Stephen's call to spread his wings and arise from the Daedalian labyrinth—"Bous Stephanoumenos! Bous Stephaneforos! (182)—is voiced in Greek and comes to him through a group of young boys who look as though they had just stepped out of foamy breakers onto one of the beaches of Cythera. In *Ulysses*, however, the novel in which Joyce famously refers to Dublin as the "Hibernian Metropolis," the connection between "snotgreen" and wine-dark seas is made explicit, most overtly through the allegorical structure that recodes the journeys of Odysseus as the modern-day peripatetics of the advertising salesman Leopold Bloom.[12]

Both *A Portrait* and *Ulysses* thus insert Dublin into a symbolic network that exceeds the span of the national imagination temporally as well as spatially. There is, I would argue, an intimate connection between this cosmopolitan ambition and the sophisticated ways in which *A Portrait* moves beyond the developmental dynamics of the traditional novel of formation. Earlier in this study, I pointed to Mikhail Bakhtin's essay "The *Bildungsroman* and Its Significance in the History of Realism" as a text that exerted a profound impact on Homi K. Bhabha's notion of a "vernacular cosmopolitanism." In that same text, Bakhtin notes of Goethe's writing that in it the "background of the world's buttresses *begins to pulsate* . . . , and this pulsation determines the more superficial movement and alteration of human destinies and human outlooks."[13] For Bakhtin, Goethe's genius lies in his ability to mediate between the cyclical experience of time characteristic of the premodern agrarian society into which he was born, and the essentially linear, progressive "historical time" that comes to dominate during the last thirty years of the eighteenth century.[14] As I have also argued, however, care needs to be taken to adequately acknowledge the invariably local and culturally "thick" nature of such mediations.

In his 1904 essay, "A Portrait of the Artist," which contains the first seeds of the novel he would complete a decade later, Joyce came up with a useful shorthand term for such localized mediations between emergent and cyclical temporalities. At the beginning of this essay, Joyce declares his dissatisfaction with all representations of personal growth premised on the "characters of beards and inches," and

---

12. James Joyce, *Ulysses*, Gabler ed. (New York: Vintage, 1986), 7.1–2, 1.78. Further references to this edition will be by chapter and line number and will appear in parentheses in the text.
13. Mikhail Bakhtin, "The *Bildungsroman* and Its Significance in the History of Realism," in *Speech Genres and Other Late Essays*, trans. Vern W. McGee (Austin: University of Texas Press, 1986), 30.
14. Bakhtin, "The *Bildungsroman* and Its Significance," 26.

thus implicitly also with traditional conceptions of the *Bildungsroman*, which valorize growth that occurs organically and in gradual increments.[15] He casts his lot instead with those who "seek through some art, by some process of the mind as yet untabulated, to liberate from the personalized lumps of matter that which is their individuating rhythm, the first or formal relation of their parts."[16] This metaphor of an "individuating rhythm" ingeniously points to a structural compromise between cyclical and progressive elements, between a temporal sequence that moves relentlessly forward and one in which individual stresses are repeated and thereby create compositional units (musical bars or, in Joyce's case, sections and chapters).

The relevance of this rhythmical metaphor is demonstrated by a little-noticed episode in the second chapter of *A Portrait*, which tells the story of Stephen's visit, along with his father, to the city of Cork in the west of Ireland. The excursion begins with a detailed description of Stephen's impressions during the journey on the Dublin-Cork night train. As the train leaves the station, the boy is overcome by a curious feeling of detachment that enforces a definite rupture between his present self and his personal recollections: "As the train steamed out of the station he recalled his childish wonder of years before and every event of his first day at Clongowes. But he felt no wonder now. He saw the darkening lands slipping past him, the silent telegraphpoles passing his window swiftly every four seconds, the little glimmering stations, manned by a few silent sentries, flung by the mail behind her and twinkling for a moment in the darkness like fiery grains flung backwards by a runner" (92). A consummate modernist subject, Dedalus is no longer capable of feeling any wonder, for wonder presupposes rootedness in familiar circumstances. Yet as he continues on toward an uncertain destination, Stephen leaves all prior allegiances behind him. He appears as a monadic entity cutting a solitary path through historical time and into the promise of modernity. As the landscape that he has known for all his life fades into darkness, his primary markers of experience become the passing telegraph poles, which no longer frame recognizable vistas but instead measure out the relentless advance of empty time at the rate of one bar every four seconds.

In a move that is typical of *A Portrait*, however, a psychosexual component is immediately added to Stephen's exhilarating experience of modernist vertigo. His self-assured demeanor on the train corresponds to a simultaneous debasement of

---

15. Joyce would, of course, have approached the *Bildungsroman* tradition (which at any rate lacked a name until Wilhelm Dilthey introduced this term to modern criticism in 1906) primarily through the impact it left on nineteenth-century French and English novels of literary realism. It does not appear that he had read Goethe by 1904, though Breon Mitchell has suggested that Stanislaus Joyce came up with the name Stephen Hero by analogy to Wilhelm Meister (i.e., "William Master"). See Breon Mitchell, "*A Portrait* and the *Bildungsroman* Tradition," in *Approaches to Joyce's "Portrait": Ten Essays*, ed. Thomas F. Baley and Bernard Benstock (Pittsburgh: University of Pittsburgh Press, 1976), 65 n. 5.

16. James Joyce, "A Portrait of the Artist," in *The Workshop of Daedalus: James Joyce and the Raw Materials for "A Portrait of the Artist as a Young Man,"* ed. Robert Scholes and Richard M. Kain (Evanston, IL: Northwestern University Press, 1965), 60.

his father, who now appears to him as stuck in the past, and as futilely clinging to experiences that history has long since condemned to irrelevancy: "Stephen heard but could feel no pity. The images of the dead were all strange to him save that of uncle Charles, an image which had lately been fading out of memory" (92). Stephen tosses his personal recollections into the darkness behind him in roughly the same way in which the night train flings backward the "fiery grains" of the provincial postal stations. His father, who still held a position of supreme respect in his life during the earlier Christmas dinner scene, now seems to him ludicrous—a weak old man who nurses the fires of past passions with occasional sips from his pocket flask. The endless succession of telegraph poles thus flanks a trail that leads Stephen not only into historical modernity, but also toward an unencumbered personal development.

But as night yields to day, Stephen's initial exhilaration has to make room for a very different, and much more depressing, experience: "The cold light of the dawn lay over the country, over the unpeopled fields and the closed cottages. The terror of sleep fascinated his mind as he watched the silent country or heard from time to time his father's deep breath or sudden sleepy movement. The neighborhood of unseen sleepers filled him with strange dread as though they could harm him: and he prayed that the day might come quickly" (92). For the first time since his evening departure, the Irish landscape becomes visible as something more than a mere abstraction, something more than a dark mass of shades broken up every four seconds by a telegraph pole. And what Stephen views through his window isn't just any landscape (and certainly not the urban agglomeration of Dublin in which he has lived for most of his life), but rather a landscape of cottages and "unpeopled fields," an almost mystical vision of rural Eire. Suddenly, the previous feeling of detachment and disjunction gives way to a definite sense of place: the experience of a locality that is steeped in custom, organic social experience, and intransigent historical continuity.

Stephen's sense of his own position in the world changes in accordance with the landscape that he glimpses outside of his window. His father's presence, so easily dismissed just a few hours ago, takes on an almost claustrophobic heaviness, and the dim outlines of the fellow passengers in his compartment inspire a strange dread in him. Stephen's experience of time changes as well. His attention is no longer held by the passing telegraph poles, which measure out the advance of historical time in a relentlessly repetitive mechanical continuity, but by his father's heavy breathing and occasional sleepy movement. The mechanical thus yields to the biological, and mere repetition is replaced by the organic cycle of pulmonary activity. Time no longer progresses but appears at a standstill.

To contain his fears, Stephen takes recourse in a sort of prayer, which, "addressed neither to God nor saint, began with a shiver, as the chilly morning breeze crept through the chink of the carriage door to his feet, and ended in a trail of foolish words which he made to fit the insistent rhythm of the train; and silently, at intervals of four seconds, the telegraphpoles held the galloping notes of the music between punctual bars" (92–93). An important change occurs over the course of these four lines. The telegraph poles that fly by outside of the window are no longer merely described as markers of a spatiotemporal contiguity, but as the "punctual bars" that create an underlying "rhythm" for the "galloping notes" of Stephen's prayer. Stephen's prayer is the direct result of his newly apprehended spatiotemporal situation, an insight that negates his earlier feelings of modernist vertigo. Clock time and circadian time, the linear and unbroken expanse of the railroad tracks and the cyclical movement of pulmonary activity, have blended to create a rhythmical structure.

Stephen's prayer provides a vivid illustration for the "synchronicity of the nonsynchronous" that Ernst Bloch diagnosed as a characteristic of modernity and employed as a conceptual weapon in the struggle with Lukácsian totality. To be more precise, it illuminates with almost uncanny precision Fredric Jameson's argument, itself inspired by Bloch, that "the subjects or citizens of the high-modern period are mostly people who have lived in multiple worlds and multiple times—a medieval *pays* to which they return on family vacations and an urban agglomeration whose elites are, at least in most advanced countries, trying to 'live with their century' and be as 'absolutely modern' as they know how."[17] Nevertheless, despite its considerable formal innovation, this passage still employs the rhetorical vocabulary of nationhood: it is precisely the recognition of an Irish landscape outside that allows Stephen to arrive at a sense of who he is. In another essay, Jameson would even go so far as to say that this recognition of place, by means of which both a psychic and a national identity come into stable focus, is what differentiates Joyce from most other modernist writers.[18]

In another passage in *A Portrait*, however, Joyce already uses the rhythmic metaphor in a quite different fashion that points beyond the nation as a construct with which to suture the psychic wound that separates emergent and cyclical temporalities. Father Arnall's sermon in the third chapter forms both the literal and the symbolic centerpiece of Joyce's novel. The priest begins his descriptions of hell with a proem reminding his students of the future that awaits them in colonial service—a future imagined as the very negation of present circumstances: "Many of the boys who sat in these front benches a few years ago are perhaps now in distant lands, in the burning tropics or immersed in professional duties or in seminaries or voyaging over the vast expanse of the deep or, it may be, already called by the great God to another life and to the rendering up of their stewardship" (117). From this proem, the sermon gathers force over the span of almost forty pages, before it culminates in an elaborate metaphor intended to dramatize the quite literally inconceivable duration of an eternity of suffering:

---

17. Fredric Jameson, *Postmodernism: Or, The Cultural Logic of Late Capitalism* (Durham, NC: Duke University Press, 1991), 366.
18. Jameson, "Modernism and Imperialism," 164–65.

> You have often seen the sand on the seashore. How fine are its tiny grains! And how many of those tiny little grains go to make up the small handful which a child grasps in its play. Now imagine a mountain of that sand, a million miles high, reaching from the earth to the farthest heavens, and a million miles broad, extending to remotest space, and a million miles in thickness: and imagine such an enormous mass of countless particles of sand multiplied as often as there are leaves in the forest, drops of water in the mighty ocean, feathers on birds, scales on fish, hairs on animals, atoms in the vast expanse of the air: and imagine that at the end of every million years a little bird came to that mountain and carried away in its beak a tiny grain of that sand. How many millions upon millions of centuries would pass before that bird had carried away even a square foot of that mountain, how many eons upon eons of ages before it had carried away all. Yet at the end of that immense stretch of time not even one instant of eternity could be said to have ended. (142)

The image of sand that needs to be cleared away from a beach has become a familiar symbol of the progressive urge ever since Goethe finished the second part of his *Faust* in 1832. But in Father Arnall's hellscape, this struggle for improvement has been converted into a futile and repetitive activity: hell quite literally is development at a standstill, a denial of the teleological promise modernity holds out to its faithful disciples.

Father Arnall's point is that only devoted service to the imperial powers of London and of Rome can overcome this image of development at a standstill. This, after all, is why he begins his sermon with references to graduates who now labor in the "burning tropics" or in seminaries. The Irish national struggle, by contrast, does not fit into his rhetoric: the imperialist logic associates the colony not with a process of gradual emergence, but only with eternal stasis. Stephen's formation over the course of the novel will largely consist of finding a middle ground between these calls: on the one hand, the summons of cultural nationalism, which in the context of the Gaelic revival is premised on continuity and repetition; and on the other, the call of imperialism, which urges him to forget where he has come from and create a new identity for himself in the slipstream of modernity. Stephen's paradoxical resolution at the end of the novel says it all: "I go to encounter for the millionth time the reality of experience and to forge in the smithy of my soul the uncreated conscience of my race" (275–76). His aspiration is for a conscience that is as yet "uncreated," but in order to achieve it he has to tread down a path that has been walked a million times before. The "rhythmical" construction of *A Portrait*, in which emergent and cyclical temporalities play an equally important part, and its cosmopolitan message are inextricably intertwined.

Dublin, Berlin, and the Globalizing Logic of the Modern City

By the time that he finished *Ulysses* eight years later, Joyce's meditations on the relationship between the local and the global had become a good deal more complex.

It is commonly acknowledged in the critical literature that the "Cyclops" chapter pivots around the encounter between the ultranationalist and anti-Semitic "citizen" and the cosmopolitan Jew (of sorts) Leopold Bloom. What is less frequently commented on, however, is the fact that both the citizen and Bloom understand Irish identity to be a global construct. The citizen does so when he says, in reference to the postfamine exodus, that "those that came to the land of the free remember the land of bondage. And they will come again and with a vengeance, no cravens, the sons of Granuaile, the champions of Kathleen ni Houlihan" (12.1372–75). Bloom, on the other hand, after a series of stumbles arrives at the definition of a nation as "the same people living in the same place . . . or also living in different places" (12.1422–28). The distinction here is that the citizen still works with an organic, albeit "rhythmical," understanding of what Ireland is: he conceives of the postfamine émigrés as the lifeblood of the nation that has been scattered all over the world in a kind of systolic expansion only to eventually return in a diastolic contraction. Bloom's definition, on the other hand, is genuinely cosmopolitan and diasporic—not so much national as it is transnational, in the sense given to that term by Arjun Appadurai.

"The same people living in different places": this phrase is not a bad definition of *Ulysses* itself. Indeed, *Ulysses* is divided into eighteen different chapters, almost none of which share the same setting, and almost all of which (as we know from the schema Joyce loaned to Valery Larbaud) take place at different times of day.[19] It would be difficult to imagine a novel that more eloquently undermines the narrative logic of simultaneous action that Benedict Anderson characterized as one of the foundational principles of national consciousness. *Ulysses* documents a single calendar day (June 16, 1904) in the history of Dublin, but Dublin does not appear as one city over the course of the entire book, nor are the people that populate it always readily discernible as one implicitly national community. There are, instead, multiple communities (the students in the Martello tower, the congregants at Dignam's funeral, the revelers at Barney Kiernan's pub, to name just a few) that inhabit discrete spaces, both geographical and textual. In addition, each of these discrete communities is described by a different textual logic, a different way of organizing experience in narrated time. There are the hectic street scenes of the "Lestrygonians" chapter, for instance, which takes place in the early afternoon in the middle of downtown Dublin and is stuffed full of information. Or the contrapuntal style of "Sirens," in which simultaneous events are played off of one another, though not in the usual way that this is done in the realist novel: instead, Blazes Boylan's jingling pockets are integrated into the musical texture of the Ormond Hotel, so that his progress down the street toward Molly's house can no longer be truly said to be separate from Bloom's own situation. Or the lazy

---

19. The exceptions, of course, are that parts of "Calypso," as well as all of "Ithaca" and "Penelope" are set in Leopold Bloom's house, and that "Telemachus," "Nestor," and "Proteus" unfold in parallel with "Calypso," "Lotus Eaters," and "Hades."

and overindulgent style of the "Eumaeus" episode, which perfectly captures the mind-set of a couple of drunkards staggering home from a pub at one o'clock in the morning.

Without these differing narrative treatments, all the individual spaces and communities of *Ulysses* would be immediately recognizable as part of a larger whole, namely turn-of-the-century Ireland. But the style of *Ulysses* prevents such ready assimilation to a common frame of reference, and not just because the dazzling array of techniques that Joyce brings to bear on his materials serves to estrange the reader. Instead, the individual communities of *Ulysses* can be said to follow different rhythmical patterns—patterns that vary according to the time of day and the place in which they are located: both "Lestrygonians" and "Eumaeus" take place in the same square mile of city streets, but the rhythm of Dublin and of its residents at 1:00 p.m. differs profoundly from that at 1:00 a.m. The city thus emerges as internally fragmented, no longer simply the largest settlement in Ireland, but rather a contested space in which multiple modes of belonging come into conflict with one another.

In this context, Joyce's definition of Dublin as a "Hibernian metropolis" takes on a new significance. As Henri Lefebvre has pointed out, "The large Mediterranean towns appear to have always lived and still to live in a regime of compromise between all the political powers. Such a 'metastable' state is the fact of the polyrhythmic."[20] "Polyrhythmicality" in this context should be understood as the simultaneous existence in close spatial proximity of lifeworlds that place differing emphases on the linear and cyclical elements that constitute historical experience. The forum, for example, in which each successive ruler reconfigures public life through a series of legal and even architectural adjustments coexists with older parts of town in which traditions pass unchanged from one generation to the next. Joyce would have had ample opportunities to observe this phenomenon in Trieste and Pola, the two colonized cities in which he wrote *Ulysses*, and what he saw undoubtedly influenced his depiction of the colonial city of Dublin. In an urban space in which national temporality is prevented from exercising a hegemonic influence, the rhythms of the city itself assert their prominence and foreground hitherto unrecognized forms of belonging that have their basis in the accidents of spatiotemporal contiguity, rather than in any sense of a shared destiny. Colonial domination, in other words, renders communities of men who gather in a pub or at a funeral into inherently meaningful units, whereas otherwise they would simply be subordinated to a larger national collective.

---

20. Henri Lefebvre, *Rhythmanalysis: Space, Time, and Everyday Life*, trans. Stuart Elden and Gerald Moore (London: Continuum, 2004), 92. For an introduction to Lefebvre's theories and some preliminary theses regarding their applicability to Joyce's works, I am sincerely indebted to Tom Sheehan, "Colonial Rhythms" (unpublished manuscript circulated at the MSA Conference, November 2005), Microsoft Word file.

In this fashion, *Ulysses* undermines the historicist foundations of traditional national thinking, according to which national communities are characterized by the preservation of a common formative drive—or what we may now call a common rhythm—through historical time. In place of this historicist logic, Joyce's novel strives to offer a textual correlative of Bloom's hypothesis that a nation is "the same people . . . also living in different places." The cosmopolitan implications of this endeavor are articulated in a number of places in the novel, perhaps most overtly in the "Ithaca" chapter, where Bloom tries to enlist the skeptical Stephen Dedalus in an ingenious "get rich quick" scheme. Bloom's proposal is described by the Joycean "arranger" in the characteristic question-and-answer format that distinguishes this episode, in which both of the central characters have returned to a tenuous sobriety after a night of boozing and are clinging to facts:

> What rapid but insecure means to opulence might facilitate immediate purchase [of a country residence]?
> A private wireless telegraph which would transmit by dot and dash system the result of a national equine handicap (flat or steeplechase) of 1 or more miles and furlongs won by an outsider at odds of 50 to 1 at 3 hr 8 m p.m. at Ascot (Greenwich time), the message being received and available for betting purposes in Dublin at 2.59 p.m. (Dunsink time). (17.1672–78)

Bloom's scheme relies on the fact that colonial Dublin was quite literally, rather than just figuratively, "left behind" by modernity and was excluded from Greenwich Mean Time, which held sway throughout the rest of the British Isles and had been made the cornerstone of the universal day by the International Meridian Conference of 1884. Dublin, like the rest of Ireland, was instead subject to Dunsink time (named after Dunsink Observatory just outside of the city), which trailed GMT by roughly twenty-five minutes and thus formed a temporal exclave within the modern system of global time zones. Because of this twenty-five-minute difference, however, it would theoretically have been possible for a gambler who received almost instantaneous information about the outcome of a horse race at Ascot to place a wager before the close of the Irish betting offices. Bloom, in other words, is proposing to turn national belatedness into a weapon by cunningly exploiting inherent structural flaws in the global financial system. His scheme is a recognizable instance of the cliché of Irish cunningness, but it is possible only because of his prior cosmopolitan recognition of the place that Ireland occupies in the world at large.

Taken together, the two dynamics that I have just described illustrate Saskia Sassen's contention that the concepts of "the national" and "the global" do not constitute discrete analytical domains but rather form "a spatiotemporal order with considerable internal differentiation and growing mutual imbrications with [one another]. Their internal differences interpenetrate in ways that are variously conflictive, disjunctive and neutralizing."[21] The arena in which this interpenetration occurs most overtly is the modern city, in which global processes shatter the integrity of national-historical time and create a number of local temporalities, which in turn undermine the universal reach of globalizing currents. Joyce's modernist technique is among other things a way to give a narrative shape to this dually disruptive process.

In reflecting on the manner in which Döblin followed on the path that Joyce had blazed for him, one encounters the obvious objection that Dublin in 1904 was a truly colonial city, whereas Berlin in the 1920s was a postimperial metropolis. Joyce experienced the fragmenting influence of colonial domination as part of his everyday reality and at a very early age rejected all organic metaphors to describe modern reality. Döblin, on the other hand, made no overt references to Germany's former status as an imperial power, and, in his manifesto "The Spirit of the Naturalist Age," written just a few years before *Berlin Alexanderplatz*, still compared modern urban centers to "coral reefs for the collective organism man."[22] For him, in other words, cities are organic entities, comprised of smaller beings that go about their errands without realizing that they each contribute to the compound life of the whole. This compound life, in turn, possesses an animating individuality of its own and is subject to a process of growth like any other living being: "Taken as a totality, the collective organism man represents a superior expression of mankind. It would be careless to say that the mighty force of the social drive that formed this collective organism arose from pure need. All that we can say is that the drive is there and possesses an incomparable strength."[23] These lines include a strong reference to Germany's historicist tradition that is entirely absent in Joyce. How, then, could any of the lessons that the Irish writer drew from the political history of his own country be applicable to Döblin's novel?

The starting point for an answer to this question can be found in Karl Scheffler's *Berlin: Destiny of a City*, which I have already mentioned as one of the most influential analyses of the German capital to appear during Döblin's lifetime. This book makes an intriguing case for Berlin as a colonial settlement. Scheffler's argument proceeds from the observation that "Berlin became what it is as the seat of power

---

21. Saskia Sassen, "Spatialities and Temporalities of the Global: Elements for a Theorization," *Public Culture* 12:1 (2000): 216. In a sense, Sassen merely rewrites in spatiotemporal terms an experiential insight at which Georg Simmel arrived in his own analysis of urban life in the early twentieth century, namely: "For the metropolis it is decisive that its inner life is extended in a wave-like motion over a broader national or international area. . . . The most significant aspect of the metropolis lies in this functional magnitude beyond its actual physical boundaries and this effectiveness reacts upon the latter and gives to it life, weight, importance and responsibility." Georg Simmel, "The Metropolis and Mental Life," in *Georg Simmel on Individuality and Social Forms*, ed. Donald N. Levine (Chicago: University of Chicago Press, 1971), 335.
22. Alfred Döblin, "Der Geist des naturalistischen Zeitalters," in *Schriften zu Ästhetik, Poetik und Literatur*, ed. Erich Kleinschmidt (Olten: Walter-Verlag, 1989), 180.
23. Döblin, "Der Geist des naturalistischen Zeitalters," 180.

[*Residenzstadt*] of a colonial country, and it remains, now as it was several hundred years ago, a colonial city" (15). He points to Berlin's geographical location at the fringes of the German Empire, in flat and sandy terrain that bears little resemblance to the landscape west of the Elbe River, and to its proximity to the Slavic cultures as the causes of a frontier mentality quite unlike the mind-set that one finds among the residents of other capital cities. Picking up on a larger current of thought that has its origins in Walther Rathenau's comparison of Berlin to Chicago, Scheffler argues further: "Berlin literally grew like a colonial city and in exactly the same way in which cities in the American and Australian outback grew in the nineteenth century. Just as the Yankee is the product of German, English, Irish, Scandinavian, and Slavic influences, the Berliner is the product of a blood mixture that includes elements from all the regions of Germany, from Holland, France, and the Slavic countries" (20). These foreign "elements" flocked to Berlin partly out of a desire to conquer and settle new land, partly because they were forcibly relocated by the Prussian electors and kings, and partly because, like the Huguenots, they were fleeing oppression in their own, ostensibly more civilized Western European cultures.

Scheffler's troubling rhetoric about "blood mixture" and his consistent denigration of the Slavic peoples as a "lazy race" (16) aside, there can be no doubt that he puts his finger on an essential aspect of Berlin's unique identity. All major cities sustain and replenish themselves through a continual influx of new residents from the provinces, but Berlin has always been an extreme case. Between 1865 and 1910, Berlin's population more than trebled, only to double again in 1920, when the surrounding suburbs were belatedly incorporated into "greater Berlin." A large percentage of these new residents (some estimates put the figure as high as 50 percent) came from East Prussia as well as from other surrounding Slavic regions such as Russia and Bohemia. This rapid influx of immigrant populations did indeed create an atmosphere that reminded more than one observer of the boomtowns of the U.S. frontier. The economist Moritz Julius Bonn, for instance, who visited Berlin in the closing years of the nineteenth century, reported: "Everything was new and extremely clean; streets and buildings were spacious, but there was a lot of tinsel meant to look like gold. The place was not unlike an oil city of the American West, which had grown overnight and, feeling its strength, insisted on displaying its wealth."[24]

In point of fact, the "local color" that Döblin works into his novel and that so many critics (Benjamin foremost among them) have praised is in reality an

---

24. I derive this quotation, as well as the figures on Berlin's population growth, from Modris Eksteins, *Rites of Spring: The Great War and the Birth of the Modern Age* (Boston: Houghton Mifflin, 1989), 74–75. It should be noted that the popular comparisons of Berlin to U.S. frontier settlements owed much more to the imagination than to experience—few Germans had actually visited the American West. And while Berlin's population growth exceeded that of London or Paris, it lagged far behind the demographic explosion of a city like Chicago, the population of which grew about tenfold during the same period.

expression of the multitude of migratory and transnational movements that converge on the Prussian capital. Few of Döblin's characters are native Berliners; almost all of them come from the territories to the east, from Silesia, Pomerania, or East Prussia, from towns like Breslau, Czernowitz, and Frankfurt on the Oder. The Berlin dialect, in which the entire book is written, similarly bears testimony to the city's tumultuous history of migration, occupation, and forced resettlement: Flemish, French, Polish, Czech, Yiddish, and Hebrew all intermingle with German to form an utterly creolized patois. The first people with whom Biberkopf engages in a meaningful human relationship following his release from prison are the Jews Nachum and Eliser, whose accent and behavior betray them as recent emigrants from a shtetl; his first girlfriend is "Polish Lina" Przyballa. Together, all these characters and the patois in which they communicate form the "individuating rhythm" of the Alexanderplatz: a vernacular form of cosmopolitanism expressed entirely through the characteristic activities of a built environment.

The subsection of the second book of *Berlin Alexanderplatz* in which Döblin describes a typical day in the urban triangle between Alexanderplatz, Rosenthaler Platz, and Hackescher Markt tellingly begins with the statement "The Rosenthaler Platz carries on a conversation" ("Der Rosenthaler Platz unterhält sich"—imprecisely translated by Eugene Jolas as "The Rosenthaler Platz is busily active"). These conversations among ordinary people are explicitly contrasted with the administrative announcements that formed the previous section, which Döblin copied verbatim from official publications of the Berlin magistrate. As a sort of transition between the two styles of writing, the very first conversation that the reader subsequently witnesses is, fittingly enough, carried out between two officials (a policeman and a street-car inspector) who momentarily forget their professional duties to have a laugh at the expense of a reckless passerby: "In the middle of the Rosenthaler Platz a man with two yellow packages jumps off from the 41, an empty taxi glides just past him, the copper looks at him, a street-car inspector appears, cop and inspector shake hands: damned lucky that fellow with his packages" (54). Needless to say, this conversation, like all those that will follow, is carried out in the local dialect and sounds even less formal in the original: "Der hat aber mal Schwein gehabt mit seine Pakete."

Döblin's Berlin thus begins where official administrative language ends, along with the temporal rhythms that it, in turn, tries to impose on the city. The "Chief Burgomaster, Controller of Hunting Licenses," may issue strict decrees as to how the citizens of Berlin should comport themselves ("Shooting must cease in summer, from April 1st to September 30th, by 7 p.m., in winter, from October 1st to March 31st, by 8 p.m." [52]), but the actual rabbit hunt that constitutes the main plot of the novel obeys different temporal laws. This conflict between state power and the life of Döblin's protagonist is portrayed in its most extreme form at an earlier point in the novel, when Franz Biberkopf receives an official notification from the chief of police regarding his recent release from prison. Once again, Döblin employs montage to contrast administrative language with the earthier tone of the Berlin residents. The notification informs Biberkopf: "According to documents in my possession, you have been convicted of assault and battery with fatal consequences, as a result of which you are to be regarded as dangerous to public safety and morality" (44). There then follows a list of forty-two administrative districts in and around the city that Döblin's protagonist is henceforth prohibited from entering. The narrator conveys Biberkopf's reaction with the succinct statement "A staggering blow, that" (45).

This passage emphasizes that the relationship between state power and city life as it is portrayed in *Berlin Alexanderplatz* in fact closely parallels the opposition between colonizer and colonized that is the basis of Joyce's *Ulysses*. Biberkopf is quite literally being resettled, with the technocratic logic that underlies many colonization efforts. And just like Joyce's character, he retreats into a subnational space created for him by his urban environment. Taken into the protective custody of a prisoner's rehabilitation society, Biberkopf settles in a part of town known to the locals as the Scheunenviertel (Barnyard Quarter), which formerly lay outside the eastern gates of the city, where Jews and other suspect arrivals from Eastern Europe were allowed to settle. The Scheunenviertel is, of course, never mentioned by name—it exists as an experience, a concretely realized example of urban cosmopolitics, not as an administrative abstraction. Indeed, state power penetrates it only imperfectly: while the police headquarters at the Alexanderplatz is compared to a "panoptical building" (583), its presence has no unifying effect on the text that would be comparable to the Tower Society initiation chamber in the seventh book of *Wilhelm Meister*.

Berlin Alexanderplatz between *Bildungsroman* and Big City Novel

The thematic affinities that connect *Berlin Alexanderplatz* to the traditional German novel of formation are, in fact, already suggested before the narrative proper actually begins. In a brief preface, the narrator summarizes Biberkopf's story as one in which "his eyes are forcibly opened in a way which I do not describe here. He is most distinctly given to understand how [his present situation] came about.... This awful thing which was his life acquires a meaning. Franz Biberkopf has been given a radical cure." And, with an optimism that recalls Morgenstern's, he also declares: "To listen to this, and to meditate on it, will be of benefit to many who, like Franz Biberkopf, live in a human skin" (2). Once the story gets under way, however, Döblin's novel is much more difficult to reconcile with traditional expectations. Franz Biberkopf is a petty crook rather than a bourgeois citizen of the kind that dominates the nineteenth-century examples of the genre. He is also middle-aged, has held a previous job as a furniture mover, has served in World War I, and has done four years time in Tegel Prison for killing his girlfriend Ida in an argument.

Perhaps most importantly, he is not particularly given to self-reflection, and the three successive catastrophes that eventually "open his eyes" (an act of personal betrayal by an acquaintance, the loss of his right arm after a close friend pushes him from a moving vehicle, and, finally, the murder of his girlfriend Mieze at the hands of that same, ostensible friend) are much more extreme than anything that Goethe's Wilhelm Meister or any of his successors had to endure.

Nevertheless, Biberkopf's trajectory, when viewed from a certain magnanimous distance, bears an unmistakable similarity to that of more traditional heroes. The four years that Döblin's hero served behind prison bars have estranged him from the world, and not just in the sense that he has to relearn simple social interactions, but also because Germany itself has changed so much. When Biberkopf entered Tegel in 1923, the Weimar Republic was just emerging from a period of hyperinflation. Industry was at a standstill, poverty and hunger were widespread, and Germany in general was marked by its war defeat. The years 1927 and 1928, however, in which *Berlin Alexanderplatz* is set, arguably saw the economic zenith of the short-lived republic. Business had been booming for the past three years, leading to comparative affluence, amply filled department stores, infrastructural developments on a massive scale, and a new symbolic ecology aimed at directing the desires of the masses. Döblin refers to Biberkopf's overwhelming difficulties with all of these changes in his opening pages, which survey the glittering shop windows lining the Seestrasse ("Let 'em blaze away, are they going to make you afraid or something, why, you can smash 'em up, can't you?" [2]), the subway construction at Rosenthaler Platz ("Just go ahead and mix with people, then everything's going to clear up" [2]), and the tawdry movie theaters that line the Münzstrasse ("On the huge poster a beet-red gentleman was standing on a staircase, while a peach of a young girl embraced his legs, she lay on the stairs, and he stood up above with a leering expression on his face" [28]). Biberkopf, in other words, has to find his place in a complex society about which he is just as ignorant as Wilhelm Meister was about his own world when he first accepted employment with the Count.

Biberkopf's ignorance of recent developments has a richly symbolic dimension as well. When he is first dumped onto the streets of Berlin after serving his time, Döblin's protagonist steels himself by quietly humming the opening lines of "The Watch on the Rhine," a nationalist and anti-French song that served as a kind of unofficial anthem of Wilhelmine Germany and enjoyed great popularity among the reactionary circles that so heavily influenced public affairs during the years following the Great War. Over the course of the book, Biberkopf will sing this song over and over again; in a pivotal scene, he bellows it at the top of his voice in a courtyard and thereby attracts the attention of Nachum the Jew. What he does not realize, however, is that his song choice is fraught with troubling overtones in the politically charged atmosphere of the late Weimar Republic. The Germany in which Biberkopf was initially socialized, and the one that he took with him into Tegel Prison, stood united behind its Kaiser; Germans from all over the social and political spectrum would have joined to sing the jingoistic chorus of "The Watch on the Rhine." To perform this song in 1928, however, means to pick sides in a frequently violent struggle over the future of the Republic—and to make a choice, furthermore, that may not be entirely advisable in the working-class Berlin neighborhoods in which Biberkopf lives out his existence.

Biberkopf's problem, in other words, is that he is unable to figure out exactly what has happened to his country (and to his city) in the past four years, and to determine a proper course of action for himself. He was quite literally overtaken by modernity while he sat in his prison cell, and he still acts in many ways according to the customs of a world that no longer exists. (This, incidentally, differentiates him from the protagonists of the great French and English *Bildungsromane* of the nineteenth century, who were almost universally creatures of the provinces. At the end of their respective stories, Balzac's Lucien, Dickens's Pip, and Flaubert's Frédérique all can and do return to the provincial towns from which they started out. Biberkopf, however, is temporally rather than geographically dislocated. He has no simpler world to which he could return.) This same problem also afflicted German society as a whole during the 1920s. The years of the Weimar Republic were a time of tremendous social, political, and economic progress: a period in German history that brought women's suffrage and the first democratic elections, did away with censorship and the more medieval aspects of the penal code, and brought the fruits of modernity to ordinary people. Yet German society as a whole never found an adequate response to these developments, never fully accepted the democratic institutions that governed it, and never embraced the new freedoms that it had been given.

In many ways, then, Biberkopf represents the tendencies of his age, internally contradictory as these might have been. This is certainly the way in which *Berlin Alexanderplatz* was interpreted by its first readers. The respectable *Frankfurter Zeitung*, which had serialized the novel, received several letters to the editor pleading to "show some consideration for the readership abroad, which should not be privy to such a view of German life."[25] Clearly these readers went beyond the reaction that Döblin anticipated in his narrator's preface: they related to Biberkopf not just as a fellow man "in human skin," but rather more specifically as a contemporary German, fearing that his frequently coarse and violent exploits might be interpreted as national characteristics in the foreign press.[26]

---

25. Hermann Kasack, "Mosaik: Briefe zu Döblins *Alexanderplatz*," in *Materialien zu Alfred Döblin, Berlin Alexanderplatz,* ed. Matthias Prangel (Frankfurt am Main: Suhrkamp, 1975), 60. This article was first published in the *Frankfurter Zeitung* of November 1, 1929.

26. These reactions may seem extreme, but it is possible to do them one better by referring to academic literary criticism. In 1968, James H. Reid published an article that interpreted Biberkopf not simply as a paradigmatic German, but rather as an allegory of Weimar Germany: newly released into the world, prone to fall in with the wrong kind of friends, saddled with territorial losses (the amputated arm), and marching into the future with headstrong determination. I will have more to say about such allegorical readings in the conclusion of this study. See James H. Reid, "*Berlin Alexanderplatz*: A Political Novel," *German Life and Letters* 21 (1968): 214–23.

If Döblin's more naïve readers thus feared *Berlin Alexanderplatz* because the novel held up a mirror to a side of themselves that they would rather not submit to greater scrutiny, Walter Benjamin criticized the work precisely because it does aim, in the end, for some kind of harmony and reconciliation. For much of the story, Biberkopf may march on with almost bovine determination, oblivious to the fact that his "friends" constantly betray him and that he, in turn, inflicts a similar kind of punishment on his long string of girlfriends, to whom he later serves not only as boyfriend, but also as pimp. But by the time that the ninth and final book comes around, he *has* reached some higher level of awareness about his life, which he immediately transforms into a resolution:

> Much unhappiness comes from walking alone. When there are several, it's somewhat different. I must get the habit of listening to others, for what the others say concerns me, too. Then I learn who I am, and what I can undertake. Everywhere about me my battle is being fought, and I must beware, before I know I'm in the thick of it.
>
> He is assistant door-man in a factory. What is fate anyway? One is stronger than I. If there are two of us, it grows harder to be stronger than I. If there are ten of us, it's harder still. And if there are a thousand of us and a million, then it's very hard, indeed.
>
> But it is also nicer and better to be with others. Then I feel and I know everything twice as well. A ship cannot lie in safety without a big anchor, and a man cannot exist without many other men. The true and the false I will know better now. Once I got myself into trouble for a single word and had to pay bitterly for it, this shan't happen to Biberkopf again. The words come rolling up to us, we must be careful not to get run over; if we don't watch out for the autobus, it'll make apple-sauce out of us. I'll never again stake my word on anything in the world. Dear Fatherland, be comfort thine, I'll watch, and use these eyes o'mine.
>
> Often they march past his window with flags and music and singing. Biberkopf watches coolly from his door, he'll not join the parade any more. Shut your trap, in step, old cuss, march along with the rest of us. But if I march along, I shall have to pay for the schemes of others. That's why I first figure out everything, and only if everything's quite O.K., and suits me, I'll take action. Reason is the gift of man, jackasses replace it with a clan. (633–34)

These are not the reflections of an analytically trained mind, nor do they remain entirely steadfast. When Biberkopf dwells for too long on the kind of "words that come rolling up to us," his thoughts are once again hijacked by "The Watch on the Rhine," and the chorus of the nationalist song ("Dear Fatherland, be comfort thine") seamlessly blends with his own mental idiom ("I'll watch and use these eyes o'mine," instead of the original "Firm stands and true the watch on the Rhine" [Lieb Vaterland, magst ruhig sein / Fest steht und treu die Wacht am Rhein]). But Biberkopf's conclusion is nevertheless clear. He renounces his prior egotism, which caused him to lay the blame for all of his problems on other people, rather than on his frequently execrable behavior, and he now acknowledges that "I must get the habit of listening to others, for what the others say concerns me, too." At the same time, he has learned to eschew the simplistic politics of community that characterize late Weimar culture and to interrogate everything that he is told. His foot may occasionally still tap to the beat of a marching drum, but his thoughts no longer automatically fall into the same rhythm.

Biberkopf's resolution, which at once affirms the value of community and stresses the necessity for each individual to maintain his or her separate identity, recalls the quotation from "The Spirit of the Naturalist Age" that identified cities as the "coral reefs for the collective organism man." Döblin's analysis of man's social impulse in that essay similarly stresses a tension between the desire of the individual to find strength in numbers and the desire of the collective to "reduce its members to specialized beings in order to internally differentiate itself"—a problem that, in turn, sounds eerily similar to the one raised in one of the foundational pieces of *Bildungsroman* criticism, Schiller's *Letters on the Aesthetic Education of Man*.[27] Döblin's approach, however, is ultimately very different from Schiller's. Whereas Schiller saw man's collective existence realized in the state, Döblin confines his discussion to cities, that is, to empirical entities held together not by law but rather by vernacular quotidian praxis. Identifying as a resident of modern-day Berlin signifies something very different from stepping forward as a citizen of ancient Athens or Sparta. It implies not submission to a specific *demos*, but rather acculturation to certain customs, rituals, and rhythms that govern everyday life. And these customs, unlike the laws of the state, change and grow organically in tune with the times; they undergo a *Bildung* of their very own.

Biberkopf's formation, then, does not result in the creation of an autonomous subject in the way that traditional *Bildungsroman* criticism imagined this process to work. Döblin's hero instead maintains a subservient yet critically reflective relationship to the collective entity of which he is an immediate part: the metropolitan identity of Berlin, not the national one of Germany or the statist one of the Prussian-led Reich. Rather than taking his cue from the ideology of imagined communities or from the institutions of an authoritarian state, he models his behavior on the *actual* community with whom he interacts on an everyday basis, the community of Berliners. This community is clearly "subnational" in one sense, since it is held together by purely local affiliations. But it is also "supranational," since Berlin is an immigrant capital, and many of the most endearing characters in Döblin's novel are neither a part of the German national imaginary, nor do they readily submit to Prussian state power.

---

27. Döblin, "Der Geist des naturalistischen Zeitalters," 180.

It is easy to read Biberkopf's relationship with the built environment that surrounds him in psychoanalytic terms, as a series of coping mechanisms meant to preserve an invariable identity against the pressures of an all-too-variable modern city. In the following passage, for instance, psychic trauma is projected outward, onto a series of rooftops and glass facades that promptly seem to separate from the houses that held them together:

> But then his glance slipped with a jerk up the house-fronts, examined them, made sure they were standing still and did not stir, although really a house like that has lots of windows and could easily bend forward. That might get the roofs started, carry them along with it, they are liable to start rocking. They might begin to shake, to rock, to jolt. The roofs could slide down, obliquely like sand, like a hat falling down from a head. Why, they're all, yes, all of them, standing obliquely over the roof-tree along the whole row. But they're nailed down fast, strong beams below and then the roofing, the tar. Firm stands and true, the watch, the watch on the Rhine. (165–66)

The same passage can, however, also be read in the opposite direction, as a merciless laying bare of the relentless pace of urban modernization by means of a prophetic vision. The visual vocabulary of *Berlin Alexanderplatz* is thus more complexly coded than it is in the masterworks of expressionist cinema, such as *The Cabinet of Dr. Caligari* (1920) or *The Blue Angel* (1930). The angled streetscapes, which tower over the protagonist and are seemingly ready to collapse at any minute, do not merely signify the pent-up anxieties that are a by-product of cultural sublimation and therefore of *internal* modernization. They are also visual correlatives of *external* urban modernization, which in turn sets into motion a complex chain of psychological responses. Biberkopf's instinctive reaction, which is once again to hum "The Watch on the Rhine," is comically inadequate to the situation with which he is confronted, and not just because the nineteenth-century lyrics about military prowess have been rendered absurd by the mechanized warfare that we know him to have witnessed at Arras. His problems also arise from the fact that the old equation, in which the psychic integrity of the bourgeois subject is matched with the territorial integrity of the nation-state, has been rendered absurd by the cityscape of modern Berlin.

The same dual movement between subjective and objective world, between individual and urban environment, can also be observed in one of the most famous passages of *Berlin Alexanderplatz*: the opening scene of book 5, in which the narrator describes the giant pile-driver that is laying down tracks for the city's newest subway line: "Boom, boom, the steam pile-driver thumps in front of Aschinger's on the Alex. It's one story high, and knocks the rails into the ground as if they were nothing at all" (216). The psychic damage that is wrought by this primordial manifestation of urban renewal becomes evident only a page later, when the narrator interrupts his description of the changes imposed on the city with an otherwise unmotivated conjugation of the verb "to beat": "They have torn down Loeser and Wolff with their mosaic sign, 20 yards further on they built it up again, and there's another branch over there in front of the station. . . . I beat everything, you beat everything, he beats everything with boxes of 50 and cardboard packages of 10, can be mailed to every country on earth, Boyero 25 pfennigs, this novelty has won us many friends, I beat everything, but I never retreat" (217–18). Yet another few pages later, the internalized violence becomes external again, when it is projected onto the steam pile-driver, which now becomes imbued with a destructive agency of its very own: "Rrr, rrr. The pile-driver thumps down, I beat everything, another rail" (222).

Far from being structural opposites in a novel that vacillates between descriptions of human subjectivity and urban environments, Döblin's protagonist and the city in which he lives thus exist in a kind of codependent relationship. Sabine Hake speaks, in this context, of metropolitan Berlin as a "production site of the modern mass individual or, to use a more accurate term, the post-humanist subject." Drawing heavily on theoretical models developed by Gilles Deleuze and Félix Guattari, she further interprets Biberkopf's strolls through the city as those of a paranoid schizophrenic, occupied with a "gradual dismantling of the oedipal structure and its replacement by an all-encompassing, but highly volatile, narcissistic complex."[28]

I myself am less willing to sacrifice the territory of classical humanism (which is, after all, the logical domain of the novel of formation) for the theoretical allure of the posthuman. Döblin's image of the city as a coral reef, and of individual human subjects as its constituent polyps, is undoubtedly posthumanist, but as I tried to show by grounding Biberkopf's struggle in the concrete reality of Weimar modernization, the literary realization of this metaphor in *Berlin Alexanderplatz* introduces (rather than forecloses) new tropes of historical emplotment. Schizophrenia, which is the name commonly given to any psychic disorder marked by the inability to maintain a coherent identity over time, is surely the opposite if not of "history" as such, then at least of "historicism" in the traditional sense of the term. If this is true, then any "schizoanalytic" reading of Döblin's text would necessarily have to pit itself against the historicist legacy of the classical *Bildungsroman*. By contrast, I would like to propose that *Berlin Alexanderplatz* stages not "urban paranoia," but rather the creation of a new rhythmic synchrony between the *Bildungsroman* hero and his environment—a synchrony premised not on the concept of the nation, but rather on that of the modern city. Cities, unlike nations, are naturally permeable and mutable entities. Except in some very rare instances that themselves do violence to what an urban environment should be (Berlin between 1961 and 1989, for instance) they aren't surrounded by demarcated borders but rather fade gradually

---

28. Sabine Hake, "Urban Paranoia in Alfred Döblin's *Berlin Alexanderplatz*," *The German Quarterly* 67:3 (Summer 1994): 347–50.

into the surrounding countryside. Nor are they generally subject to the same kind of emotional and ideological cathexis that nation-states are; transformative change is, instead, an important source of pride for the typical inhabitant of a modern metropolis. Döblin's challenge, then, was to create the same kind of relationship between his protagonist Franz Biberkopf and the city of Berlin that the nineteenth-century *Bildungsroman* found in the homology of the individual subject and the nation.

From the very beginning, the technical vocabulary used to describe modernist city texts has owed a heavy debt to the discipline of psychoanalysis, which emerged alongside the twentieth-century metropolis. "Shock," "trauma," "rupture," "paranoia," and even "schizophrenia" figure large in such accounts. Occluded in many discussions is the positive role that urban environments can play in the structuring of human experience. Far from being merely the source of countless essentially random shock experiences, the modern city is instead a place where different communities, classes, and ethnicities intermingle, rendering identities fluid and forcing individuals into a constant dialogue with their surroundings. Unlike the nation, which is an imaginative construction premised on a theoretical ideal of existential homogeneity, the modern city takes shape through the practical and quotidian experience of existential *multiplicity*. This "vernacular" quality manifests itself not only on the level of content (e.g., in the fact that a typical modernist city text features a much more diverse set of characters than a realist country-house novel, or even a work by Dickens), but also on the level of form. The competing experiences that characterize the metropolis require different kinds of temporal organization, and thus each possesses what Joyce himself called an "individuating rhythm." This polyrhythmic complexity works against the totalizing logic of the traditional *Bildungsroman*, but it need not negate the genre altogether. Joyce and Döblin instead embrace the chaos of the urban environment and use it to shape a new kind of formative fiction.

The Slaughterhouse and the Train Car

Unlike Wilhelm Meister, who eventually penetrates into the panoptical tower that has been surveilling, administrating, and recording his life, Franz Biberkopf never settles his differences with the Prussian state. He remains an inscrutable cipher for both the police and the medical professionals who examine him after his arrest following Mieze's murder and a barroom brawl. Biberkopf's epiphany instead takes place in the closed ward of the Buch insane asylum—another locus of state power, to be sure, but also a place where the state confines those over whom it implicitly acknowledges having lost all dominion. In this borderline space—a "heterotopia" rather than a panopticon, to stay with the language of Michel Foucault—Biberkopf struggles with death and experiences a feverish vision of the city's Eastern hinterland that leads him toward his final realization of who he truly is:

So let it come—the night, however black and nothing-like it be. So let them come, the black night, those frost-covered acres, the hard frozen roads. So let them come: the lonely, tile-roofed houses whence gleams a reddish light; so let them come: the shivering wanderers, the drivers on the farm wagons traveling to town with vegetables and the little horses in front. The great flat silent plains crossed by suburban trains and expresses which throw white light into the darkness on either side of them. So let them come—the men in the station, the little girl's farewell to her parents, she's traveling with two older acquaintances, going across the big water, we've got our tickets, but good Lord, what a little girl, eh, but she'll get used to it over there, if she's a good little girl it'll be all right. So let them come and be absorbed: the cities which lie along the same line, Breslau, Liegnitz, Sommerfeld, Guben, Frankfurt on the Oder, Berlin, the train passes through them from station to station, from the stations emerge the cities, the cities with their big and little streets. Berlin with Schweidnitzer Strasse, with the Grosse Ring of the Kaiser-Wilhelm Strasse, Kurfürstendamm, and everywhere are homes in which people are warming themselves, looking at each other with loving eyes, or sitting coldly next to each other; dirty dumps and dives where a man is playing the piano. (607–8)

The generic status of this dream fragment is difficult to decide. Clearly, it does not belong to the same Homeric or biblical register that characterizes so many of the novel's "epic" intrusions. Perhaps its closest analogue is the long description of the slaughterhouses in the fourth book of *Berlin Alexanderplatz*, a passage to which it indeed bears a strong resemblance. Both the slaughterhouse narrative and the dream fragment tell the story of migratory train travels from the east to the west, from the provinces into urban centers: on the one hand, the voyage of "specimens of the genus sheep, hog, ox, from East Prussia, Pomerania, Brandenburg, West Prussia" (174); on the other, the journey of a young Silesian girl to Berlin and, presumably, from there on further west to Scheffler's cities of the "American outback." In both passages, the city is also characterized first and foremost as a succession of rings made up of broad streets like the Kaiser-Wilhelm Strasse, the Kurfürstendamm, and the Landsberger Allee, and of railway tracks.

In the slaughterhouse passage, however, these city streets resemble fortifications. To the modern reader, they likely recall descriptions of concentration camps, or perhaps the inner-German border of 1961–89: "Along Eldenaer Strasse run the dirty-gray walls topped with barbed wire. The trees outside are bare, it is winter, the trees have sent their sap into the roots, to wait for spring." The atmosphere here is depressed, characterized by opportunism and cruelty: "Slaughter wagons roll up at a smart gallop, with yellow and red wheels, prancing horses in front. A skinny horse runs along behind a wagon, from the sidewalk somebody calls 'Emil,' they bargain about the old nag, 50 marks and a round for the eight of us, the horse turns, trembles, nibbles at a tree, the driver tears it away, 50 marks and a round, Otto, otherwise we'll let it drop" (173). Döblin's prose also veers back into monologic bureaucratese: the narrator meticulously lists lot sizes ("47.88 hectares, equal to 118.31 acres") and real-estate prices ("27,083,492 marks were sunk into this construction, of which sum the cattle-yard cost 7,682,844 marks, and the slaughterhouse 19,410,648 marks" [173]). We learn that the stockyards employ an administrative staff of 17 and a further 258 employees. If the slaughterhouse is a synecdoche for the city as a whole, then it is a city of the worst kind, in which urban space has simply been turned into an administrative unit.

Franz Biberkopf's fever dream, on the other hand, presents a very different kind of city image, even though it employs many of the same descriptive elements. The streets are not fortified enclosures but instead sprout organically from train tracks that in turn connect them to a far-reaching communications network. Horses trot gaily in front of farm wagons loaded with vegetables, not with the carcasses of fellow beasts. And human beings, at least some of them, have homes to go back to, private retreats where they can gather warmth and strength. This is the positive side of Döblin's vision of the city as a giant coral reef, in which the overall entity is only as alive as the multitude of its constituent parts.

This fever dream of a train journey represents the pivotal point in Franz Biberkopf's development into a man who has been "bent straight" (2), just as the train journey to Cork represents a pivotal point in Stephen Dedalus's autopoiesis. In either case, the "frost-covered acres" and "hard-frozen roads" that glide by outside the windows represent not only a landscape (though they represent that, too) but also an emotional attachment that needs to be overcome through a new form of spatial organization, a new way of dwelling and being. For Stephen Dedalus, this attempt takes the form of Parisian exile, and thus of another journey from the periphery to the center; it wasn't until *Ulysses* that Joyce fully realized the power of native Irish spaces to articulate a "vernacular" critique of national belonging. On the other hand, a spatial dislocation is never an option for Franz Biberkopf, who, like his creator, is entirely the product of a metropolitan environment.

What makes city spaces so attractive to cosmopolitan projects is, of course, the fact that they offer spaces in which people who might otherwise never encounter one another can mingle. For the *Bildungsroman*, this means in concrete terms not only a new openness toward hitherto unknown subject matter, but also an opportunity for a break with the historicist logic that characterizes nineteenth-century examples of the genre. Modern cities do not submit to the developmental logic according to which imagined communities come into being through the experience of a common trajectory through time; instead, they present both individuals and local communities with a chance to organize around "individuating rhythms." Both Joyce and Döblin dramatize this search for an individuating rhythm in their novels. Modernist devices such as montage and stream of consciousness allow them to play with the ways in which narrative transforms time into experiences, while the use of local idioms, such as the Berlin patois, enables them to escape the administrative grip of the twentieth-century state. Of course, Joyce, in transitioning from

A Portrait to *Ulysses*, also decided to leave the *Bildungsroman* conventions behind, and to focus his gaze on a single day in the life of Dublin. But Döblin's strong belief in the organic life of cities allowed him to situate Berlin itself on a new kind of developmental trajectory. Just as Biberkopf turns from a delusional fool into a man of modest wisdom, the city itself turns from an uncompromising slaughterhouse into a welcoming environment. With this move, Döblin shows that human historicity and the time of the city, *Bildungsroman* and *Großstadtroman* are ultimately reconcilable to one another, and he also proves that the characteristic nonsynchronicity of the Weimar Republic can be read as a symptom of an emergence into a properly global modernity.

Conclusion

Apocalipsis cum figuris: Thomas Mann and the *Bildungsroman* at the Ends of Time

On July 2, 1947, the *Neue Zürcher Zeitung* published a short essay celebrating the seventieth birthday of the novelist Hermann Hesse, written by his friend and colleague Thomas Mann. Mann spends most of his time discussing Hesse's novel *The Glass Bead Game*, which had appeared in 1943 and to which Mann refers not only as a "work of old age" (*Alterswerk*), but also as a "late work of dangerously advanced spiritualization."[1] Such descriptions might appear cruelly inappropriate given the occasion, but it is important to remember that Mann ultimately always meant himself when he was talking about other writers. Indeed, seventieth birthdays formed a neuralgic point of sorts for the German author, who had once predicted that he himself would die at that age—and who almost seemed disappointed when the event came and went in 1945 without any attending fatal accident. It thus should have surprised no one when Mann, only a few months after his laudatory article, published his own "work of old age": a "glass bead game played with black pearls," as he inscribed his presentation copy to Hesse. The novel in question, of course, was *Doctor Faustus: The Life of the German Composer Adrian Leverkühn as Told by a Friend*.

If Mann's use of the epithet *Alterswerk* can be justified by pointing to the mature age that both Hesse and his reviewer had reached at this point in their lives, his

---

1. Quoted in Volker Michels, ed., *Materialien zu Hermann Hesses "Das Glasperlenspiel"* (Frankfurt am Main: Suhrkamp, 1973), 1:276.

reference to a "dangerously advanced spiritualization," operative not only in *The Glass Bead Game*, but also, one infers, in *Doctor Faustus*, seems to set up entirely different terms. Something larger is at stake here, something having to do with the spirit of the times, from which both of the modernist masters draw and which they, in turn, shape through their works. Thomas Mann's exegetes were quick to pick up on this dimension. One of the earliest responses to his novel, Erich Kahler's "The Secularization of the Devil" (1948), already refers to the "final chapter of a terminal *oeuvre*" and praises Mann for having brought the "representative symbol, not only of German but of Western culture, up to date."[2] Georg Lukács and Hans Mayer, writing from the Marxist tradition, speak of an "epilogue to the whole [bourgeois] development after 1848" and of a book "that dissolve[s] the form of the bourgeois novel."[3]

These latter two formulations express a view of the modernist novel that already informed Walter Benjamin's critique of Döblin, and that regards the increasingly digressive works of that period as a natural antithesis to the novels built around strong characters that were produced in the nineteenth century, the *Bildungsroman* in particular. On this view, a view that continues to inform standard genre surveys, the novels of Mann and Hesse form the logical endpoint of the *Bildungsroman* tradition as a whole. And yet one need not turn to grand arguments about the rise and fall of bourgeois culture to understand that there is a more immediate occasion for the artistic endgame presented in *Doctor Faustus*: 1945, the year of Mann's seventieth birthday, may have come and gone without his death, but it *did* see the demise of the Third Reich, an event that the author actively hastened through his work as a political essayist and broadcaster for the BBC, even as he looked into the future with skepticism and anxiety. *Doctor Faustus* again and again announces itself as a work that deliberates on the consequences of an absolute annihilation—not only materially, but also culturally—and inquires into the role that literary narration might play in circumventing this crisis. Serenus Zeitblom, wondering whether any of his manuscript pages will survive the aerial bombardment of the Allies, is a transparent cipher for Thomas Mann, not at all convinced that future generations will still turn to his stories, just as Zeitblom's resolve to tell Leverkühn's story despite the fact that nobody performs his compositions mirrors Mann's unwavering fealty to German culture even in the face of its perversion through Hitler.

The basic dilemma that informed Mann's thinking during this period—the realization that *everything* that presently existed in Germany would have to come

---

2. Erich Kahler, "The Secularization of the Devil: Thomas Mann's *Doctor Faustus*," in *The Orbit of Thomas Mann* (Princeton, NJ: Princeton University Press, 1969), 30, 38. In the original German manuscript, Kahler speaks rather more forcefully of an "Endbuch des Endwerks" and an "Endschrift der Endschriften."

3. These quotes are, respectively, from Georg Lukács, "The Tragedy of Modern Art," in *Essays on Thomas Mann*, trans. Stanley Mitchell (London: Merlin Press, 1964), 52, and from Hans Mayer, *Thomas Mann* (Frankfurt am Main: Suhrkamp, 1980), 312.

to an end in order to allow Germany to once again live—finds expression in a powerful temporal metaphor in the novel: that of the apocalypse, alluded to again and again over the course of the work, and most obviously inscribed in the title of Adrian Leverkühn's polyphonic masterpiece, the *Apocalipsis cum figuris*. In its original Christian sense, apocalyptic temporality is characterized by an extreme version of the Blochian "synchronicity of the non-synchronous." It implies a simultaneity of all of creation in the act of judgment before God. Apocalyptic temporality in this sense, however, is the exact inverse of historicism as I have defined it over the course of this study. *Doctor Faustus* can thus be said to express an endpoint of the classical *Bildungsroman* in more than one way. Besides the attack on the liberal subject that was already diagnosed by Lukács and Mayer, it also stages an attack on the formative novel's characteristic structure of temporal unfolding. Mann's apocalypse of the novel is an apocalypse also of historicism.

The intellectual engagement with the legacy of German historicism is another thing that ties Mann's novel to Hesse's and thus points to a more general tendency of the times. Both of these works pit aesthetic formalism, conceived as an ideology of timeless perfection, against humanistic historicism, conceived as an ideology of perfection through time. In *Doctor Faustus*, this conflict is staged between Adrian Leverkühn, the advocate of a dodecaphonic style, and his amanuensis Serenus Zeitblom, who struggles to show how Leverkühn's mature compositions have roots in much earlier biographical stages. Mann's novel also transposes this same conflict onto the level of form, and a long-standing debate in the critical literature has raged around the question of whether *Doctor Faustus* is best read as a humanist *Bildungsroman*, or as a literary adaptation of the "apocalyptic" compositional technique invented by Adrian Leverkühn.[4] This question is further connected to a larger investigation into the role that *Bildung* and historicism more generally may have played in the German catastrophe. Leverkühn's musical growth from a late romantic idiom, in which motifs develop over time, toward a stringent dodecaphonic style is explicitly connected to the German slide toward fascism (for instance, in the chapters juxtaposing the description of the Kridwiss circle with that of the *Apocalipsis*). Exactly 150 years after the publication of *Wilhelm Meister's Apprenticeship*, Mann thus revisited the complex knot of temporal emplotment, national identity formation, and character development that already occupied Goethe, although he

---

4. A partial list of the most important critics arguing for a "dodecaphonic" interpretation of *Doctor Faustus* would include Erich Kahler, Gunilla Bergsten, and Russell A. Berman. See Gunilla Bergsten, *Thomas Mann's "Doctor Faustus": The Sources and Structure of the Novel*, trans. Krishna Winston (Chicago: University of Chicago Press, 1963), 166–200; and Russell A. Berman, *The Rise of the Modern German Novel: Crisis and Charisma* (Cambridge, MA: Harvard University Press, 1986), 261–86. Although the matter is far from settled, the consensus seems to have shifted against such a reading. For an intelligent critique, see Ritchie Robertson, "Accounting for History: Thomas Mann, *Doktor Faustus*," in *The German Novel in the Twentieth Century: Beyond Realism*, ed. David Midgley (Edinburgh: Edinburgh University Press, 1993) 128–48.

did so from exile and in full awareness of the fact that the Germany that Goethe helped build was lying in ruins.

A similar constellation of ideas, combined with an even more explicit appeal to Goethe and his legacy, can be found in yet a third book that an aging member of Germany's intellectual elite concluded shortly after the end of the Second World War. Friedrich Meinecke's *The German Catastrophe* (1946) was one of the first, and for many years the most widely read, analyses of Hitler's rise to power, and it was written by arguably the last great practitioner of German historicist thought. Unlike the novels of Mann and Hesse, however, Meinecke's treatise has not withstood the test of time, and today the explanations and justifications it offers ring hollow, as does its famous concluding call for the creation of nationwide "Goethe Communities" under whose guidance the Germans might be lead to once again embrace their humanist past. It is precisely these failures that can help a contemporary reader understand the difficult situation in which historicist thinking found itself during the mid-1940s, and thus also lead to a better understanding of the *Bildungsroman* at its frequently declared endpoint.

The Crisis of Historicism and the German Catastrophe

The origins of the so-called crisis of historicism (to use a phrase coined by Ernst Troeltsch in 1922) reach back a quarter century before the publication of *The German Catastrophe* to the years immediately subsequent to another world war. Both Meinecke and Mann were participants in this earlier intellectual debate, Meinecke through his book on Machiavellianism, *Die Idee der Staatsräson in der neueren Geschichte* (1924), and Mann through his lecture "On the German Republic" (1922). Both of these works set out to defend German intellectual life against charges of what Mann succinctly called an "inwardness protected by power" (*machtgeschützte Innerlichkeit*) that had supposedly been brought on in part by an excessive fealty to the historicist tradition.

One of the central tenets of historicism is that human beings who share a culture, language, or even just geographic location will frequently undergo the same formative process and thus find themselves on a communal journey through historical time. This formative process is best described with organic rather than mechanical metaphors, because its shape derives not from universal laws or first principles, but rather from variable local conditions.[5] The twentieth-century "crisis of historicism" is, at its heart, the product of an increasing unease with the consequences of such an organic approach. If history does indeed manifest itself in a

---

5. This second point is the source of frequent confusion in English, where for many years the most influential text on the subject was Karl Popper's *The Poverty of Historicism* (Boston: Beacon Press, 1957), which is actually an attack on Hegel's attempts to elucidate a universal law behind the formative drive that was postulated by eighteenth-century historicism.

large variety of locally grown forms, influenced by a number of factors that would be impossible to replicate in different settings, then what is to stop historical contemplation from sliding into mere relativism? How, in other words, are historians supposed to derive prescriptive insights from an endless temporal flux? These questions proved extremely vexatious to a generation of scholars caught between a lingering philosophical idealism on the one hand, and the pressures of the nascent social sciences on the other. Men such as Dilthey, Troeltsch, and Meinecke sought to allay their unease with variations of what, in my discussion of Herder, I called the "panentheistic" approach to history—the belief, in other words, that while history is apperceptible only in the manifest form of various entelechies, various *Bildungen*, it nevertheless has an underlying universal character. Friedrich Meinecke, for instance, defined the "principle of historicism" as the recognition that "[historical constructs] are not merely recurring types subject to general laws, but also possess an individual and totally unique character, much like every person conforms to the general category of the 'human being' yet at the same time differs from all other people and is therefore an incomparable individual."[6]

As Georg Iggers points out, the 1920s marked a decisive break with this sort of panentheistic thinking: "The concept of *Geschichtlichkeit* (historicity), which began to dominate German philosophic discussion after the appearance of Martin Heidegger's *Being and Time*, marked the negation of classical historicism. As a doctrine, *Geschichtlichkeit* assumes—as did historicism—that man has no nature, only a history. But it rejects the idea that history has objective existence of its own; rather it sees history as an inseparable aspect of man."[7] Central to the post–World War I debates about historicism, however, was a more practical concern sparked by the specter of relativism: if the conduct of states was to be evaluated not by their adherence to general laws, but rather by their conformity to national entelechies, then all too often history and philosophy became merely the handmaidens of established powers. If the German Empire, for instance, was more autocratic than most

---

6. Friedrich Meinecke, "Klassizismus, Romantizismus und historisches Denken," in *Werke*, ed. Hans Herzfeld, Carl Hinrich, and Walther Hofer, vol. 4, *Zur Theorie und Philosophie der Geschichte*, ed. Eberhard Kessel (Stuttgart: K. F. Koehler Verlag, 1959), 265. In his study *From History to Sociology: The Transition in German Historical Thinking,* Carlo Antoni similarly explains how Ernst Troeltsch, influenced by his academic training as a theologian, "concluded, therefore, that in the apparent anarchy [of history] one could discover the 'profound divinity' of the human spirit, could discover that faith in God was essentially identical in all its forms, and could find that this faith progressed, i.e. gained in energy and purity, in the degree to which man became disengaged from his original bonds of nature (*Naturgebundenheit*)." Antoni hastens to add: "In so arguing, however, he did not mean to imply an agreement with the Hegelian concept of becoming. On the contrary, like Ranke, he wished to allow all of the historical formations to retain their individuality and peculiar value: succession ought not 'mediate' the individual, nor was it to be considered as a continuous and inevitable growth. Nor did the hierarchy of 'formations' coincide completely with mere chronological succession." Carlo Antoni, *From History to Sociology: The Transition in German Historical Thinking*, trans. Hayden V. White (Detroit: Wayne State University Press, 1959), 52.

7. Georg Iggers, *The German Conception of History: The National Tradition of Historical Thought from Herder to the Present* (Middletown, CT: Wesleyan University Press, 1968), 243.

other Western powers, then surely this circumstance could be explained by the fact that the German national character differed from that of England or France. To call for democratic reforms following the example of these other countries would therefore constitute a logical fallacy. Germany would have to follow its own path into the future.

In his early writings, Meinecke effectively arrived at a kind of feedback loop between spirit and power, the intelligentsia and the governing classes, in which the former propped up the latter for as long as power would, in turn, create and protect an environment in which culture might flourish. Mann articulated a very similar position in his *Confessions of a Nonpolitical Man* (1918). Following the cataclysmic defeat in the war, which revealed to all who were willing to pay attention the utter incompetence of the Wilhelmine establishment, such a position was no longer tenable; Meinecke's book on Machiavellianism thus was an attempt to resolve a newly discovered tension between spirit and power through the conceptual category of the "reason of state." Mann similarly groped for a new and more critical relationship between intellectuals and the state in his lecture "On the German Republic," which attracted an audience of restless conservatives but proved to be a robust defense of the young Weimar Republic.

On the level of historical methodology, the most immediate response to the trauma of the war was Oswald Spengler's monumental expression of cultural pessimism, *The Decline of the West* (1918). Spengler's main thesis was that world history consists of the successive rise and fall of different cultures that each possess a distinctive morphology; as the title of his work already implies, the early twentieth century coincides with the decline of Western civilization. Spengler's work illustrates yet another aspect of the intellectual crisis under discussion here, namely historicism's reluctance to think across cultural boundaries—its inability, in other words, to adopt a cosmopolitan perspective. Troeltsch, for instance, much like Spengler, divided the civilizations of the world into a number of different "cultural circles" (*Kulturkreise*). Each of these circles possesses what Troeltsch called an "individual totality," a spiritual reality that is uniquely and totally its own and could never be completely apprehended by somebody not born into it. There is an obvious paradox in the idea of a scholar who argues so vigorously that our upbringing imposes strict epistemic limitations and yet feels so confident in drawing up boundaries between foreign cultures, and as Carlo Antoni comments, "[Troeltsch] differs from Spengler and Keyserling, who penetrated into similar alien cycles, only in the consciousness of his incompetence, his prudence, or (if one wishes) his modesty. In reality, Troeltsch's history of Europeanism is only a revision of that chapter in *The Decline of the West* which deals with our own civilization."[8]

In the context of the 1920s, however, methodological concerns coexisted with practical ones, and the more progressive among the Weimar intellectuals came

---

8. Antoni, *From History to Sociology*, 83.

to the abrupt realization that the thesis that Germans would never be truly able to understand the French or the British—and would, in turn, not be understood by them—presented an obstacle preventing full integration into the new political order of Europe. In order to lead their country back into the house of civilized nations, Germans would need to not only talk to their neighbors, but also prove themselves willing to learn from them. The disjunctive "and" in the title of Meinecke's early *Cosmopolitanism and the National State* (1908) would have to be turned into a conjunctive one. Thomas Mann's awkward speculations in his lecture "On the German Republic" regarding the elective affinities between Novalis and Walt Whitman, principal examples of what he four years earlier had still described in Manichaean terms as "German culture" and "Western civilization," illustrate his newfound interest in cosmopolitan thinking.

This is the background one has to keep in mind when evaluating *The German Catastrophe* and its relevance for Mann's own reengagement with historicism in *Doctor Faustus*. In many ways, the same issues that vexed the intellectual discourse of the Weimar years find a quickened expression in Meinecke's attempt to account for Hitler. It is instructive here to compare Meinecke's position to that of Max Horkheimer and Theodor Adorno, who produced their own, now much better-known, theory of fascism almost concurrently (*Dialectic of Enlightenment* appeared in 1947). Horkheimer and Adorno, of course, were Marxists and thus naturally approached the totalitarian terror of the Nazis as the heightened expression of a tendency they proclaimed to be latent in capitalist modernity as a whole: that of driving the division between subject and object to such an extreme that enlightenment dialectically reverts into myth. They were also Jewish and had thus experienced at first hand the Nazi ploy to whip up a nationalist frenzy through the deliberate exclusion of an "enemy within" and the division of the German people into "Aryan" and "Semitic" races. Meinecke, by contrast, clung to the historicist belief that events as profoundly transformative as the rise of the Third Reich had to be an expression of an individual national entelechy. He also, though an unwavering opponent of the Nazis who retired from public life and moved into inner emigration after the Reichstag burned down, never relinquished his identification with the German people, to whom he always refers in the first person plural throughout his book.

The introductory paragraph of Meinecke's study encapsulates his conflicted position:

> Will one ever fully understand the monstrous experience which fell to our lot in the twelve years of the Third Reich? We have lived through them, but up to now we—every one of us without exception—have understood them only incompletely. This or that side of our fate, to be sure, has stood before our eyes, often in glaring light, apparently free from any uncertainty. But who is able to explain completely how it all fits together and how it was interwoven with deeper causes; how the boundless illusion

to which so many succumbed in the first years of the Third Reich necessarily changed into the boundless disillusionment and collapse of the final years? German history is rich in difficult riddles and unfortunate turns. But for our comprehension the riddle that confronts us today and the catastrophe through which we are now living surpass all previous occurrences of similar kind.[9]

Any number of questions could be asked in response to this argument. To whom does the pronoun "one" (*man*) in the first sentence refer, and what is its relationship to the "we" that is used throughout the rest of the paragraph? Why does Meinecke not mention the millions of casualties that the twelve years of the Reich caused in Germany, or the many millions more who fell victim to its wars of aggression and to the Holocaust? Was Nazism truly "fated," and, if it was, how does this fate relate to the "deeper causes" that Meinecke also mentions? Did "boundless illusion" really "necessarily" change into "boundless disillusionment" during the final years (or even months, or days) of the war? And to what "previous occurrences of similar kind" might this supposedly unique historical event be compared?

Meinecke's struggle (a struggle that was also Thomas Mann's) clearly lies in the attempt to reconcile his anti-Nazism with his German patriotism, all the while staying true to the historicist doctrine, which holds that historical events have an individual basis in the cultural bedrock from which they sprung, and that they cannot be explained away as the product of abstract processes like "modernity" or "capitalist rationalization." His solution is problematic, to say the least. "[The] question of the German catastrophe broadens at the same time to a question which extends beyond Germany to the destiny of the West [*abendländisches Schicksal*] in general," Meinecke argues. He continues: "Hitler's National Socialism, which brought us directly to this abyss, is not a phenomenon deriving from merely German evolutionary forces, but has also certain analogies and precedents in the authoritarian systems of neighboring countries" (1). The key word in these sentences is "merely," for Meinecke avoids the devastating conclusion that Nazism might indeed be the logical outcome of centuries of "German evolutionary forces" by instead attributing it to the interplay of what his chapter title already calls the "two waves of the age." These two "waves," we learn, are socialism and nationalism; the first is egalitarian, universal, and aims for a "millennial kingdom of human happiness" (*tausendjähriges Reich neuen Menschenglücks*); the second is exclusive, local, and aims not for "a fundamental social revolution but the increase of the political power of the nation" (3). Both waves, however, are characteristic of the epigenesis of the West; unlike his colleagues in the Frankfurt school, Meinecke isn't trying to work out a theory of modernity as a whole, but chronicling the fate of only one cultural circle.

---

9. Friedrich Meinecke, *The German Catastrophe: Reflections and Recollections*, trans. Sidney B. Fay (Cambridge, MA: Harvard University Press, 1950), xi. Further references to this edition will appear in parentheses in the text.

Nazism can now be explained as a phenomenon that results from the particular way in which these two waves interacted in the German context. In Germany, Meinecke claims, the nationalist movement had seized a hold fifty years before the socialist one and had brought with it a new materialism and an obsession with power that stood in stark contrast to the idealism of Goethe's generation. This "new realism," which expressed itself most forcefully in Prussian militarism, found powerful amplification in the machine age and "put an end to the way of living aimed solely at the advancement and enrichment of one's own individuality. It directed attention more to corporate living in masses, to the structure of society and to the nation as a whole" (9). As the nineteenth century progressed, the national movement thus focused less and less on the "nation" as a grouping of like-minded individuals, and more and more on the "mass" as a faceless, anonymous entity. Socialism, meanwhile, which originally took the proletarian mass as its basic subject of analysis, had moved more and more in the opposite direction, until it had come to focus on the nation in the works of the national-social (not to be confused with "national-socialist") politician Friedrich Naumann in the 1890s. It is the interaction of these two larger tendencies—the renunciation of subjective idealism for base realism and power politics on the one hand, and the inability to formulate political utopianism in terms outside of the nation on the other—that according to Meinecke led to an eventual catastrophe during the Weimar years.[10] As he summarizes it,

> [We stood in 1914] at the main turning-point in the evolution of the German people. The man of Goethe's day was a man of free individuality. He was at the same time a "humane" man, who recognized his duty toward the community to be "noble, helpful, and good" and carried out his duty accordingly. He lived and developed at first in the synthesis of classical liberalism and then of the national socialism of the Naumann stamp. He became ever more strongly bound with the social needs of the masses and with the political requirements of the state; that is, he became ever more tightly and concretely united with the community of people and state that enveloped him. (26)

Although Meinecke acknowledges the unique nature of the Third Reich, his insistence on telling the story of its rise as an interplay of larger forces lends his story a strangely abstract quality. "Socialism" and "nationalism," in this account, are towering forces that stand both above and beyond German history, which merely provides the grounds for their local manifestations; the responsibility for the rise of Nazism thus somehow surpasses the country. It is surely no coincidence that Meinecke attributes to socialism the desire for a "millennial kingdom of human happiness" and thus subtly connects it to one of the best-known Nazi epithets for their

---

10. For a more thorough analysis of Meinecke's etiology of Nazism in *The German Catastrophe* and contemporaneous writings, see Mark W. Clark's *Beyond Catastrophe: German Intellectuals and Cultural Renewal after World War II, 1945–1955* (Lexington, MA: Lexington Books, 2006), 33–35.

state.[11] This abstract take on German guilt is also responsible for the passages of Meinecke's text that are most liable to make the contemporary reader uncomfortable, namely his consistent treatment of Hitler as something external and foreign. The Germans, as Meinecke states quite clearly, weren't responsible for creating the totalitarian ideology of Nazism, but only for foolishly succumbing to its virulent influence: "The German people were not fundamentally diseased with criminal sentiments but were only suffering for a while with a severe infection from poison administered to it" (95). This approach, in turn, allows Meinecke to maintain a pronounced victim's mentality; his book focuses myopically on the destruction that the Third Reich brought on Germany without so much as commenting on either its wars or the Holocaust. Meinecke also ignores the simple fact that in Nazism, German citizens were exploited and killed because of their race, creed, political beliefs, or sexual orientation, perhaps because it casts serious doubts on his narrative of German history as a unified national entelechy.

This regrettable stance also colors the final prescriptive passages of *The German Catastrophe*, which today remain the best-known sections of the book. Meinecke wrote his book at a time when "re-education" and "de-Nazification" were the watchwords of Allied policy, and in 1948 accepted the call to become founding rector of the Free University of Berlin, which had been built in the western part of the city as a deliberate counterpoint to the former Friedrich Wilhelm (and future Humboldt) University in the Soviet Zone of Occupation. And yet Meinecke does not stake Germany's path to reconciliation and recovery on renewed engagement with the Enlightenment legacy of the Western Allies. Instead, he calls for a return to the values of Goethean humanism—for a return, in other words, to German virtues as they existed *before* the dual waves of socialism and nationalism began to exert their corrosive influence. To this end, he proposes the creation "in every German city and larger village" of communities "of like-minded friends of culture which I should like best to call Goethe Communities." To these Goethe Communities "would fall the task of conveying into the heart of the listeners through sound the most vital evidences of the great German spirit, always offering the noblest music and poetry together" (120). It is a telling solution, in which masterpieces of culture are enlisted to distribute the Pentecostal message of the great and undying "German spirit."

In Meinecke's defense, his project intends to do more than merely burnish the legacy of the past in the hopes that its glory will outshine the crimes of the present. He also aims to reintegrate Germany into a cosmopolitan dialogue of cultures:

---

11. At a much later point in the analysis, Meinecke will also draw a comparison to the "millennial kingdom" of the Anabaptists in Münster in 1535. This reference is surprising, especially as it is simply made to illustrate Meinecke's uncharacteristically pathos-laden assertion that there is no "great, new, existence-changing idea . . . in which Satan has not insinuated himself both as driver and as beneficiary" (*The German Catastrophe*, 71). But this only heightens the intriguing parallel to Mann's *Doctor Faustus*, in which a similar comparison is drawn between the fanaticism of Hitler and that of Martin Luther.

"Four decades ago, in the field of political history, I tried to show that cosmopolitanism and the modern idea of the national state were not originally rigid contrasts, but existed together for mutual enrichment. . . . Today, after a generation of the most tremendous revolutions, let us recognize that for Occidental cultural life a similar dialectic is applicable" (118). In outlining the details of this dialectic, however, Meinecke maintains a somewhat one-sided focus on Germany's export contributions to what for him is an exclusively Western marketplace of ideas, and he also insists that all genuine masterworks have to meet the standards of national purity first: "What is more powerful than Goethe's *Faust* and how powerfully has it cast its radiance upon the Occident! Whatever springs from the very special spirit of a particular people and is therefore inimitable is likely to make a successful universal appeal. . . . In order to exert a universal influence, [however,] spiritual possessions of this kind must always blossom forth naturally, uniquely and organically out of any given folk spirit" (118). Hybridity, adaptation, or collaborative exchange across national borders are clearly unknown entities to Meinecke, whose understanding of culture remains as rigid and monolithic as his conception of the German people and the uniform fate that has supposedly befallen them.

Zeitblom and the Burden of History

Meinecke's essay represents one possible response to the end of the Third Reich, a response in which the values of historicism align with those of the inner emigration to chart out a path toward redemption that simultaneously leads back to a lost cultural heritage. *Doctor Faustus* is obviously a very different book from *The German Catastrophe*, and yet Mann grappled with many of the same problems as his slightly older contemporary. Indeed, Serenus Zeitblom, the retired schoolteacher who narrates the novel, at times sounds a lot like Meinecke. In sentences that could easily be borrowed from *The German Catastrophe*, Zeitblom waxes about the "spirit and claims of our historical development," and he too is fond of words such as "becoming, development, destiny."[12] Zeitblom furthermore has difficulties reconciling his strident anti-Nazism with his love of country and seems uncertain whether to pray for the victory or the defeat of the German armed forces. He also persistently speaks about Germany in the first person plural, even though it is clear that the reigning powers have driven him into inner emigration, and that his sons would not hesitate to turn against him should they learn about the book that he is secretly writing. Like Meinecke's *The German Catastrophe*, finally, Zeitblom's biography of Adrian Leverkühn is a Janus-faced work that looks with uncertainty into the future even as it tries to account for past evils.

---

12. Thomas Mann, *Doctor Faustus: The Life of the German Composer Adrian Leverkühn as Told by a Friend*, trans. John E. Woods (New York: Alfred A. Knopf, 1997), 6, 28. All further references to this edition will appear in parentheses in the text.

As an etiology of Nazism, however, *Doctor Faustus* suffers from serious problems, problems that to some extent also parallel those of *The German Catastrophe*. First, the equation "Leverkühn = Hitler Germany" seems to slander the dodecaphonic technique that ranks as the fictional composer's greatest achievement, by comparing the move away from tonality to a departure from the principles of liberal democracy. This may appear to be a fairly esoteric matter, but Arnold Schoenberg's virulent reaction to what he regarded as an instance of plagiarism and character assassination on Mann's part demonstrates that it can nevertheless have serious consequences in the real world. Inversely, the retelling of the German move toward Nazism as a lone composer's descent into madness might be taken to trivialize acts of almost unspeakable horror. Finally, and perhaps most seriously, the central conceit of Mann's story, namely the pact with the devil, once again implies an externality of evil. Leverkühn, and by extension Germany as a whole, can certainly be declared guilty for signing the infernal contract, but the source of the evil lies elsewhere. Indeed, Meinecke's own formulation of a "severe infection" that befell a German people who were nevertheless "not fundamentally diseased" finds an uncanny echo in *Doctor Faustus*, in which Mann's hero finalizes the pact by voluntarily contracting syphilis.

In short, Zeitblom can plausibly be faulted for fleeing from collective historical responsibility into the comforting realm of myth. As critics have noted, the same charge could be levied against many other novels (especially by authors from an older generation) that were published during the immediate postwar years.[13] After all, Hesse's *The Glass Bead Game* also tends toward the mythical, even if here the myth is disguised as a futuristic fantasy. Zeitblom, however, is precisely *not* Mann. In a letter to Paul Amann, Mann instead described his character as "a parody of myself," and in his long essay "The Creation of *Doctor Faustus*" he further ruminated on the ways in which he employed Zeitblom's humanist style "only in parody."[14] Indeed, Mann himself on several occasions confirmed that he had put as much of himself, if not more, into the character of Leverkühn as he had into Zeitblom. Much like Gustav Aschenbach or Hans Castorp in earlier tales, Zeitblom thus is a distorted mirror image of his creator, to be treated with some sympathy, but also to be held at an ironic distance.

The exact nature of this parody is complex. Mann obviously pokes fun at his own love of sententious phrases and sometimes unquestioning reverence for the traditional humanist canon. Beyond that, however, we can also see in Zeitblom a sophisticated critique of historicist thinking. That the "crisis of historicism" formed an important part of Mann's intellectual formation and occupied him especially

---

13. See, e.g., Judith Ryan, *The Uncompleted Past: Postwar German Novels and the Third Reich* (Detroit: Wayne State University Press, 1983).

14. Quoted in Jürgen Scharfschwerdt, *Thomas Mann und der deutsche Bildungsroman: Eine Untersuchung zu den Problemen einer literarischen Tradition* (Stuttgart: W. Kohlhammer, 1967), 245.

during the years leading up to the composition of *Doctor Faustus* has by now been fairly well established in the critical literature. Birger Solheim, for instance, argues in a comprehensive study that "[when] he wrote the *Confessions of a Nonpolitical Man*, Thomas Mann's thought was under the spell of historicism in a number of ways," and goes on to list no less than twelve such identifying characteristics, including a tendency to relate individual phenomena to more holistic categories, such as "state," "people," or "nation," and a preference for monadic conceptions of history, in which little or no room is allotted to intercultural communication.[15] According to Solheim, Mann broke with historicism shortly afterward, when he read *The Decline of the West* and came to the conclusion that the only appropriate response to Spengler's characteristic fatalism was precisely parody and ironic self-distance.

Evidence uncovered by Martin Travers, however, suggests that Mann's personal debate over the uses and abuses of historicism continued well into the 1930s and 1940s and was far from resolved after the encounter with Spengler. Travers identifies two quite diverse influences on Mann's thought during this period but does not fully consider the obvious tensions that result from them. The first such influence is the aforementioned historian Erich Kahler, with whom Mann carried out an intensive correspondence that lasted from 1931 to the novelist's death in 1955. In his very first letter to Mann, Kahler speaks of his ambition "to undertake an elemental rethinking of the essence of Germanism. I don't mean a 'German History' or a 'Psychology of the German', but a graphic summary of what we can call specifically German."[16] Mann was at first noncommittal, but he took notice when Kahler published *The German Character in the History of Europe* (1937). However, parallel to this fructifying relationship ran a second influence, which Travers locates in Mann's study of *Heritage of Our Times*. In Bloch, Mann encountered the notion of the "synchronicity of the non-synchronous" as an antidote to historicism.

The conflict between these two very different interpretations of the German character greatly contributes to the parodic dimensions of Mann's novel. Zeitblom is from the beginning committed to providing not merely a biography of Leverkühn, but also an entelechy. When he describes the early music lessons that he and his friend received from Hanne the milkmaid, for instance, Zeitblom isn't content to merely record that the rounds that Hanne taught them awoke in his friend an appreciation for music as the artistic organization of time. He also has to add: "None of us was aware that under the direction of a milkmaid we were already moving on a comparatively high plane of musical culture, a branch of imitative

---

15. Birger Solheim, *Zum Geschichtsdenken Theodor Fontanes und Thomas Manns: oder, Geschichtskritik in "Der Stechlin" und "Doktor Faustus"* (Würzburg: Königshausen & Neumann, 2004), 146.

16. Quoted in Martin Travers, "Thomas Mann, *Doktor Faustus*, and the Historians: The Function of 'Anachronistic Symbolism,'" in *The Modern German Historical Novel: Paradigms, Problems, and Perspectives*, ed. David Roberts and Philip Thomson (New York: Berg, 1991), 155.

polyphony, which first had to be discovered in the fifteenth century before it could provide us with amusement." And he concludes: "In recalling Adrian's burst of laughter [which the rounds elicited from the boy], I find in retrospect that within it lay knowledge and the initiate's sneer" (32). That the two young students could not possibly appreciate the complexity of what they were doing is irrelevant; Zeitblom is showing his readers that the first musical lesson that Leverkühn received was already a lesson in polyphony, and thus in the particular technique that he would later revive and lead to new heights in works such as the *Apocalipsis*. A dual optic is at work here, and a gaze that sees in events only their surface meaning (a child's burst of laughter) combines with one that reinterprets these events in the light of later experiences (the burst is actually an initiate's sneer).

Given the parameters of his own narrative, it is thus all the more telling that Zeitblom shows such reluctance in acknowledging the devilish nature of Leverkühn's pact. What vexes Zeitblom—the dignified philologist who believes that "in the worthy realm of the humanities one is safe from all . . . spooks" (23)—isn't merely that a medieval legend should suddenly turn out to have a modern and all too real counterpart, but also that Leverkühn's bargain imputes an inevitable nature to all that he has done. Tellingly, Mann has chosen an organic metaphor: Leverkühn's creative career begins when he willingly contracts syphilis, and his accomplishments grow at the same rate that the bacteria spread in his brain. The composer thus merely acts out what the devil has already planted within him; he cannot depart from the path that will lead him into madness by, for instance, saving the life of his nephew Nepomuk Schneidewein. Zeitblom's reluctance to confront the demonic pact head-on even though he subscribes to a similar fatalism provides a neat compression of the same dilemma that also plagued Friedrich Meinecke. Like Meinecke, Zeitblom arranges past experiences according to a set heuristic, and also like Meinecke, he shies away from the full extent of the damning conclusion to which this heuristic would seem to commit him.

This damning conclusion, of course, is not only that his old friend has sold his soul to the devil, but also that the German nation may have done likewise. Indeed, Zeitblom has consistently drawn parallels between Leverkühn's career as a composer and the state of his country. The two men's early disagreements over whether the libretto for Leverkühn's opera *Love's Labour's Lost* should be written in German or English, for instance, occur simultaneously with the heated debates about Germany's place in Europe that divide the members of their student fraternity at Halle. And Leverkühn's fateful turn to the "barbarism" of early modern polyphony in the *Apocalipsis cum figuris* coincides with his membership in the protofascist "Kridwiss circle," whose intellectual leader, Chaim Breisacher, extols the virtues of the primitive, including those of theocratic government. Leverkühn's aloof nature forestalls readings of men like Breisacher as straightforward influences on the composer; instead, they formulate social and political views whose basic structure uncannily mirrors that of Leverkühn's advances within music theory.

Mann's diaries make clear that he partially patterned Breisacher on Oswald Spengler, and indeed Breisacher displays both the intellectual range and the cultural pessimism of his model: "He was a polyhistor, who could talk about anything and everything, a philosopher of culture, whose opinions, however, were directed against culture insofar as he affected to see all of history as nothing but a process of decline. The most contemptuous word from his mouth was 'progress'" (295). Breisacher's preferences for the primitive, the unadulterated, and the strong are also rooted in Spengler, as are his polemics exalting Mosaic Law over the New Testament. These opinions simultaneously mark the point, however, where the developmental logic of historicism (even if the development in question here is an inverse one, a devolution) yields to something else altogether. Breisacher has formulated the operative logic of fascism, whereby the productive forces of modernity are harnessed through the structuring intervention of myth: a controlled recourse to the "synchronicity of the non-synchronous."

The description of the Kridwiss circle thus forms a pivotal moment in Mann's text. It marks the point at which historicist thinking, hijacked by the cultural pessimism produced by a lost world war, turns cynical and abandons its own basic commitment to temporal continuity. Instead, the past is to be brought into the present so as to better control the future. Unlike traditional conservatism, which simply believes in the persistence of core values throughout time, the Kridwiss circle is open to radical change in the areas of political and social organization. It merely believes that such changes should be dressed in the rhetoric and the symbolism of the past so as to make them more palatable to the gullible masses.

The same turn toward cynicism and myth can also be found in the form of Zeitblom's narrative. In many critical summaries, Zeitblom's habit of showing how early episodes in Leverkühn's biography already carry within them the seeds of later developments has simply been filed away as an example of the leitmotivic technique that Mann first developed around the turn of the century and had already applied with great success to artistic biographies in works such as *Tonio Kröger* (1903) and *Death in Venice* (1912).[17] To some extent, of course, this is true. But a leitmotif is unthinkable without the notion of temporal growth or development, and without what I have earlier called a "dual optic" employed by the reader. In order to become a "motif," an idea needs to have a discrete identity *and* be recognizable as merely one more variant of a larger ideational cluster that gains in complexity over time. In addition to the many motifs that are undeniably present in *Doctor Faustus*, however, Zeitblom is also battling with an entirely different form of temporal emplotment in which individual instances of "motifs" seem entirely identical to one another and thus suggest stasis rather than development. This second form of emplotment is foreshadowed rather early, when Zeitblom describes

---

17. See, for instance, Kahler, "The Secularization of the Devil," 32–33, as well as Bergsten, *Thomas Mann's "Doctor Faustus,"* 168–78.

Leverkühn's native farmstead, Buchel, near Kaisersaschern and mentions that it included a "massive old linden tree" of some significance to the family history: "This beautiful tree, fixed forever in my memory, was somewhat in the way of the wagons maneuvering in the courtyard, I suppose, and I have heard that as a young man each heir would argue with his father that common sense required its removal, only later, then, as owner of the farm, to defend the tree against the same demands from his own son" (14).

It is perhaps idle to speculate about whether any relationship exists between this linden tree and the one that acquires such significance as a symbol of German destiny at the end of *The Magic Mountain*. In the context of Buchel, at any rate, the massive trunk clearly represents an obstacle to the rationalization of work processes (even if only in the most primitive sense) and also acquires a kind of talismanic significance by which the natural succession of generations is turned from a course of rebellion to one of stasis. A similar turn from successive change to stasis is effected in Zeitblom's shuddering realization that Adrian's later domicile at Pfeiffering "very strangely resembled, even replicated, the framework of his childhood" (29), which, he believes, "says something unsettling about a man's inner life" (30). The analogy that Zeitblom chooses to support his displeasure is telling as well: "It reminds me, rather, of a man of my acquaintance who, although externally robust and sporting a beard, was so high-strung that whenever he fell ill—and he tended to be sickly—he would only allow a pediatrician to treat him. Moreover, the doctor into whose care he put himself was so short that he, quite literally, could never have measured up to a medical practice with adults" (30). Hitler, after all, was also known for his short stature.

In moving from a leitmotivic technique that stresses growth and development to one in which continuities between earlier developmental stages are privileged, Zeitblom is giving a narrative shape to the essential fatalism that underlies so much historicist thought during its late phase in the twentieth century. In connecting Adrian's conscious choice of a residence that closely resembled his childhood home to the story of the man who required help from a pediatrician, he is furthermore emphasizing the intellectually infantilizing implications of this fatalism, and possibly also giving it a political subtext. In *Doktor Faustus*, the plot of the traditional *Bildungsroman*, in which the protagonist performatively enacts the nation's voyage into an open future, hence gradually yet inevitably modulates into a different dynamic, in which the protagonist allegorically acts out an inevitable destiny. Through the means of literature, then, Thomas Mann illustrates how historicism, the mode of thought that stood behind the traditional *Bildungsroman*, can easily slide into something altogether darker. After all, every entelechy is premised on the idea that complexly developed forms contain within them the residues of earlier larval stages. All that is required to move from an optimistic celebration of open development to a pessimistic embrace of cultural determinism is a slight change in optic, a change that was all too commonly performed in Germany during the interwar period.

Dodecaphony and Antihistoricism

Leverkühn's compositional technique takes this impasse of historicism as its starting point. With his archetypal German composer, Mann created a vehicle through which to contemplate the possibilities of an antihistoricist style, a way of arranging narrative elements in time that avoids the dynamic of the traditional *Bildungsroman*. Leverkühn's turn toward polyphony and his later invention of dodecaphony take aim against homophony as the organizing principle of musical development—and, by extension, also against history. In his various theoretical pronouncements, the composer frames this struggle as one of barbarism versus culture, myth versus enlightenment, and identifies Beethoven as the pivotal figure who stands between the two. He inherits this thought from his teacher, Wendell Kretzschmar, who argues in one of his public lectures: "[Beethoven] had been the grand master of a profane epoch of music, in which art had emancipated itself from the cultic to the cultural" (64).

Leverkühn at once admires and detests Beethoven, an ambivalent relationship that is best summarized through his various pronouncements on the Ninth Symphony. He admires Beethoven because the older composer raised music from mere craftsmanship into a spiritual vehicle; at the same time, however, he also detests the romantic genius, whose elevation of "mere musicality" into "the realm of general intellect" (152) went hand in hand with a congruent elevation of human freedom into the noblest goal of musical expression, a shift best expressed in the triumphant "Ode to Joy" that concludes the Ninth Symphony. The Ninth Symphony breaks with the sonata form that had governed symphonic writing during the classical period, and instead recasts its materials in the form of a developmental narrative. This is evident in at least two different ways. First, the symphony opens in an indeterminate key on an empty fifth chord; it concludes, in an equally unprecedented manner, with a grand choral movement. As Nietzsche might say (and few other people influenced Mann's understanding of music as profoundly as Nietzsche did), the symphony thus celebrates the triumph of Apollonian *logos* over Dionysian *mythos*. Second, the final choral movement recapitulates the structure of the previous three movements in miniature, thereby giving the symphony the shape of an entelechy, in whose final flowering can still be found the remnants of earlier developmental stages.

According to Leverkühn, "culture" as it expresses itself in musical romanticism in general, and in Beethoven in particular, thus differs from the "cultic" in two important ways. First, it no longer contents itself with the mere craftsmanship and musicality that characterized the music of the classical period, aiming instead for a general celebration of the human spirit. Secondly, it elevates freedom—and with it inventiveness and human subjectivity—into the vehicle through which this celebration will be achieved. Nineteenth-century compositions reach for such freedom by dispensing with the "strict style" of earlier periods and focusing instead on development through variation: "Development had been a small part of the sonata, a modest refuge for subjective illumination and energy. With Beethoven it becomes universal, the center of the entire form, which, even where it remains given of convention, is absorbed by the subjective and newly created in freedom" (204). Musical "development created in freedom," however, is but one more instance of a *Bildung* or entelechy, for "freedom becomes the principle of a comprehensive economy, which allows music nothing accidental and develops the most extreme diversity out of materials that are always kept identical. Where there is nothing unthematic left, nothing that might not prove it has been derived from a single abiding constant, one can scarcely still speak of a free style of composition" (204).

The influence of Thomas Mann's musical adviser, Theodor W. Adorno, hangs heavy over these lines, which essentially propose that culture and freedom, when pushed to their extreme, are bound to dialectically revert into cultic control. Leverkühn's own compositions can be interpreted as an ongoing effort to come to terms with this paradox, although his solutions become ever more extreme as his syphilitic infection progresses. Early on—in a phase that reaches from roughly 1910, when he moves beyond his early experiments with musical impressionism, to 1919, when he concludes the *Apocalipsis*—Leverkühn seeks to improve on the polyphonic tendencies of Beethoven's late works by leading them back to a more rigorous application of counterpoint: "True counterpoint demands the simultaneity of independent voices. Counterpoint designed as melodic harmony, such as that in late Romantic works, is none at all" (204–5). Already in the Brentano cycle, however, he grasps for a more radical solution, which will eventually lead to his implementation of dodecaphony in his final work, *The Lamentation of Doctor Faustus*. This symphonic cantata, in which human voices are drowned out by the music of the orchestra, is conceived as an explicit antithesis to the "Ode to Joy," as Leverkühn confesses:

"I have discovered that it ought not be."

"What ought not be, Adrian?"

"The good and the noble," he replied, "what people call human, even though it is good and noble. What people have fought for, have stormed citadels for, and what people filled to overflowing have announced with jubilation—it ought not be. It will be taken back. I shall take it back."

"I don't quite understand, my dear fellow. What do you want to take back?"

"The Ninth Symphony," he replied. And then came nothing more, even though I waited. (501)

It is clear that Leverkühn's compositional struggles carry a significance that reaches far beyond the musical arena. At stake here are such deeper questions as the meaning of culture and the importance of freedom in ensuring human development. And the "late romantic" solution that Mann's composer rejects is in many ways similar to the historicist thought of Meinecke and, by extension, of Zeitblom. It seeks to cast human thought into the shape of an ongoing development that at once gives and obeys its own laws, thereby stressing the underlying thematic unity behind a seemingly free and entirely subjective process. Leverkühn's experiments with polyphony can consequently also be interpreted as an attack on historicist thinking: his demand for a "simultaneity of independent voices," for instance, represents a break with the monadism of orthodox historicism. More importantly, his turn backward toward early modern compositional devices negates the notion of artistic progress. This final impulse leads eventually to his invention of the dodecaphonic method, which not only eliminates all subjectivity from music but also turns an inherently time-bound art form into what is, on at least one level, an expression of intellectual stasis. In the "strict style" that Leverkühn describes to Zeitblom (and later implements in the *Lamentation*), all musical materials are simple variations (derived through the three basic operations of transposition, retrograde, and inversion) of an unchanging underlying tone row.

Mann himself was the first person to recognize the obvious similarities between Leverkühn's endeavors and the art of fellow modernist writers, or at least a certain critical view of those writers. His English wasn't good enough to read *Ulysses* in the original, and he apparently did not have access to a German translation in America, but in "The Creation of *Doctor Faustus*" he quotes a sentence from Harry Levin's *James Joyce: A Critical Introduction* (1941) that made a deep impression on him just as he was struggling with the twenty-second chapter of his novel, in which Leverkühn first describes the dodecaphonic method: "The best writing of our contemporaries is not an act of creation, but an act of evocation, peculiarly saturated with reminiscences."[18] Levin's salvo against artistic creation echoes T. S. Eliot's insistence, in "Tradition and the Individual Talent" (1919), that a great writer must first develop the feeling that "the whole of the literature of Europe from Homer and within it the whole of the literature of his own country has a simultaneous existence and composes a simultaneous order."[19] Levin, furthermore, called *Ulysses* a "novel to end all novels" and joined Eliot in arguing that Joyce had ended literature's subservience to subjective individuality by creating an impersonal "modern epic." Leverkühn's dodecaphonic compositions are "epic" in this specialized sense of the word as well. Joyce's Odyssean parallels, which force artistic inventiveness into a strictly pre-given frame, correspond to Leverkühn's all-powerful twelve-tone rows. As a result, neither *Ulysses* nor *The Lamentation of Doctor Faustus* can be unambiguously read as the product of an individual creative mind; in both works, furthermore, the forward drive of conventional narrative and music is subordinated to the "simultaneous order" of myth.

---

18. Thomas Mann, "Die Entstehung des *Doktor Faustus*," in *Gesammelte Werke in dreizehn Bänden*, ed. Peter de Mendelssohn (Frankfurt am Main: Fischer, 1990), 11:204.
19. T. S. Eliot, *Selected Prose of T. S. Eliot*, ed. Frank Kermode (Orlando, FL: Harcourt, 1975), 38.

From here it was just a short step—first taken by Erich Kahler but most influentially repeated by Gunilla Bergsten and Hans Mayer—to the argument that *Doctor Faustus* itself is an example of a modern epic. This argument in turn implies a decisive break not only with nineteenth-century realism, but more specifically also with the *Bildungsroman* tradition.[20] If Leverkühn's actions are already predetermined by mythic correspondences, then there can be no free development, no *Bildung*, and thus also no *Bildungsroman*. Serenus Zeitblom's worst fear, namely that beginning and end of his tale might become coterminous in the moment of apocalypse and thereby imply that Leverkühn's destiny was inevitable, would thus have come to fruition.

There is reason to be skeptical about such a reading, however. Mann's self-identification with Joyce was superficial at best and seems to have arisen mainly out of a need to reassure himself that his work was still relevant, that it hadn't succumbed to tepid traditionalism and vulgar populism. In the very same breath in which he praises Joyce, he also once again stresses his own parodic ambitions, thereby highlighting that his gaze was turned backward, toward tradition, even if his basic intent was to subvert it. And surely it could not have been otherwise, for like Friedrich Meinecke during these years, Mann was entirely preoccupied with the etiology of the "German Catastrophe." The enormity of the events that were unfolding before his very eyes prevented him from taking refuge in the formal experiments of the avant-garde.[21]

More important than these biographical considerations, however, are certain formal ones that arise from the conclusion of *Doctor Faustus*. Immediately before the masterful description of Leverkühn's symphonic cantata, in which the principles of the "strict style" are fully realized for the first time, Mann has his

---

20. As Hans Mayer argues, "The epical works of Proust, Joyce, Kafka, Faulkner, and Musil correspond as epics to the process that Adrian Leverkühn's music passes through in the Faustus-novel. That is the reason why the Faustus-novel itself had to take on a new form as an epic picture. In the same way in which the Faust problem represented a 'taking back' [*Zurücknahme*] of Goethe's world tragedy, so both its outer composition and its inner form represent a 'taking back' of *Wilhelm Meister's Apprenticeship*." Hans Mayer, *Von Lessing bis Thomas Mann: Wandlungen der bürgerlichen Literatur in Deutschland* (Pfullingen: Neske, 1959), 403.

21. As Ritchie Robertson writes in this context, "Modernism is an art of fragmentation. But what does the artist do when faced with real, physical fragmentation? In the period from 1943 to 1945, when Mann was writing his novel, he was aware of fragmentation in space: the destruction of German cities, the division of its territory among four invading armies. And he was also aware of fragmentation in time, since recent German history seemed to consist of alarming discontinuities: defeat in 1918, the establishment of a fragile democracy, and its transformation into a Fascist state resting on mass support and committed to brutal internal repression and external aggression. Modernism by itself could neither register nor explain the enormity of these events. If he was going to explore the origins of the German catastrophe in its cultural and intellectual history, Mann needed an art of continuity" ("Accounting for History," 128). Somewhat strangely, however, Robertson goes on to argue: "For a novelist like Mann, Germany's history could only be grasped by a device foreign to both Realism and Modernism, namely myth," as if modernism and myth had never been related to one another by figures as diverse as T. S. Eliot and Theodor W. Adorno.

composer deliver a final defiant address to the devil, the import of which calls into question the gravity of what is to come. Certain that he himself will go to hell, Leverkühn nevertheless consoles himself that his nephew Nepomuk Schneidewein will just as certainly be saved: "And may eternities be rolled twixt my place and his, I will yet know that he is in the place from whence You, foul filth, were cast out. And that will be the cooling water upon my tongue and a hosanna to mock You in my foulest curse!" (500). Human freedom thus asserts itself at the very moment in which predetermination appears to be the strongest.[22] The most interesting thing about these lines, however, is that they do not simply negate the allegorical correspondences that have progressively subverted the novel's claim to be a *Bildungsroman*, but rather turn them inside out. Indeed, Leverkühn's final act of defiance even as his mind caves in to madness *also* has an allegorical correspondence, but this one not from the medieval Faust chapbook, but rather from Goethe's *Faust, Part I*, which concludes with the redemption of Gretchen. In the end, then, "strict style" finds its nemesis in Goethe's romantic celebration of unfettered personal striving. Leverkühn's challenge to the devil consequently suggests what Mann's audience in 1947 already knew to be a fact: that a time would come when the Ninth Symphony would once again replace *The Lamentation of Doctor Faustus* as the most appropriate spiritual expression of the German people.[23]

Georg Lukács provides an alternate reading of *Doctor Faustus* that stresses the novel's continuities with, as well as its departures from, the classical *Bildungsroman* tradition. In his essay "The Tragedy of Modern Art," he argues: "Even if we understand form in the widest possible sense there is nothing in common between [Mann's *Doctor Faustus*] and the Wilhelm Meister novels. . . . Despite the similarities in the problem and certain individual incidents it bears no resemblance to Goethe's works. The parallel is rather one of inner development which, translated into form, appears as an antithesis."[24] For Lukács, the outward differences in form are caused by material differences between Goethe's early and Mann's late bourgeois societies. Here, however, I wish to suggest that they result instead from a changed relationship to the legacy of historicism. Just as *Wilhelm Meister's Apprenticeship*, which moves beyond the eighteenth-century novel in its depiction of a hero who changes in dynamic accord with a changing world around him, gave a form to the "temporalization of history," so *Doctor Faustus*, which threatens historical movement with apocalyptic simultaneity, gives a form to the "crisis of historicism" of the mid-twentieth century.

---

22. Compare also the words that Leverkühn speaks a little later at Nepomuk's deathbed, drawn from the conclusion of Shakespeare's *The Tempest*, when Prospero releases Ariel from bondage: "Then to the elements. Be free, and fare thou well!" (503)

23. It is interesting to remember in this context that in the first years after the war the "Ode to Joy" was frequently intoned on public occasions as a substitute national anthem.

24. Lukács, *Essays on Thomas Mann*, 50.

Like Meinecke, then, Mann ultimately looks back toward Goethe in an attempt to find a remedy for troubled times.²⁵ The similarities end there, however. Meinecke's own position was one of full identification with the German people, mixed with the conviction that Nazism had been an external evil imposed by world-historical forces on an otherwise sound nation. As a result, his appeal to Goethe took the form of a true return to origins, and he regarded classical German humanism as an uncorrupted good. Thomas Mann, influenced in part by the dialectical thinking of his musical adviser, but more importantly also by his own exile experiences, thought very differently about the matter. Deprived of his citizenship, forced to live in hotel rooms and depend on private, institutional, and governmental patronage, he quickly acquired a much more conflicted understanding of what it meant to be German, an understanding perhaps best expressed by his famous statement in the *New York Times* of February 22, 1938: "[Exile] is hard to bear. But what makes it easier is the realization of the poisoned atmosphere in Germany. That makes it easier because it's actually no loss. Where I am, there is Germany. I carry my German culture in me. I have contact with the world and I do not consider myself fallen."²⁶ In an ingenious move, Mann simultaneously declares the duality of German culture (a "poisoned atmosphere" back home versus a redemptive version inside him) *and* its unity, because the inner Germany is the only one that matters. In a move that should be all too familiar by now, Mann here decouples national culture, which is portable, from the state institutions that attempt to control it, and unconsciously reproduces Goethe's formula for world literature. He remains defiantly German but understands this identity as the product of a cosmopolitan exchange of art and ideas.

Over the following years, Mann would significantly deepen his reflections on the contemporary meaning of German identity, first in the essay "Brother Hitler" (1938) and then in his masterful address "Germany and the Germans," delivered in Coolidge Auditorium at the Library of Congress on May 29, 1945. The latter in part resembles a reader's guide to Mann's as-yet-unfinished Faustus novel and is thus particularly suited to shed light on the compositional mysteries of this work. Mann's concluding insight follows:

> There are *not* two Germanys, a good one and a bad one, but only one, whose best turned into evil through devilish cunning. Wicked Germany is merely good Germany

---

25. As Jürgen Scharfschwerdt argues, "Viewed from [the perspective of the *Bildungsroman* critic], *Doctor Faustus* contains the question of a different future. When Leverkühn compares himself to Goethe's Wilhelm Meister, for instance, he thereby not only highlights the fundamental difference between his own situation and that of Wilhelm Meister, but by the specific nature of this correspondence also indirectly and in a very general fashion poses the question of a new future for the *Apprenticeship*, i.e. he interrogates the historical reality that gave rise to Goethe's novel and Wilhelm Meister's formative development" (*Thomas Mann und der deutsche Bildungsroman*, 244).

26. The phrase "Where I am, there is Germany" occurs in a number of Mann's writings of this period. See in this context Hermann Kurzke, *Thomas Mann: Das Leben als Kunstwerk* (Frankfurt am Main: Fischer, 1999), 450–51.

gone astray, good Germany in misfortune, in guilt, and in ruin. For that reason it is quite impossible for one born there simply to renounce the wicked, guilty Germany and to declare: "I am the good, the noble, the just Germany in the white robe; I leave it to you to exterminate the wicked one." Not a word of all that I have just told you about Germany or tried to indicate to you came out of alien, cool, objective knowledge, it is all within me, I have been through it all.[27]

While Thomas Mann, much like Meinecke, thus fully identifies with the German people, he also goes one courageous step further by accepting responsibility for the evils of Nazism, acknowledging that they have undeniable roots in German nature. At the same time, however, he resists the notion that Nazism was the inevitable product of a fundamentally diseased national character. Instead, "wicked Germany" is "good Germany gone astray, good Germany in misfortune, in guilt, and in ruin."

A similar dynamic is also at work in *Doctor Faustus*. Serenus Zeitblom and Adrian Leverkühn represent antithetical outlooks on life (humanistic culture versus cultic control), they formulate antithetical compositional principles (freedom in development versus "strict style"), and they summarize antithetical positions vis-à-vis history (historicism as an expression of creative striving versus historicism as the cause of fatalist resignation). And yet Mann neither takes sides with one of these positions, nor does he pit them against one another in a relentless struggle. Instead, as his "The Creation of *Doctor Faustus*" reiterates again and again, he approaches his novel under the guiding light of parody: a style of writing, in other words, in which utterances relentlessly foreground their own significance and, precisely in so doing, revert to their opposite. Zeitblom's attempt to portray Leverkühn's life through the form of the *Bildungsroman*, in which mature achievements can be traced back to earlier immature expressions, eventually modulates into the timelessness of allegorical correspondence. Simultaneously, Leverkühn's attempts to circumvent individuality and historicity through a modernist "strict style" guided by myth lead him to the greatest myth of them all: the romantic myth of human freedom.

Transposed to the level of genre analysis, these parodic reversals reveal Thomas Mann's struggles with the narrative form that for 150 years had been the single dominant vehicle by which German poets reflected on their place in history. Cognizant of the "crisis of historicism," Mann gave a powerful literary shape to his fear that a narrow-minded allegiance to the notion of national entelechies could lead to unspeakable evil. Equally cognizant, however, that the modernist ambition to replace development with myth as a structuring narrative principle had dangerous political implications, he rejected the "strict style" that he himself described so well

---

27. Thomas Mann, *Thomas Mann's Addresses Delivered at the Library of Congress: 1942–1949* (Washington, DC: Library of Congress, 1963), 64–65.

as a possible solution for his "work of dangerously advanced spiritualization." *Doctor Faustus* remains, in the end, *The Life of the German Composer Adrian Leverkühn as Told by a Friend*. After reading it, however, the simple notion of the integrity of a life, so fundamental to the more ambitious construction of the German *Bildungsroman*, is called into question. In more ways than one, *Doctor Faustus* really is what Thomas Mann said it was under the pretense of delivering a verdict on Hesse: a "work of old age" and a "late work of dangerously advanced spiritualization." It is, in short, a novel apocalypse: the moment in which the *Bildungsroman* submits to a final judgment—but also the moment in which it is resurrected in the ultimate act of redemption.

The Fiction of Closure: Some Reflections on Allegory and World Literature

Thomas Mann marks the endpoint of most traditional surveys of the German *Bildungsroman* just as surely as Johann Wolfgang von Goethe marks their beginning. My own study repeats this basic structure not because I believe the *Bildungsroman* to somehow come to a conclusion with Mann, but rather because *Doctor Faustus* explicitly returns to the historicist roots of the genre and thereby allows me to claim for my work the semblance of closure and totality that the novel of formation perennially undermines as mere fiction. History, in truth, always goes on, and so does the history of the *Bildungsroman*.

In this last section of the book, I nevertheless want to return to one of the methodological premises with which I began my study, and ask whether there isn't something final about *Doctor Faustus* after all, something that marks an irrevocable turning point in the formative tradition. I have in mind here the relationship between normativity and performativity, between theories that treat the *Bildungsroman* as an allegorical vehicle for the revelation of some essential trait (be it "national character," the "symbolic form of modernity," or "humanity as such") and my own approach, which sees the genre as an attempt to impose narrative meaning on the basically random movements of a larger collective through historical time. *Doctor Faustus* is, as the preceding sections have shown, an allegorical narrative. Adrian Leverkühn isn't just any random character; he *is* Germany, in the sense that specific episodes in his artistic biography can be mapped onto equally specific episodes in German history.

At least two problems immediately arise in this context, however. The first is that Mann's allegory is undeniably polysemous, pairing each signifier with a number of different signifieds. Thus Leverkühn's life can be matched with concurrent events in German intellectual culture between 1900 and 1933, but also with events in Nietzsche's biography during the late nineteenth century and with broader epochs in German history from the Middle Ages to the present. Fredric Jameson has even applied the early Christian model of a fourfold exegetical scheme to *Doctor Faustus*, thereby refuting the necessary link between Leverkühn's biography and the development of "modern society" that is demanded by Jed Esty's notion of the "soul-nation allegory."[28] Indeed, how precisely would one measure such a social trajectory? Over the span of a thousand years, as is suggested by the equation drawn between Leverkühn's childhood home at Kaisersaschern and the figure of Otto III, Holy Roman Emperor from 996 to 1002, or just over the span of fifty, which is roughly the period covered by the novel? Related to this is a second problem, namely that *Doctor Faustus* breaks with the "aesthetic ideology" supposedly at work in the classical *Bildungsroman* by not moving toward a vision of plenitude and fulfillment, but rather one of madness and catastrophe. Mann's novel presents an etiology of fascism, and thus ultimately of a modernity that (to borrow from Horkheimer and Adorno) has turned in on itself, collapsing into its opposite. The same problems that Jeffrey L. Sammons uncovered at the heart of the formative tradition, leading him to declare the *Bildungsroman* a "missing genre," render this particular text a literary triumph.

Doctor Faustus thus represents an unusual form of allegorical narrative, one that attacks the very notion of a referential stability on which allegory is originally founded. And yet I would nevertheless argue that this novel, far from representing merely an extreme example of modernist literary vertigo (another sense in which we might read Mann's reference to a "late work of dangerously advanced spiritualization"), actually succeeds in articulating a cogent critique of the peculiar conditions that would come to dominate literary production in the second half of the twentieth century. *Doctor Faustus* does not merely diagnose a lacuna at the heart of traditional historicism; it also looks as resolutely into the future as any other *Bildungsroman* did before it.

To understand why this is so, it is necessary to delve even further into the perplexing layers of allegorical meaning that structure this novel. According to Jameson, the narrative level that we would ordinarily associate with the "literal" or "referential" in conventional texts, namely the biography of Adrian Leverkühn, should actually be read as a first layer of allegory. The only thing that is literal in the novel is the account of its own creation, namely Zeitblom's bracketing narrative about his authorial struggles in Freising near the end of the Second World War. The reason for this is that Zeitblom was rarely actually present during the most important formative episodes of Leverkühn's adult life. He is thus forced to abandon the mimetic pretensions of traditional realist narrative (according to which the descriptive sentences possess a kind of indexical force, rendering a true and literal representation of what was actually there) and substitute for them a series of "just-so" stories that logically and consistently represent how events *could* have been.

It is possible to translate Jameson's insight about a fundamental shift from mimesis to diegesis in *Doctor Faustus* into the vocabulary of theatrical representation,

---

28. Fredric Jameson, "Allegory and History: On Reading *Doktor Faustus*," in *The Modernist Papers* (London: Verso, 2007), 113–33.

and to thereby connect it to my understanding of the *Bildungsroman* as a "performative" genre that does not merely aim to represent, but rather strives to construct an ordered historical reality. Indeed, Zeitblom's constant assurances and disclaimers about what he did and did not witness bear a distinct resemblance to the antitheatricality of much modernist drama (and of Brechtian "epic theater" in particular), which also tries to assure the audience of the meaningfulness of what it is about to enact even as it abjures the conventions of traditional "realist" staging. In other words, unlike traditional allegorical narratives, which simply demand to be taken at face value, *Doctor Faustus* reminds its readers of the performative character of what is about to transpire, and thereby emphasizes that meaning is something to be created rather than merely revealed over the course of the narrative.

Jameson further points out that Zeitblom's remove from the narrative is fundamentally also that of Thomas Mann as he tried to narrate the historical destiny of the German people from the vantage point of an émigré in Pacific Palisades. Mann ultimately, and perhaps somewhat naïvely, sought to cut through this Gordian knot of entwined allegories with the declaration "Where I am, there is Germany." But merely by making such a statement, Mann already testified to a condition that is now widely recognized as one of the distinguishing features of world literature in the late twentieth century, namely the increasing dual remove between writers and the national communities for which they purport to speak on the one hand, and between writers and their intended audience on the other. Over the last half century, it has practically become a norm for writers, especially those who hail from developing countries or from linguistic groups that aren't large enough to sustain an independent publishing industry, to write not for a national community, but for an amorphous international audience. At the same time, censorship, political oppression, or simple poverty frequently makes it impossible for many national communities to read the novels in which their own historical trajectory is ostensibly depicted. Thomas Mann, celebrated in America as the cultural ambassador of a nation that could, in turn, listen to his words only in the form of "enemy broadcasts," is perhaps the first fully formed example of this intellectual condition, just as *Doctor Faustus* is the first mature literary reflection on it.

Roughly twenty-five years ago, in an address written to celebrate the birth of the literature program at Duke University, Fredric Jameson faulted previous students of what he called "Third-World Literature" for their tendency to reductively interpret foreign national traditions according to a simple allegorical schema based on the protagonists' efforts to acquire an education under conditions of colonial domination.[29] *Doctor Faustus*, on the other hand, suggests a different way in which we might conceptualize the relationship between allegory and the novel

---

29. Fredric Jameson, "On Literary and Cultural Import-Substitution in the Third World: The Case of the Testimonio," in *The Real Thing: Testimonial Discourse and Latin America*, ed. Georg M. Gugelberger (Durham, NC: Duke University Press, 1996), 173.

of formation: not as a means to render visible what Jameson called the "life-and-death struggle with first-world cultural imperialism," but rather as an attempt by deracinated writers to draw attention to the performative nature of their own literary activity.[30] The contemporary global *Bildungsroman* insists on its poetic fidelity to the historical rhythm of the community from which it has ostensibly sprung, but in the very act of this insistence also acknowledges the quite different conditions under which it was actually created and will inevitably also be consumed. In this way, nationalism and cosmopolitanism become one and the same, and the *Bildungsroman* affirms a place in world literature that in reality it possessed all along.

---

30. Fredric Jameson, "Third-World Literature in the Age of Multi-National Capitalism," *Social Text* 15 (1986): 68.

Bibliography

Adelung, Johann Christoph. *Grammatisch-kritisches Wörterbuch der hochdeutschen Mundart.* 3rd ed. Leipzig, 1811. Münchener DigitalisierungsZentrum der Bayerischen Staatsbibliothek. http://lexika.digitale-sammlungen.de/adelung/online/angebot.
Anderson, Amanda. *The Powers of Distance: Cosmopolitanism and the Cultivation of Detachment.* Princeton, NJ: Princeton University Press, 2001.
Anderson, Benedict. *Imagined Communities: Reflections on the Origin and Spread of Nationalism.* London: Verso, 1983.
——. *The Spectre of Comparisons: Nationalism, Southeast Asia, and the World.* London: Verso, 1998.
Antoni, Carlo. *From History to Sociology: The Transition in German Historical Thinking.* Trans. Hayden V. White. Detroit: Wayne State University Press, 1959.
Appadurai, Arjun. *Modernity at Large: Cultural Dimensions of Globalization.* Minneapolis: University of Minnesota Press, 1996.
Appiah, Kwame Anthony. *Cosmopolitanism: Ethics in a World of Strangers.* New York: Norton, 2006.
Aristotle. *Poetics.* Trans. Richard Janko. Indianapolis: Hackett Publishing Company, 1987.
Auerbach, Erich. *Mimesis: The Representation of Reality in Western Literature.* Trans. Willard R. Trask. Princeton, NJ: Princeton University Press, 1968.
Bakhtin, Mikhail. "The *Bildungsroman* and Its Significance in the History of Realism." In *Speech Genres and Other Late Essays*, trans. Vern W. McGee and ed. Caryl Emerson and Michael Holquist, 10–59. Austin: University of Texas Press, 1986.
Bayly, C. A. *The Birth of the Modern World, 1780–1914: Global Connections and Comparisons.* Oxford: Blackwell Publishers, 2003.

Beddow, Michael. *The Fiction of Humanity: Studies in the Bildungsroman from Wieland to Thomas Mann.* Cambridge: Cambridge University Press, 1982.

Beecroft, Alexander. "World Literature without a Hyphen: Towards a Typology of Literary Systems." *New Left Review* 54 (2008): 87–100.

Beer, Gillian. *Darwin's Plots: Evolutionary Narrative in Darwin, George Eliot, and Nineteenth-Century Fiction.* Cambridge: Cambridge University Press, 1983.

Benjamin, Walter. "Crisis of the Novel." In *Selected Writings*, trans. Rodney Livingstone et al. and ed. Michael W. Jennings, Howard Eiland, and Gary Smith, vol. 2, *1927–1930*, 299–304. Cambridge, MA: Harvard University Press, 1999.

———. *Illuminations.* Trans. Harry Zohn. Ed. Hannah Arendt. New York: Schocken, 1968.

Bergsten, Gunilla. *Thomas Mann's "Doctor Faustus": The Sources and Structure of the Novel.* Trans. Krishna Winston. Chicago: University of Chicago Press, 1963.

Berlin, Isaiah. *The Roots of Romanticism.* Princeton, NJ: Princeton University Press, 2001.

Berman, Russell A. *The Rise of the Modern German Novel: Crisis and Charisma.* Cambridge, MA: Harvard University Press, 1986.

Bhabha, Homi K. "Unsatisfied: Notes on Vernacular Cosmopolitanism." In *Postcolonial Discourses: An Anthology*, ed. Gregory Castle, 39–52. Oxford: Blackwell, 2001.

Blanckenburg, Friedrich von. *Versuch über den Roman.* Stuttgart: Metzler, 1965. Facsimile of the original edition of 1774.

Bloch, Ernst. "Discussing Expressionism." In *Aesthetics and Politics*, ed. Ronald Taylor, 16–27. London: Verso, 1980.

———. *Heritage of Our Times.* Trans. Neville Plaice and Stephen Plaice. Berkeley: University of California Press, 1990.

———. "Non-Synchronism and the Obligation to Its Dialectics." Trans. Mark Ritter. *New German Critique* 11 (Spring 1977): 22–38.

Bloom, Harold. *The Anxiety of Influence: A Theory of Poetry.* New York: Oxford University Press, 1973.

Bollenbeck, Georg. *Bildung und Kultur: Glanz und Elend eines deutschen Deutungsmusters.* Frankfurt am Main: Insel Verlag, 1994.

Bramsted, Ernest K. *Aristocracy and the Middle-Classes in Germany: Social Types in German Literature, 1830–1900.* Chicago: University of Chicago Press, 1964.

Brooks, Peter. *The Novel of Worldliness.* Princeton, NJ: Princeton University Press, 1969.

———. *Realist Vision.* New Haven, CT: Yale University Press, 2005.

Bruford, W. H. *The German Tradition of Self-Cultivation: 'Bildung' from Humboldt to Thomas Mann.* Cambridge: Cambridge University Press, 1975.

Brunner, Otto, Werner Conze, and Reinhart Koselleck, eds. *Geschichtliche Grundbegriffe: Historisches Lexikon zur politisch-sozialen Sprache in Deutschland.* 8 vols. Stuttgart: Klett, 1972–97.

Buckley, Jerome. *Season of Youth: The Bildungsroman from Dickens to Golding.* Cambridge, MA: Harvard University Press, 1974.

Castle, Gregory. *Reading the Modernist Bildungsroman.* Gainesville: University Press of Florida, 2006.

Cheah, Pheng. "Introduction Part II: The Cosmopolitical–Today." In *Cosmopolitics: Thinking and Feeling beyond the Nation*, ed. Pheng Cheah and Bruce Robbins, 20–44. Minneapolis: University of Minnesota Press, 1998.

———. *Spectral Nationality: Passages of Freedom from Kant to Postcolonial Literatures of Liberation.* New York: Columbia University Press, 2004.

Clark, Mark W. *Beyond Catastrophe: German Intellectuals and Cultural Renewal after World War II, 1945–1955*. Lexington, MA: Lexington Books, 2006.

Clifford, James. *Routes: Travel and Translation in the Twentieth Century*. Cambridge, MA: Harvard University Press, 1997.

Cocalis, Susan. "The Transformation of *Bildung* from an Image to an Ideal." *Monatshefte* 70 (1978): 399–414.

Cohen, Margaret. *The Sentimental Education of the Novel*. Princeton, NJ: Princeton University Press, 1999.

Cohen, Margaret, and Carolyn Dever, eds. *The Literary Channel: The Inter-National Invention of the Novel*. Princeton, NJ: Princeton University Press, 2002.

Cooppan, Vilashini. "Ghosts in the Disciplinary Machine: The Uncanny Life of World Literature." *Comparative Literature Studies* 41:1 (2004): 10–36.

Diderot, Denis. *Selected Writings on Art and Literature*. Trans. Geoffrey Bremner. London: Penguin Classics, 1994.

Dilthey, Wilhelm. *Selected Works*. Ed. Rudolf A. Makkreel and Frithjof Rodi. Vol. 5, *Poetry and Experience*. Princeton, NJ: Princeton University Press, 1985.

Dimock, Wai Chee. "Literature for the Planet." *PMLA* 116 (2001): 173–88.

Döblin, Alfred. *Berlin Alexanderplatz: The Story of Franz Biberkopf*. Trans. Eugene Jolas. New York: Frederick Ungar, 1983.

———. "Der Geist des naturalistischen Zeitalters." In *Schriften zu Ästhetik, Poetik und Literatur*, ed. Erich Kleinschmidt, 168–90. Olten: Walter-Verlag, 1989.

Dumont, Louis. *Homo aequalis II: L'idéologie allemande; France-Allemagne et retour*. Paris: Éditions Gallimard, 1991.

Eksteins, Modris. *Rites of Spring: The Great War and the Birth of the Modern Age*. Boston: Houghton Mifflin, 1989.

Eliot, George. *Daniel Deronda*. New York: Oxford World's Classics, 1988.

Eliot, T. S. *Selected Prose of T. S. Eliot*. Ed. Frank Kermode. Orlando, FL: Harcourt, 1975.

Esty, Jed. "The Colonial *Bildungsroman*: *The Story of an African Farm* and the Ghost of Goethe." *Victorian Studies* 49.3 (2007): 407–30.

———. *Unseasonable Youth: Modernism, Colonialism, and the Fiction of Development*. New York: Oxford University Press, 2011.

Fauser, Markus. *Intertextualität als Poetik des Epigonalen*. Munich: Wilhelm Fink, 1999.

Foucault, Michel. *Discipline & Punish: The Birth of the Prison*. New York: Vintage, 1977.

Fraiman, Susan. *Unbecoming Women: British Women Writers and the Novel of Development*. New York: Columbia University Press, 1993.

Freytag, Gustav. *Debit and Credit*. Trans. L. C. Cummings. Reprint, New York: Howard Fertig, Inc., 1990.

———. *Soll und Haben: Roman in sechs Büchern*. Waltrop: Manuscriptum, 2002.

Fries, Marilyn Sibley. "The City as Metaphor for the Human Condition: Alfred Döblin's *Berlin Alexanderplatz* (1929)." *Modern Fiction Studies* 24 (1978): 41–64.

Fritzsche, Peter. *Stranded in the Present: Modern Time and the Melancholy of History*. Cambridge, MA: Harvard University Press, 2004.

Gellner, Ernest. *Nations and Nationalism*. Ithaca, NY: Cornell University Press, 1983.

Gilbert, Sandra M., and Susan Gubar. *The Madwoman in the Attic: The Woman Writer and the Nineteenth-Century Literary Imagination*. New Haven, CT: Yale University Press, 1979.

Goethe, Johann Wolfgang von. *Collected Works*. Ed. Victor Lange, Eric A. Blackall, and Cyrus Hamlin. 12 vols. New York: Suhrkamp, 1983–89.

———. *Conversations with Eckermann (1823–1832)*. Trans. John Oxenford. San Francisco: North Point, 1984.
———. *Xenien und Votivtaveln*. In *Werke: Weimarer Ausgabe*, vol. I/5.1, *Gedichte, Fünfter Theil, Erste Abtheilung*, 203–313. Weimar: Böhlau, 1893.
Hadley, Michael. *The German Novel in 1790: A Descriptive Account and Critical Bibliography*. Bern: Herbert Lang, 1973.
Hake, Sabine. "Urban Paranoia in Alfred Döblin's *Berlin Alexanderplatz*." *The German Quarterly* 67:3 (Summer 1994): 347–50.
Hardt, Michael, and Antonio Negri. *Empire*. Cambridge, MA: Harvard University Press, 2000.
Hegel, Georg Wilhelm Friedrich. *Aesthetics: Lectures on Fine Art*. Trans. T. M. Knox. 2 vols. Oxford: Clarendon Press, 1975.
Heiderich, Manfred W. *The German Novel of 1800: A Study of Popular Prose Fiction*. Bern: Peter Lang, 1982.
Henry, Nancy. *George Eliot and the British Empire*. Cambridge: Cambridge University Press, 2002.
———. "George Eliot and Politics." In *The Cambridge Companion to George Eliot*, ed. George Levine, 138–58. Cambridge: Cambridge University Press, 2001.
Herder, Johann Gottfried. *Philosophical Writings*. Trans. Michael N. Forster. Cambridge: Cambridge University Press, 2002.
———. *Sämmtliche Werke*. Ed. Bernhard Suphan. 33 vols. Berlin: Weidmannsche Buchhandlung. 1877–1913.
Hohendahl, Peter Uwe. *Building a National Literature: The Case of Germany, 1830–1870*. Trans. Renate Baron Franciscono. Ithaca, NY: Cornell University Press, 1989.
Howe, Susanne. *Wilhelm Meister and His English Kinsmen: Apprentices to Life*. New York: Columbia University Press, 1930.
Hubrich, Peter Heinz. *Gustav Freytags "Deutsche Ideologie" in "Soll und Haben."* Kronberg im Taunus: Scriptor, 1974.
Humboldt, Wilhelm von. "Über die Aufgabe des Geschichtsschreibers." In *Gesammelte Werke*, ed. Alexander von Humboldt and Carl Brandes, 1:1–25. Photomechanical reprint, Berlin: Walter de Gruyter, 1988.
Hunt, Lynn. *The Family Romance of the French Revolution*. Berkeley: University of California Press, 1992.
Iggers, Georg. *The German Conception of History: The National Tradition of Historical Thought from Herder to the Present*. Middleton, CT: Wesleyan University Press, 1968.
Immermann, Karl. *Die Epigonen: Familienmemoiren in neun Büchern, 1823–1835*. Ed. Peter Hasubek. Munich: Winkler Verlag, 1981.
———. *Die Jugend vor fünfundzwanzig Jahren*. In *Werke in fünf Bänden*, ed. Benno von Wiese, vol. 4, *Autobiographische Schriften*, 357–547. Frankfurt am Main: Athenäum. 1973.
Jacobs, Jürgens. *Wilhelm Meister und seine Brüder: Untersuchungen zum deutschen Bildungsroman*. Munich: Fink, 1972.
Jameson, Fredric. *The Modernist Papers*. London: Verso, 2007.
———. "On Literary and Cultural Import-Substitution in the Third World: The Case of the Testimonio." In *The Real Thing: Testimonial Discourse and Latin America*, ed. Georg M. Gugelberger, 172–91. Durham, NC: Duke University Press, 1996.
———. *The Political Unconscious: Narrative as a Socially Symbolic Act*. Ithaca, NY: Cornell University Press, 1981.

———. *Postmodernism: Or, The Cultural Logic of Late Capitalism*. Durham, NC: Duke University Press, 1991.

———. *A Singular Modernity: Essay on the Ontology of the Present*. London: Verso, 2002.

———. "Third-World Literature in the Age of Multi-National Capitalism." *Social Text* 15 (1986): 65–88.

Joyce, James. "A Portrait of the Artist." In *The Workshop of Daedalus: James Joyce and the Raw Materials for "A Portrait of the Artist as a Young Man,"* ed. Robert Scholes and Richard M. Kain, 56–74. Evanston, IL: Northwestern University Press, 1965.

———. *A Portrait of the Artist as a Young Man*. London: Penguin, 1993.

———. *Ulysses*. Gabler ed. New York: Vintage, 1986.

Kahler, Erich. "The Secularization of the Devil: Thomas Mann's *Doctor Faustus*." In *The Orbit of Thomas Mann*, 20–43. Princeton, NJ: Princeton University Press, 1969.

Kant, Immanuel. "An Idea Towards a Universal History in a Cosmopolitan Sense." In *Theories of History*, ed. Patrick Gardiner, 22–34. New York: Free Press, 1959.

Kasack, Hermann. "Mosaik: Briefe zu Döblins *Alexanderplatz*." In *Materialien zu Alfred Döblin, Berlin Alexanderplatz*, ed. Matthias Prangel, 60–61. Frankfurt am Main: Suhrkamp, 1975.

Klopstock, Friedrich Gottlieb. *Ausgewählte Werke*. Ed. Karl August Schleiden. Munich: Carl Hanser Verlag, 1962.

Kontje, Todd. *The German Bildungsroman: History of a National Genre*. Columbia, SC: Camden House, 1993.

———. *Private Lives in the Public Sphere: The German Bildungsroman as Metafiction*. University Park: Pennsylvania State University Press, 1992.

Kopp, Kristin. "Ich stehe jetzt hier als einer von den Eroberern: *Soll und Haben* als Kolonialroman." In *150 Jahre "Soll und Haben": Studien zu Gustav Freytags kontroversem Roman*, ed. Florian Krobb, 225–38. Würzburg: Königshausen & Neumann, 2005.

Koselleck, Reinhart. *Futures Past: On the Semantics of Historical Time*. Trans. Keith Tribe. New York: Columbia University Press, 2004.

Kurzke, Hermann. *Thomas Mann: Das Leben als Kunstwerk*. Frankfurt am Main: Fischer, 1999.

Lämmert, Eberhard. "Zum Wandel der Geschichtserfahrung im Reflex der Romantheorie." In *Geschichte: Ereignis und Erzählung*, ed. Reinhart Koselleck and Wolf-Dieter Stempel, 503–15. Munich: Wilhelm Fink Verlag, 1973.

Lauster, Martina. "Einführung." In *Deutschland und der europäische Zeitgeist*, ed. Martina Lauster, 9–26. Bielefeld: Aisthesis, 1994.

Leavis, F. R. *The Great Tradition: George Eliot, Henry James, Joseph Conrad*. New York: New York University Press, 1963.

Lefebvre, Henri. *Rhythmanalysis: Space, Time, and Everyday Life*. Trans. Stuart Elden and Gerald Moore. London: Continuum, 2004.

Lewis, Pericles. *Modernism, Nationalism, and the Novel*. Cambridge: Cambridge University Press, 2000.

———. *Religious Experience and the Modernist Novel*. Cambridge: Cambridge University Press, 2010.

Löwith, Karl. *Meaning in History: The Theological Implications of the Philosophy of History*. Chicago: University of Chicago Press, 1949.

Lukács, Georg. *The Theory of the Novel: A Historico-Philosophical Essay on the Epic Forms of Great Literature*. Trans. Anna Bostock. Cambridge, MA: MIT Press, 1971.

———. "The Tragedy of Modern Art." In *Essays on Thomas Mann*, trans. Stanley Mitchell, 47–97. London: Merlin Press, 1964.

Mahoney, Dennis. "The Apprenticeship of the Reader: The *Bildungsroman* of the 'Age of Goethe.'" In *Reflection and Action: Essays on the Bildungsroman*, ed. James Hardin, 97–117. Columbia: University of South Carolina Press, 1991.

———. "The French Revolution and the *Bildungsroman*." In *The French Revolution and the Age of Goethe*, ed. Gerhart Hoffmeister, 127–43. Hildesheim: Georg Holms AG, 1989.

Mann, Thomas. *Doctor Faustus: The Life of the German Composer Adrian Leverkühn as Told by a Friend*. Trans. John E. Woods. New York: Alfred A. Knopf, 1997.

———. *Gesammelte Werke in dreizehn Bänden*. Ed. Peter de Mendelssohn. Frankfurt am Main: Fischer, 1990.

———. *Thomas Mann's Addresses Delivered at the Library of Congress: 1942–1949*. Washington, DC: Library of Congress, 1963.

Mannheim, Karl. *Essays on the Sociology of Knowledge*. London: Routledge, 1952.

Marx, Karl, and Friedrich Engels. *The Communist Manifesto*. London: Penguin, 1986.

May, Anja. *Wilhelm Meisters Schwestern: Bildungsromane von Frauen im ausgehenden 18. Jahrhundert*. Königstein im Taunus: Helmer, 2006.

Mayer, Hans. *Thomas Mann*. Frankfurt am Main: Suhrkamp, 1980.

———. *Von Lessing bis Thomas Mann: Wandlungen der bürgerlichen Literatur in Deutschland*. Pfullingen: Neske, 1959.

Meinecke, Friedrich. *The German Catastrophe: Reflections and Recollections*. Trans. Sidney B. Fay. Cambridge, MA: Harvard University Press, 1950.

———. *Historism: The Rise of a New Historical Outlook*. New York: Herder and Herder, 1972.

———. "Klassizismus, Romantizismus und historisches Denken." In *Werke*, ed. Hans Herzfeld, Carl Hinrich, and Walther Hofer, vol. 4, *Zur Theorie und Philosophie der Geschichte*, ed. Eberhard Kessel, 264–78. Stuttgart: K. F. Koehler Verlag, 1959.

Mendelssohn, Moses. "Ueber die Frage: Was heißt aufklären?" In *Gesammelte Schriften: Jubiläumsausgabe*, ed. Alexander Altmann and Eva J. Engel, 6.1:113–20. Reprint, Stuttgart: Friedrich Frommann Verlag, 1971.

Meyer, Susan. *Imperialism at Home: Race and Victorian Women's Fiction*. Ithaca, NY: Cornell University Press, 1996.

Michels, Volker. *Materialien zu Hermann Hesses "Das Glasperlenspiel."* 2 vols. Frankfurt am Main: Suhrkamp, 1973.

Midgley, David. *Writing Weimar: Critical Realism in German Literature, 1918–1933*. New York: Oxford University Press, 2000.

Miles, David H. "The Picaro's Journey to the Confessional: The Changing Image of the Hero in the German *Bildungsroman*." *PMLA* 89 (1974): 980–92.

Mill, John Stuart. *On Liberty*. London: Penguin, 1974.

Minden, Michael. *The German Bildungsroman: Incest and Inheritance*. Cambridge: Cambridge University Press, 1997.

———. "Problems of Realism in Immermann's *Die Epigonen*." *Oxford German Studies* 16 (1985): 66–80.

Mitchell, Breon. *James Joyce and the German Novel, 1922–1933*. Athens, OH: Ohio University Press, 1976.

———. "*A Portrait* and the *Bildungsroman* Tradition." In *Approaches to Joyce's "Portrait": Ten Essays*, ed. Thomas F. Baley and Bernard Benstock, 61–76. Pittsburgh: University of Pittsburgh Press, 1976.

Montebello, Philippe de. "'And What Do You Propose Should Be Done with Those Objects?'" In *Whose Culture Is It? The Promise of Museums and the Debate over Antiquities*, ed. James Cuno, 55–70. Princeton, NJ: Princeton University Press, 2009.

Moretti, Franco. "Conjectures on World Literature." *New Left Review* 1 (2000): 54–68.

———. *The Way of the World: The Bildungsroman in European Culture*. Trans. Albert Sbragia. New ed. London: Verso, 2000.

Morgenstern, Karl. "On the Nature of the *Bildungsroman*." Trans. Tobias Boes. *PMLA* 124 (2009): 647–59.

Neubuhr, Elfried. "Einführung." In *Begriffsbestimmung des literarischen Biedermeier*, ed. Elfriede Neubuhr, 1–12. Darmstadt: Wissenschaftliche Buchgesellschaft, 1974.

Norton, Robert E. *The Beautiful Soul: Aesthetic Morality in the Eighteenth Century*. Ithaca, NY: Cornell University Press, 1995.

Osterhammel, Jürgen. *Die Verwandlung der Welt: Eine Geschichte des 19. Jahrhunderts*. Munich: C. H. Beck, 2009.

Ozouf, Mona. "Revolution." In *A Critical Dictionary of the French Revolution*, ed. François Furet and Mona Ozouf and trans. Arthur Goldhammer, 806–17. Cambridge, MA: Harvard University Press, 1989.

Petrey, Sandy. *Realism and Revolution: Balzac, Stendhal, Zola, and the Performances of History*. Ithaca, NY: Cornell University Press, 1988.

Pfau, Thomas. "Of Ends and Endings: Teleological and Variational Models of Romantic Narrative." *European Romantic Review* 18:2 (April 2007): 231–41.

Ping, Larry L. *Gustav Freytag and the Prussian Gospel: Novels, Liberalism, and History*. Frankfurt am Main: Peter Lang, 2006.

Popper, Karl. *The Poverty of Historicism*. Boston: Beacon Press, 1957.

Qualls, Barry. "George Eliot and Religion." In *The Cambridge Companion to George Eliot*, ed. George Levine, 119–37. Cambridge: Cambridge University Press, 2001.

Ramponi, Patrick. "Orte des Globalen: Zur Poetik der Globalisierung in der Literatur des deutschsprachigen Realismus (Freytag, Raabe, Fontane)." In *Poetische Ordnungen: Zur Erzählprosa des deutschen Realismus*, ed. Ulrich Kittstein and Stefani Kugler, 17–60. Würzburg: Königshausen & Neumann, 2007.

Redfield, Marc. *Phantom Formations: Aesthetic Ideology and the Bildungsroman*. Ithaca, NY: Cornell University Press, 1996.

Reid, James H. "*Berlin Alexanderplatz*: A Political Novel." *German Life and Letters* 21 (1968): 214–23.

Richards, Robert J. *The Romantic Conception of Life: Science and Philosophy in the Age of Goethe*. Chicago: University of Chicago Press, 2002.

Robbins, Bruce. *Secular Vocations: Intellectuals, Professionalism, Culture*. New York: Verso, 1993.

Robertson, Ritchie. "Accounting for History: Thomas Mann, *Doktor Faustus*." In *The German Novel in the Twentieth Century: Beyond Realism*, ed. David Midgley, 128–48. Edinburgh: Edinburgh University Press, 1993.

Rosenkranz, Karl. "Einleitung über den Roman." In *Zur Geschichte des deutschen Bildungsromans*, ed. Rolf Selbmann, 100–119. Darmstadt: Wissenschaftliche Buchgesellschaft, 1988.

Ryan, Judith. *The Uncompleted Past: Postwar German Novels and the Third Reich*. Detroit: Wayne State University Press, 1983.

Safranski, Rüdiger. *Romantik: Eine deutsche Affäre*. Munich: Hanser, 2007.

Said, Edward. *The World, the Text, and the Critic*. Cambridge, MA: Harvard University Press, 1983.

Saint-Amour, Paul K. "Airwar Prophecy and Interwar Modernism." *Comparative Literature Studies* 42:2 (2005): 130–61.

Sammons, Jeffrey L. "The Bildungsroman for Nonspecialists: An Attempt at a Clarification." In *Reflection and Action: Essays on the Bildungsroman*, ed. James N. Hardin, 26–45. Columbia: University of South Carolina Press, 1991.

———. "Heuristic Definition and the Constraints of Literary History: Some Recent Discourses on the *Bildungsroman* in English and German." In *Dazwischen: Zum transitorischen Denken in Literatur-und Kulturwissenschaft*, ed. Andreas Härter et al., 173–82. Göttingen: Vandenhoeck & Ruprecht, 2003.

———. "The Mystery of the Missing *Bildungsroman*, or: What Happened to Wilhelm Meister's Legacy?" *Genre* 14:1 (1981): 229–46.

———. "The Nineteenth-Century German Novel." In *German Literature of the Nineteenth Century*, ed. Clayton Koelb and Eric Downing, 183–206. Columbia, SC: Camden House, 2005.

———. *Six Essays on the Young German Novel*. Chapel Hill: University of North Carolina Press, 1972.

Sassen, Saskia. "Spatialities and Temporalities of the Global: Elements for a Theorization." *Public Culture* 12:1 (2000): 215–32.

Schaarschmidt, Ilse. "Der Bedeutungswandel der Begriffe 'Bildung' und 'bilden' in der Literaturepoche von Gottsched bis Herder." In *Beiträge zur Geschichte des Bildungsbegriffs*, ed. Franz Rauhut and Ilse Schaarschmidt, 28–36. Weinheim: Verlag Julius Belz, 1965.

Scharfschwerdt, Jürgen. *Thomas Mann und der deutsche Bildungsroman: Eine Untersuchung zu den Problemen einer literarischen Tradition*. Stuttgart: W. Kohlhammer, 1967.

Scheffler, Karl. *Berlin: Ein Stadtschicksal*. Berlin: Fanei & Walz Verlag, 1989.

Schiller, Friedrich. *Letters on the Aesthetic Education of Man*. Trans. Elizabeth M. Wilkinson and L. A. Willoughby. In *Essays*, ed. Walter Hinderer and Daniel O. Dahlstrom, 86–178. New York: Continuum, 1993.

Schlegel, Friedrich. *Philosophical Fragments*. Trans. Peter Firchow. Minneapolis: University of Minnesota Press, 1991.

Schor, Naomi. *George Sand and Idealism*. New York: Columbia University Press, 1993.

Schwartz, Frederic J. "Ernst Bloch and Wilhelm Pinder: Out of Sync." *Grey Room* 3 (2001): 54–89.

Scott, Walter. *Waverley*. London: Penguin, 1980.

Sheehan, Tom. "Colonial Rhythms." Unpublished manuscript, circulated at MSA conference, November 2005. Microsoft Word file.

Shuttleworth, Sally. *George Eliot and Nineteenth-Century Science: The Make-Believe of a Beginning*. Cambridge: Cambridge University Press, 1987.

Simmel, Georg. "The Metropolis and Mental Life." In *Georg Simmel on Individuality and Social Forms*, ed. Donald N. Levine, 324–39. Chicago: University of Chicago Press, 1971.

Slaughter, Joseph R. *Human Rights, Inc.: The World Novel, Narrative Form, and International Law*. New York: Fordham University Press, 2007.

Solheim, Birger. *Zum Geschichtsdenken Theodor Fontanes und Thomas Manns: oder, Geschichtskritik in "Der Stechlin" und "Doktor Faustus."* Würzburg: Königshausen & Neumann, 2004.

Spiegel, Gabrielle M. "Genealogy: Form and Function in Medieval Historical Narrative." *History and Theory* 22:1 (1983): 43–53.

Spitzer, Alan B. *The French Generation of 1820*. Princeton, NJ: Princeton University Press, 1987.

Stahl, Ernst Ludwig. *Die religiöse und die humanitätsphilosophische Bildungsidee und die Entstehung des deutschen Bildungsromans im 18. Jahrhundert*. Bern: Paul Haupt, 1934.

Steinecke, Hartmut. "The Novel and the Individual: The Significance of Goethe's *Wilhelm Meister* in the Debate about the *Bildungsroman*." In *Reflection and Action: Essays on the Bildungsroman*, ed. James Hardin, 69–96. Columbia: University of South Carolina Press, 1991.

———. "Die 'Zeitgemässe' Gattung: Neubewertung und Neubestimmung des Romans in der jungdeutschen Kritik." In *Untersuchungen zur Literatur als Geschichte*, ed. Vincent J. Günther, 325–46. Berlin: Erich Schmidt Verlag, 1973.

Stendhal. *The Red and the Black*. Trans. Robert M. Adams and ed. Susanna Lee. New York: Norton, 2008.

Süss, Wilhelm. "Karl Morgenstern: Ein kulturhistorischer Versuch." *Acta et Commentationes Universitatis Tartuensis (Dorpatensis)* 16.B (1929): 1–160.

Swales, Martin. *The German Bildungsroman from Wieland to Hesse*. Princeton, NJ: Princeton University Press, 1978.

———. *Studies of German Prose Fiction in the Age of European Realism*. Lampeter, Wales: Edwin Mellen Press, 1995.

Travers, Martin. "Thomas Mann, *Doktor Faustus*, and the Historians: The Function of 'Anachronistic Symbolism.'" In *The Modern German Historical Novel: Paradigms, Problems, and Perspectives*, ed. David Roberts and Philip Thomson, 145–59. New York: Berg, 1991.

Vogl, Joseph. *Kalkül und Leidenschaft: Poetik des ökonomischen Menschen*. Munich: Sequenzia Verlag, 2002.

Vosskamp, Wilhelm. *Der Roman des Lebens: Die Aktualität der Bildung und ihre Geschichte im Bildungsroman*. Berlin: Berlin University Press, 2009.

Walkowitz, Rebecca. *Cosmopolitan Style: Modernism beyond the Nation*. New York: Columbia University Press, 2008.

Werber, Niels. *Die Geopolitik der Literatur: Eine Vermessung der medialen Weltraumordnung*. Munich: Carl Hanser Verlag, 2007.

Wieland, Christoph Martin. "Über das Historische im Agathon." In *Werke*, ed. Gonthier-Luis Fink, Manfred Fuhrmann, et al., vol. 3, *Geschichte des Agathon*, ed. Klaus Manger, 573–85. Frankfurt am Main: Deutscher Klassiker Verlag, 1986.

Wilde, Oscar. *The Artist as Critic: Critical Writings of Oscar Wilde*. Ed. Richard Ellmann. Chicago: University of Chicago Press, 1969.

Windfuhr, Manfred. "Der Epigone: Begriff, Phänomen und Bewußtsein." *Archiv für Begriffsgeschichte* 4 (1959): 182–209.

Wohlfarth, Marc E. "Daniel Deronda and the Politics of Nationalism." *Nineteenth-Century Literature* 53:2 (1998): 188–210.

Index

academia, world of, 2, 4–5, 35–36
Acton, Lord, 123
Adams, Robert M., 85
Addresses to the German Nation (Fichte, 1808), 18
Adelung, Johann Christoph, 47–48
Adorno, Theodor W., 161, 172, 179
Adventures of Telemachus, The (Fénelon, 1699), 53
aesthetic theories of Hegel, 13–18, 21–22
allegory, *Bildungsroman* as, 20–21, 175, 178–80
almanac, history viewed as, 55–58
Amann, Paul, 166
American Civil War in *Daniel Deronda,* 117, 119, 120
American outback cities, Berlin compared to, 142, 152
American settler fiction, *Debit and Credit* compared to, 113
Anderson, Benedict, 29, 33, 64, 68, 113–14, 138
Antoni, Carlo, 159n6, 160
Anxiety of Influence, The (Bloom, 1973), 40
apocalyptic temporality of *Doctor Faustus,* 155–58, 178
Appadurai, Arjun, 2, 41, 138
Aristotle and Aristotelianism, 56, 57

asynchronicity, Bloch's model of, 27, 45, 75, 130–31, 136, 154, 157, 167, 169
Auerbach, Erich, 76–77, 78, 80
Austen, Jane, 55, 101, 116
Awkward Age, The (*Flegeljahre;* Paul, 1804), 17

Bakhtin, Mikhail, 6, 29–30, 133
Balzac, Honoré de, 45, 73–74, 78, 85, 87, 99, 101, 146
"Battle of the Nations," Leipzig, 82
Bayly, C. A., 79
Beddow, Michael, 24, 26
Beer, Gillian, 119
Beethoven, Ludwig van, 171–72
Being and Time (Heidegger, 1927), 159
Benjamin, Walter, 26, 33, 34n53, 56, 128–29, 142, 147, 156
Bentham, Jeremy, 43
Berlin, Isaiah, 52
Berlin Alexanderplatz (Döblin, 1929), 3, 8, 128–54; colonial city, Berlin as type of, 141–44; historicism of, 150; montage, use of, 130, 131, 144, 154; *Portrait of the Artist* compared and contrasted, 130–31, 153–54 (see also *Portrait*

Berlin Alexanderplatz (continued)
  of the Artist as a Young Man, A); time,
  narrative treatment of, 129–30; train-based
  slaughterhouse and dream sequence narratives
  in, 151–53; *Ulysses* and, 130–33, 137–41,
  144, 153–54, 173; urban environments and
  Bildungsroman tradition, 8, 128–29, 144–51,
  153–54; vernacular cosmopolitanism of, 143,
  153; "The Watch on the Rhine" (song) in,
  145–46, 147, 149; Weimar Republic in, 145–46,
  148, 150, 154
Berlin: Destiny of a City (Scheffler, 1910), 129,
  141–42
Berlin: Symphony of a Large City (film, 1927), 129
Bhabha, Homi K., 32–34, 64, 94, 133
Bildung, development of concept of, 46–53
Bildungsroman: as allegory, 20–21, 175,
  178–80; concept of term as inaugurated by
  Morgenstern, 1–3; defined, 1; essentialist
  versus universalist theories of, 3–5, 19–22,
  23, 35, 74–75, 103; genealogy of narrative
  and communal identity in, 9, 38–42, 69;
  generational consciousness and, 75–76, 82;
  logical endpoint of, 156, 173, 178; narrative
  voice in, 37–38; national literature, concept
  of, 4–5, 35–36; performative understanding
  of, 5, 7, 8, 28–31, 34, 42, 59–60, 68–69,
  178–81; "phantom" or "spectral" character
  attributed to, 4, 7, 25–26; totality, teleology,
  and objectivity/normativity, Hegel's aesthetics
  of, 13–16; urban environments and tradition
  of, 8, 128–29, 132–33, 144–51, 153–54;
  vernacular cosmopolitanism and, 1–3, 31–38;
  world literature and, 4–5, 9, 35–38. *See also*
  historicism; idealism; nationalism; *and specific
  Bildungsromane*
biology and *Bildung,* 50
Blanckenburg, Friedrich von, 14, 27, 58
Bloch, Ernst, 26–27, 30, 34n53, 45, 75, 130, 136,
  157, 167
Bloom, Harold, 280
Blue Angel, The (film, 1930), 149
Blumenbach, Johann Friedrich, 49, 50–51, 60, 68
Bollenbeck, Georg, 48
Bonn, Moritz Julius, 142
Border Herald, The (*Die Grenzboten;* literary
  journal), 103–4
Bourgeois Gentleman, The (Molière, 1670), 83
Bramsted, Ernest K., 93
Brecht, Bertolt, 26, 180
British realist literature, 73
Brontë, Charlotte, *Jane Eyre* (1847), 37

Brooks, Peter, 78
"Brother Hitler" (Mann, 1938), 176
Büchner, Georg, 73
Buckley, Jerome Hamilton, 132
Buddenbrooks (Mann, 1901), 102
Burney, Fanny, *Evelina* (1778), 54–55, 57
Burschenschaften, 60, 81n19

Cabinet of Dr. Caligari, The (film, 1920), 149
capitalism, merchant, as cultural good, *Debit and
  Credit* (Freytag, 1855) addressing, 103–9, 115–16
Carlsbad Decrees, 6, 60
Cassirer, Ernst, 24
Charterhouse of Parma, The (Stendhal, 1839), 73
Cheah, Pheng, 4n7, 23n24, 24n25, 25–26, 31
cinema, German, urban environments in, 129,
  149
cities. *See* urban environments
Clarissa (Richardson, 1748), 54
colonial and postcolonial literature: allegorical
  understanding of *Bildungsroman* and,
  20; Berlin as colonial city in *Berlin
  Alexanderplatz,* 141–44; genealogical approach
  to *Bildungsroman* and, 40–41; nation,
  Bildungsroman protagonist as personification
  of, 23n24; "phantom" or "spectral" character
  attributed to *Bildungsroman* and, 26; *Portrait of
  the Artist* as novel of colonial modernity, 130,
  131–37; *Ulysses,* colonial modernity of, 137–41.
  See also imperialism, modern
Confessions of a Nonpolitical Man (Mann, 1918),
  160, 167
Conversations with Eckermann (Goethe, 1827),
  35, 36
cosmopolitanism, vernacular. *See* vernacular
  cosmopolitanism
Cosmopolitanism and the National State
  (Meinecke, 1908), 161
cultural memory studies, 79
Cyropedia (Xenophon), 53

Daniel Deronda (Eliot, 1876), 3, 8, 101–7;
  American Civil War in, 117, 119, 120;
  aristocrats, attitudes toward, 120–21;
  chief characteristics of, 101; compared and
  contrasted with *Debit and Credit,* 3, 101–2,
  126 (see also *Debit and Credit*); doubling of
  Daniel and Gwendolen in, 118–19; Jews,
  attitudes toward, 101–2, 118, 120–27;
  liberal nationalism, crises of, 102–3; modern
  imperialism, as response to rise of, 8,
  102–3, 116–18, 127; Morant Bay rebellion

(1865), Jamaica, in, 102–3, 117, 119, 120; proto-Zionism in, 8, 102n1, 122; religion and nationalism, revitalization of, 121–27; Social Darwinism in, 8, 119–21; vernacular cosmopolitanism and, 103, 120–22, 125, 127; women, attitudes toward, 101–2, 118
Darwin, Charles, 119
Death in Venice (Mann, 1912), 169
Debit and Credit (Freytag, 1855), 3, 8, 101–27; agricultural section of, 113; American settler fiction, compared to, 113; aristocrats, attitudes toward, 107–8, 110, 115–16; compared and contrasted with *Daniel Deronda*, 3, 101–2, 126 (see also *Daniel Deronda*); cultural improvement, economic development, and colonialism, nexus between, 109–12; Jews, attitudes toward, 101–2, 107; liberal nationalism, crises of, 102–3; "long-distance nationalism" of, 113–15; merchant capitalism as cultural good in, 103–9, 115–16; modern imperialism, as response to rise of, 8, 102–5, 109–12, 114–16; Poland, Prussian occupation of, 104–5, 109–11; vernacular cosmopolitanism and, 103, 107, 108, 109, 112; women, attitudes toward, 101–2; "worldliness," attempts to link *Debit* to discourses of, 105n6, 108, 111–12
Decline of the West, The (Spengler, 1918), 160, 167
Defoe, Daniel, 62–63
De generis humani (Blumenbach, 1781), 50
Deleuze, Gilles, 150
Descent of Man, The (Darwin, 1871), 119
Dialectic of Enlightenment (Horkheimer and Adorno, 1947), 161
Dickens, Charles, 25, 37, 39–40, 73, 78, 85, 101, 146, 151
Diderot, Denis, 57
Dilthey, Wilhelm, 19, 21, 77, 80, 134n15, 159
Dimock, Wai Chee, 36
Döblin, Alfred: "The Spirit of the Naturalist Age" (1924), 141, 148. See also *Berlin Alexanderplatz*
Doctor Faustus (Mann, 1947), 8–9, 155–81; allegorical nature of, 21, 175, 178–80; apocalyptic temporality of, 155–58, 178; culture, freedom, and development in, 171–78; dodecaphony in, 157, 166, 171–73, 177; German identity and, 165, 167, 176–77, 179; historicism and, 157–58, 161, 165–70, 173, 175, 176; Kridwiss circle in, 157, 168–69; logical endpoint of *Bildungsroman* tradition and, 156, 173, 178; Meinecke and *The German Catastrophe*, 8, 158–66, 168, 174; myth in modern world, role of, 171, 173, 177; parodic aspects of, 166–67, 174, 177; performative understanding of *Bildungsroman* and, 178–81; *Wilhelm Meister* and, 9, 157–58, 175–76; World War II, Nazis, and Hitler, 156, 158, 161–66, 170, 176–77, 179
dodecaphony in *Doctor Faustus*, 157, 166, 171–73, 177
Dorpat, University of, 1–2

Eichendorff, Joseph von, 24
Eliot, George: concept of universal sequence and, 119n16; human bonds, ability to depict, 101; *The Mill on the Floss* (1860), 25. See also *Daniel Deronda*
Eliot, T.S., 173
Emma (Austen, 1815), 55
Engels, Friedrich, 27, 111–12
Enlightenment, 2, 47, 48
epigenesis, 50
Epigones, The (Immermann, 1836), 3, 8, 73–100; compared and contrasted with *The Red and the Black*, 82, 88–89, 91, 94, 95–96 (see also *Red and the Black, The*); definition and etymology of "epigone," 90–91; development of realist literature and, 73–76; family dynamics in, 96–98; generational consciousness and, 75–76, 81–82, 96; myth in modern world, role of, 99–100; national literature, concept of, 76–79, 82; picaresque and fragmented nature of, 88–89, 91–93; post-Napoleonic political geography, read as response to, 8, 76, 91–100; vernacular cosmopolitanism of, 79–82, 94; *Wilhelm Meister*, self-consciously imitative of, 73, 74, 89, 95
Erziehungsroman, 46
Essay on the Novel (Blankenburg, 1774), 58
essentialist versus universalist views of *Bildungsroman*, 3–5, 19–22, 23, 35, 74–75, 103
Esty, Jed, 9, 20, 21, 23, 25–26, 179
Evelina (Burney, 1778), 54–55
evolutionary theory and Social Darwinism in *Daniel Deronda*, 8, 119–21
expressionism debate, 26–27, 130

family romance: concept of, in *Wilhelm Meister*, 65–68; in *The Epigones* and *The Red and the Black*, 96–98
Faust (Goethe, 1832), 137, 165
Fénelon, François, 53
Fernandez de Lizardi, José Joaquín, 29
Fichte, Johann Gottlieb, 13, 18, 28, 58, 62

Fielding, Henry, 53–54, 55, 57, 73
film, German, urban environments in, 129, 149
First World War, 158, 160
Flaubert, Gustave, 25, 39–40, 132, 146
Foucault, Michel, 43, 45n3, 151
France: July Monarchy, 78; July Revolution (1830), 99; realist literature of (*see also* realist literature; *Red and the Black, The*)
Franche-Comté, setting of *The Red and the Black* in, 84
Franz Sternbald's Wanderings (Tieck, 1798), 17
Frederick William III (king of Prussia), 1
Freischütz, Der (Weber, 1821), 93
French Revolution, 17, 18, 58, 65, 80, 81, 83
Freytag, Gustav. See *Debit and Credit*
Fries, Marilyn Sibley, 129, 130, 133
Fritzsche, Peter, 8, 79–80, 94

Gellner, Ernest, 3, 31
genealogy of narrative and communal identity in *Bildungsroman*, 9, 38–42, 69
General Encyclopedia of the Arts and Sciences (Jablonski, 1748), 55–56
generational consciousness, 75–76, 81–82, 96
German Catastrophe, The (Meinecke, 1946), 8, 158, 161–66, 168, 174
German film, urban environments in, 129, 149
German historicism. See historicism
German idealism. See idealism
Germany: apocalyptic temporality of *Doctor Faustus* and, 156–57; essentialist versus universalist views of *Bildungsroman*, 3–5, 19–22; Holy Roman Empire, 16, 17, 18, 33, 60, 78, 82, 84, 91, 95; Mann's *Doctor Faustus* and German identity, 165, 167, 176–77, 179; Poland, Prussian occupation of, in *Debit and Credit*, 104–5, 109–11; political division, consequences of, 6, 8, 29–30; realist literature, development of, 73–76; revolution of 1848 in, 102–3, 104–5, 110; romantic nationalism of, tensions and contradictions within, 1–2, 20; Wars of Liberation in, 17, 60; Weimar Republic in *Berlin Alexanderplatz*, 145–46, 148, 150, 154; *Wilhelm Meister* as representation of "German life, German thought and the morals of our time," 1, 28, 52, 63–64, 68–69; World War I, 158, 160; World War II, Nazis, and Hitler, 156, 158, 161–66, 170, 176–77, 179
"Germany and the Germans" (Mann, 1945), 176–77
Geschichtlichkeit. See historicism
Glass Bead Game, The (Hesse, 1946), 37, 155–57, 166

globality, attempts to link *Debit and Credit* (Freytag, 1855) to discourses of, 105n6, 108, 111–12
globalization, Morgenstern's life as demonstration of, 2, 7
Goethe, Johann Wolfgang von: Bakhtin's analysis of, 29–30, 133; *Conversations with Eckermann* (1827) and concept of world literature, 35, 36; *Faust* (1832), 137, 165; *Italian Journey* (1817), 29; Joyce's exposure to, 134n15; *Wilhelm Meister's Wandering Years* (1821; revised version, 1829), 68; *Xenias* (1797), 30–31. See also *Wilhelm Meister's Apprenticeship*
"Goethe Communities," Meinecke's call for, 158, 164–65
Golden Mirror, The (Wieland, 1773), 53
Goyert, Georg, 131
Grammatico-Critical Dictionary of the High German Dialect (Adelung, 1774), 47–48
Great Expectations (Dickens, 1860–61), 25, 37, 146
Green Henry (Keller, 1879–80), 24, 37, 38
Guattari, Félix, 150

Hake, Sabine, 150
Hamlet scenes in *Wilhelm Meister,* 44, 60–61, 63, 65
Hardt, Michael, 111–12
Hardy, Thomas, 25
Hegel, Georg Wilhelm Friedrich, 3, 13–18, 21–22, 57, 59, 60, 115, 158n5, 159n6
Heidegger, Martin, 159
Heine, Heinrich, 73
Heinrich von Ofterdingen (Novalis, 1800), 17
Henry, Nancy, 116–17n12, 126
Herder, Johann Gottfried, 49, 51–52, 58, 60, 68, 159
Heritage of Our Times (Bloch, 1934), 26–27
Hesse, Hermann, 37, 155–58, 166, 178
historicism, 6, 7, 43–69; almanac, history viewed as, 55–58; of *Berlin Alexanderplatz*, 150; *Bildung*, development of concept of, 46–53; colonies, clash between lingering forms of historicity and new mechanical temporality in, 130; concept of, 48–49; contested narrative construct, *The Red and the Black*'s view of history as, 82–88; crisis of, 157–62, 166–67, 175; *Doctor Faustus* and, 157–58, 161, 165–70, 173, 175, 176; generational consciousness and, 75–76, 81–82, 96; *die Geschichte/Geschichten*, 55; Humboldt's theory of history and, 18–19; idealism and, 45, 59, 62, 68; of Meinecke, 48n10, 56, 161–65; nationalism, Herder's

connection to, 52–53; novels influenced by, 53–60; problems of idealist theory, as means of resolving, 26–31; relativism and, 159–60; structural change from hypotaxis to parataxis in *Wilhelm Meister* as expression of logic of, 43–46, 61, 67; *Ulysses* undermining, 140; urban environments and, 8; vernacular cosmopolitanism and, 33–34, 79–82, 160–61; of *Wilhelm Meister,* 5–6, 58, 68–69. *See also* time and temporality
History of Agathon, The (Wieland, 1766/1773), 53–55, 57, 60
History of Tom Jones, The (Fielding, 1749), 54
Hitler, Adolf, 156, 158, 161, 162, 164, 166, 170, 176
Hoffmann, E. T. A., 17
Holocaust, 162, 164
Holy Roman Empire, 16, 17, 18, 33, 60, 78, 82, 84, 91, 95
Homer, 14, 152, 173
Horkheimer, Max, 32, 161, 179
Human Comedy (Balzac, 1839), 45, 73
human rights law and *Bildungsroman,* 24, 26
Humboldt, Wilhelm von, 18–19, 28, 60
Hunt, Lynn, 65

idealism: German nationalist movement contrasted with, 163; historicism and, 45, 59, 62, 68; national or universal ideal, telos of *Bildung* associated with, 19–24; panentheistic approach to history and, 159; philosophical concept of *Bildung* and, 15–16; problematic fit of actual *Bildungsromans* with theories of, 4, 24, 26–28; realist literature and, 77n7, 81n19
"Idea Towards a Universal History in a Cosmopolitan Sense, An" (Kant, 1784), 31, 56
Idee der Staatsräson in der neueren Geschichte, Die (Meinecke, 1924), 158
Iggers, Georg, 159
Imagined Communities (Anderson, 1983), 29
Immermann, Karl Leberecht: generational consciousness of, 81–82; *The Youth of Twenty-Five Years Ago* (1840), 82, 96. See also *Epigones, The*
imperialism, modern: *Debit and Credit* and *Daniel Deronda* as responses to, 8, 102–5, 109–12, 114–18, 127; links between modernism and rise of imperialism, 130. *See also* colonial and postcolonial literature
Indian Summer (Stifter, 1857), 24
"In Praise of Richardson" (Diderot, 1762), 57

international human rights law and *Bildungsroman,* 24, 26
Italian Journey (Goethe, 1817), 29

Jablonski, Johann Theodor, 55–56
Jamaica, Morant Bay rebellion (1865) in, 102–3, 117, 119, 120
James, Henry, 101
James Joyce: A Critical Introduction (Levin, 1941), 173
Jameson, Fredric, 9, 20, 21, 40, 68, 130, 136, 178–81
Jane Eyre (Brontë, 1847), 37
Jena-Auerstedt, battle of, 18, 82
Jews and Judaism: in *Berlin Alexanderplatz,* 143; in *Debit and Credit* and *Daniel Deronda,* 101–2, 107, 118, 120–27; Meinecke's historicism and, 161–62, 164
Jolas, Eugene, 143
Joyce, James: *Bildungsroman* tradition and, 134n15; Mann and, 173–74; *Ulysses* (1918–20), 130–33, 137–40, 144, 153–54, 173. See also *Portrait of the Artist as a Young Man, A*
Jude the Obscure (Hardy, 1895), 25
July Monarchy, 78
July Revolution (1830), 99

Kahler, Erich, 156, 157n4, 167, 174
kalokagathia, 7, 49, 51, 54
Kant, Immanuel, 18, 31–32, 47n6, 56–57
Keller, Gottfried, *Green Henry* (1879–80), 24, 37, 38
Keyserling, Hermann Graf, 160
Klopstock, Friedrich Gottlieb, 48–51
Kontje, Todd, 4n6, 17, 39
Koselleck, Reinhart, 49, 55
Kridwiss circle in *Doctor Faustus,* 157, 168–69

Lang, Fritz, 129
Larbaud, Valery, 138
Lauster, Martina, 79, 80
Leaflets on German Art and Letters (Von deutscher Art und Kunst: Einige fliegende Blätter; Herder, 1773), 51–52
Leavis, F. R., 118
Lefebvre, Henri, 139
Letters on the Aesthetic Education of Man (Schiller, 1795), 16–18, 148
Levin, Harry, 173
Life and Opinions of the Tomcat Murr, The (Hoffmann, 1819–21), 17
life force, biological concept of, 50
Life of Henri Brulard (Stendhal, 1835–36), 82

Index

Louis Philippe (king of France), 99
Louis XIV (king of France), 84, 85
Louis XV (king of France), 87
Louis XVI (king of France), 86
Louis XVIII (king of France), 86
Löwith, Karl, 54–55
Lukács, Georg, 21–22, 26, 30, 57, 75, 130, 136, 156, 157, 175
Luther, Martin, 33, 164n11

M (film, 1931), 129
Madame Bovary (Flaubert, 1856), 25
Magic Mountain, The (Mann, 1924), 24, 170
Mann, Thomas: on *Bildungsroman,* 19–20, 21; "Brother Hitler" (1938), 176; *Buddenbrooks* (1901), 102; characters and other authors as ciphers for, 155, 156, 166; *Confessions of a Nonpolitical Man* (1918), 160, 167; *Death in Venice* (1912), 169; German identity and, 165, 167, 176–77, 179; "On the German Republic" (1922), 158, 161; "Germany and the Germans" (1945), 176–77; Goethe and, 9; *The Magic Mountain* (1924), 24, 170; Meinecke and, 8, 158–65; *Tonio Kröger* (1903), 169. See also *Doctor Faustus*
Mannheim, Karl, 75–76, 82n20, 87, 97, 99–100
Mansfield Park (Austen, 1814), 116
Marguerite of Navarre, 86, 96
Marx, Karl, 27, 57, 111–12
Marxism, 21, 26–27, 30, 75, 111–12, 130, 156, 161
Mayer, Hans, 156, 157, 174
Meinecke, Friedrich: *Cosmopolitanism and the National State* (1908), 161; *The German Catastrophe* (1946) and Mann's *Doctor Faustus,* 8, 158, 161–66, 168, 174; "Goethe Communities," call for, 158, 164–65; historicism of, 48n10, 56, 161–65; *Die Idee der Staatsräson in der neueren Geschichte* (1924), 158
Meister Eckhart, 47
Mendelssohn, Moses, 47, 48
merchant capitalism as cultural good, *Debit and Credit* (Freytag, 1855) addressing, 103–9, 115–16
Messiah, The (Klopstock, 1773), 49
Metropolis (film, 1927), 129
Mill, John Stuart, 119
Mill on the Floss, The (Eliot, 1860), 25
Mimesis (Auerbach, 1968), 76–77, 78
Minden, Michael, 26n35, 38, 97n35
modernity: *Berlin Alexanderplatz,* narrative treatment of time in, 129–30; in *The Epigones,* 92–93; logical endpoint of *Bildungsroman* tradition and, 156, 173, 178; Moretti's concept of, 130–31; myth in modern world, role of, 99–100, 171, 173, 177; nationalism as narrative response to, 64; nonsynchronicity, Bloch's model of, 27, 45, 75, 130–31, 136, 154, 157, 167, 169; as performative, 68–69; *Portrait of the Artist* as novel of colonial modernity, 130, 131–37; *Ulysses,* colonial modernity of, 137–41; *Wilhelm Meister* and, 67, 68–69; youth as symbolic form of, 22–23. See also imperialism, modern
Molière, 83
montage, Döblin and Joyce's use of, 130, 131, 144, 154
Montebello, Philippe de, 36
Morant Bay rebellion (1865), Jamaica, 102–3, 117, 119, 120
Moretti, Franco, 22–24, 36–38, 41–42, 74, 76, 130–33
Morgenstern, Karl: Biberkopf in *Berlin Alexanderplatz* compared to, 144; concept of *Bildungsroman* inaugurated by, 1–3, 27–28, 59; Hegel compared, 13; Herder, influence of, 52; historicism and, 6, 59; performative understanding of *Bildungsroman,* 5, 28; tension between romantic nationalism and cosmopolitanism in life and situation of, 2, 7, 28, 30, 60; on *Wilhelm Meister,* 1, 5–6, 28, 52, 59–60, 63
movies, German, urban environments in, 129, 149
Mundt, Wilhelm, 29
myth in modern world, role of, 99–100, 171, 173, 177

Napoleonic Wars, European legacy of, 1, 8, 60, 76, 79, 82, 84–87
narrative voice in *Bildungsroman,* 37–38
nationalism: association of telos in *Bildung* with nation, 16–24; cosmopolitanism, relationship to, 31–32; crisis of historicism and, 157–62; family romances and, 65; formation of human communities in *Wilhelm Meister* and, 60–65; generational consciousness and, 75; "German life, German thought and the morals of our time," *Wilhelm Meister* as representation of, 1, 28, 52, 63–64, 68–69; historicism and nationalism, Herder's connection of, 52–53; "long-distance nationalism" of *Debit and Credit,* 113–15; modernity, as narrative response to, 64; problem of idealist concept and, 26–31; vernacular cosmopolitanism and, 1–3, 181

national literature, concept of, 4–5, 35–36, 76–78
Nazis, Hitler, and World War II, 156, 158, 161–66, 170, 176–77, 179
Negri, Antonio, 111–12
Neoplatonic understanding of *Bildung,* 47
Nicholas Nickleby (Dickens, 1838–39), 73
Nietzsche, Friedrich, 129, 171, 178
Ninth Symphony (Beethoven), 171, 175
nonsynchronicity, Bloch's model of, 27, 45, 75, 130–31, 136, 154, 157, 167, 169
normativity, idealist theory of *Bildungsroman* and, 16–24
normativity/objectivity, as element of Hegel's literary aesthetics, 13–16
Novalis, 17, 24, 28, 58–59, 81, 161

objectivity/normativity, as element of Hegel's literary aesthetics, 13–16
"Ode to Joy" (Beethoven), 171, 172
Old Man Goriot (Balzac, 1835), 74
Oliver Twist (Dickens, 1837–39), 73
On the Formative Drive (*Über den Bildungstrieb*; Blumenbach, 1781), 50
"On the German Republic" (Mann, 1922), 158, 161
"On the Task of the Historian" (Humboldt, 1821), 18
Osterhammel, Jürgen, 79
Otto III (Holy Roman Emperor), 179

panentheistic thinking, 52, 69, 159
Panopticon, 43, 151
Paul, Jean, 17
performative understanding of *Bildungsroman,* 5, 7, 8, 28–31, 34, 42, 59–60, 68–69, 178–81
Petrey, Sandy, 87
Pfau, Thomas, 26, 27
Pickwick Papers (Dickens, 1836–37), 73
Pietism, concept of *Bildung* in, 47, 48, 50, 54
Pinder, Wilhelm, 27n38, 75
"Plan for an Academy for the Cultivation of the Heart and Mind of Young People" (Wieland, 1758), 49–50, 51
Plato and Platonism, 49, 52, 54
Poetry and Experience (Dilthey, 1906), 19, 21, 77
Poland, Prussian occupation of, in *Debit and Credit,* 104–5, 109–11
Portrait of the Artist as a Young Man, A (Joyce, 1914), 3, 8, 128–54; *Berlin Alexanderplatz* compared and contrasted, 130–31, 153–54 (see also *Berlin Alexanderplatz*); as *Bildungsroman,* 132–34; colonial modernity of, 130, 131–37; conjunction, disjunction, and "individuating rhythm" in, 131–37; idealist theory of *Bildungsroman,* failure to fit into, 25; sermon of Father Arnall in, 136–37; train narrative in, 134–36, 153; *Ulysses* and, 130–33, 137–41, 144, 153–54, 173; urban environments and *Bildungsroman* tradition, 8, 132–33, 151, 153–54; vernacular cosmopolitanism of, 133, 137, 153
postcolonial literature. *See* colonial and postcolonial literature
Preisendanz, Wolfgang, 77–78
proto-Zionism in *Daniel Deronda,* 8, 102n1, 122

Ramponi, Patrick, 105n6
Ranke, Leopold von, 81n19, 159n6
Rathenau, Walther, 142
realist literature: *Bildungsroman* compared to other forms of, 34; development of, 73–76; evolutionary theory, challenge posed by, 119; narrative realism in *Robinson Crusoe* compared to *Wilhelm Meister,* 62–63; national divisions in, 76–79; vernacular cosmopolitanism of, 79–82; Wieland on, 53–54
Red and the Black, The (Stendhal, 1830), 3, 8, 73–100; colors in title, significance of, 83–84; compared and contrasted with *The Epigones,* 82, 88–89, 91, 94, 95–96 (see also *Epigones, The*); contested narrative construct, history viewed as, 82–88; development of realist literature and, 73–76; family dynamics in, 96–98; generational consciousness and, 75–76, 81–82, 96; idealist theory of *Bildungsroman* and, 25; myth in modern world, role of, 99–100; narrative voice in, 38; national literature, concept of, 76–79, 82; post-Napoleonic political geography, read as response to, 8, 76, 84–87, 93–100; publication of, 73; vernacular cosmopolitanism of, 35, 79–82, 94
Redfield, Mark, 4n7, 21, 24, 25
relativism and historicism, 159–60
religion and nationalism, revitalization of, in *Daniel Deronda,* 121–27
re-volutionary temporality in *Wilhelm Meister,* 62–63, 66
Richardson, Samuel, 54, 55, 57, 73
Rimbaud, Arthur, 132
Rizal, José, 29
Robbins, Bruce, 34
Robinson Crusoe (Defoe, 1719), 62–63

Index

Rowlandson, Mary, 114
Ruttmann, Walter, 129

Said, Edward, 105n6, 116
Saint-Simon, Henri, 87
Sammons, Jeffrey L., 4, 25, 38, 39, 77n7, 92n30, 179
Sassen, Saskia, 140–41
Scheffler, Karl, 129, 141–42, 152
Schelling, Friedrich, 58
Schiller, Friedrich, 16–18, 30, 81, 148
Schlegel, August Wilhelm, 49, 81
Schlegel, Caroline, 28
Schlegel, Friedrich, 6, 49, 58–59, 62, 65
Schlegel, Johann Adolf, 49
Schmidt, Julian, 19, 103–4
Schneider, Ferdinand Joseph, 77
Schoenberg, Arnold, 166
Schor, Naomi, 77n7
Science of Knowledge (Fichte, 1804), 58, 62
Scott, Sir Walter, 57–58
Second World War, Nazis, and Hitler, 156, 158, 161–66, 170, 176–77, 179
"Secularization of the Devil, The" (Kahler, 1948), 156
Shaftesbury, Lord, 48, 49
Shakespeare, William, 60, 175n22
Shuttleworth, Sally, 119
Simmel, Georg, 141n21
Slaughter, Joseph R., 4n7, 23n24, 24, 25n30, 26
Social Darwinism in *Daniel Deronda*, 8, 119–21
socialism, Meinecke on, 162–64
Solheim, Birger, 167
Sonderweg hypothesis, 20
Spalding, Johann Joachim, 48
Spengler, Oswald, 160, 167, 169
Spiegel, Gabrielle M., 39
"Spirit of the Naturalist Age, The" (Döblin, 1924), 141, 148
Stendhal: *The Charterhouse of Parma* (1839), 73; generational consciousness of, 81–82; *Life of Henri Brulard* (1835–36), 82; on novels and theater after French Revolution, 83; sociological complexity, association with, 101. See also *Red and the Black, The*
Stifter, Adalbert, 24
Swales, Martin, 78

teleology, as element of Hegel's literary aesthetics, 13–16
theater after French Revolution, Stendhal on, 83
Theory of the Novel, The (Lukács, 1916), 21–22

Tieck, Ludwig, 17, 81
time and temporality: apocalyptic temporality of *Doctor Faustus*, 155–58, 178; *Berlin Alexanderplatz*, narrative treatment of time in, 129–30; colonies, clash between lingering forms of historicity and new mechanical temporality in, 130; genealogy of narrative and communal identity in *Bildungsroman*, 9, 38–42, 69; generational consciousness, 75–76, 81–82, 96; nonsynchronicity, Bloch's model of, 27, 45, 75, 130–31, 136, 154, 157, 167, 169; re-voluntionary temporality in *Wilhelm Meister*, 62–63, 66; time zones as problems of literature, 6, 30, 140. See also historicism
"To My Friends" ("Auf meine Freunde"; Klopstock), 49
Tonio Kröger (Mann, 1903), 169
totality, as element of Hegel's literary aesthetics, 13–16
Tower Society and Archive in *Wilhelm Meister,* 7, 14, 21, 37, 43–46, 61–62, 64–68, 74, 89, 95, 144
trade as cultural good, *Debit and Credit* (Freytag, 1855) addressing, 103–9, 115–16
"Tragedy of Modern Art, The" (Lukács), 175
translation studies, 5
"transnation," 2
Travers, Martin, 167
Troeltsch, Ernst, 158–60

Ulysses (Joyce, 1918–20), 130–33, 137–41, 144, 153–54, 173
universalist versus essentialist views of *Bildungsroman*, 3–5, 19–22, 23, 35, 74–75, 103
urban environments: Berlin as colonial city in *Berlin Alexanderplatz*, 141–44; *Bildungsroman* tradition and, 8, 128–29, 132–33, 144–51, 153–54; in German film, 129, 149; in *Ulysses*, 137–41

Vensky, Georg, 48
vernacular cosmopolitanism: of *Berlin Alexanderplatz,* 143, 153; concept of, 31–38; of *Daniel Deronda,* 103, 120–22, 125, 127; *Debit and Credit* and, 103, 107, 108, 109, 112; of *The Epigones* and *The Red and the Black,* 79–82, 94; historicism and, 33–34, 79–82, 160–61; nationalism and, 1–3, 181; of *Portrait of the Artist,* 133, 137, 153; of realist literature, 79–82; of *Ulysses,* 131, 133, 138, 140; in *Wilhelm Meister,* 65–69
Vico, G. B., 48n10, 56
Vienna, Congress of, 60, 84, 91, 92, 94

Vogl, Joseph, 60
Vosskamp, Wilhelm, 20, 21, 24n27

Walkowitz, Rebecca, 32
"Watch on the Rhine, The" (song) in *Berlin Alexanderplatz*, 145–46, 147, 149
Waverley (Scott, 1814), 57–58
Weber, Carl Maria von, 93
Weimar Classicism, 9, 91
Weimar Republic in *Berlin Alexanderplatz*, 145–46, 148, 150, 154
Werber, Niels, 111–12
Westphalia, Treaty of, 31
Wieland, Christoph Martin, 2, 48–51, 53–54, 57–58, 60, 81
Wilde, Oscar, 45
Wilhelm Meister's Apprenticeship (Goethe, 1795–96), 3, 7; allegorical nature of *Bildungsroman* and, 21; *Berlin Alexanderplatz* compared, 145, 151; "Confessions of a Beautiful Soul" novella within, 44, 67; *The Epigones* and, 73, 74, 89, 95; as family romance, 65–68; formation of human communities in, 60–65; genealogical approach to *Bildungsroman* and, 38, 40, 41; "German life, German thought and the morals of our time," as representation of, 1, 28, 52, 63–64, 68–69; *Hamlet* scenes in, 44, 60–61, 63, 65; historicism and, 5–6, 58, 68–69; Homeric characters compared to, 14; idealist theories of *Bildungsroman* and, 19, 23–24, 28–29; Lukács on, 22; Mann's *Doctor Faustus* and, 9, 157–58, 175–76; Mignon in, 65, 67–68, 89; modernity and, 67, 68–69; Morgenstern on, 1, 5–6, 28, 52, 59–60, 63; narrator in, 37; as paradigmatic *Bildungsroman*, 1; as political program, 17; *Portrait of the Artist* and, 134n15; re-volutionary temporality in, 62–63, 66; *Robinson Crusoe* (Defoe, 1719) compared, 62–63; Schlegel on, 58; structural change from hypotaxis to parataxis as expression of logic of historicism, 43–46, 61, 67; Tower Society and Archive in, 7, 14, 21, 37, 43–46, 61–62, 64–68, 74, 89, 95, 144; vernacular cosmopolitanism of, 65–69
Wilhelm Meister's Wandering Years (Goethe, 1821; revised version, 1829), 68
Windfuhr, Manfred, 90
Wohlfarth, Marc E., 120, 121n20
Wolf, Friedrich August, 2
Wolff, Christian, 50
women, attitudes of *Daniel Deronda* and *Debit and Credit* toward, 101–2, 118
world history, 79
"worldliness," attempts to link *Debit and Credit* (Freytag, 1855) to discourses of, 105n6, 108, 111–12
world literature, 4–5, 9, 35–38
World War I, 158, 160
World War II, Nazis, and Hitler, 156, 158, 161–66, 170, 176–77, 179

Xenias (Goethe, 1797), 30
Xenophon, 53

youth as symbolic form of modernity, 22–23
Youth of Twenty-Five Years Ago, The (Immermann, 1840), 82, 96

Zeitgeist, 75
Zionism and *Daniel Deronda*, 8, 102n1, 122